THE CITIES OF UMBRIA

BY

EDWARD HUTTON

WITH TWENTY ILLUSTRATIONS IN COLOUR BY
A. PISA
AND TWELVE OTHER ILLUSTRATIONS

FIFTH EDITION

METHUEN & CO. LTD.
36 ESSEX STREET W.C.
LONDON

First Published . . . . . . August 1905
Second Edition . . . . . . January 1906
Third Edition, Revised . . . May 1908
Fourth Edition . . . . . . September 1910
Fifth Edition 1913

TO ALICE

In hoc saltem libro inveniam faciem tuam

May 21, 1904

CONTENTS

PAGE

THE UMBRIAN SCHOOL OF PAINTING

UMBRIA MYSTICA

LIST OF ILLUSTRATIONS

IN COLOUR

FROM PHOTOGRAPHS BY MESSRS. ALINARI

PREFACE

ONE day of sunshine, mysterious and full of silence, as I was wandering among the hills about Fiesole, where hundreds of years ago Lorenzo of the Medici held his court, and, as I have been told, Botticelli first saw La Bella Simonetta in the spring, out of the splendour and sweet spaciousness of that gentle world, or perhaps from the cypresses that crown the soft round hills with mystery, there came to me an old chant, older, perhaps, than Christianity, that I had heard years and years ago when I was a child at Perugia, that city under the Apennines where they still guard the wedding-ring of the Blessed Virgin. It was an old tune that seemed to bear in its few notes all the romance of that world so long ago with its lovely gods; something of the simple and correct beauty of all that; and yet to suggest an underlying sadness and regret of the beauty that had passed away. A sudden longing seized me as I lay under the olives to hear the Mass sung in that bleak old church, to look once more on the Umbrian Hills, and to see the light that never was in any Tuscan vale, flooding the valley of Spoleto, and the countless indestructible cities. And as I lay there watching a peasant, whose clear-cut features proclaimed his race, sow his seed broadcast, as of old, over the plough-land, while behind him and above him the vines flung themselves from myrtle to myrtle under the profound and soft sky, I determined to set out that night for Umbria, the true Italia Mystica, whose saints have captured the world, whose valleys have beckoned many armies towards Rome. Once more I would see Assisi, that Italian Nazareth, early in the morning, and follow the road towards Foligno, the city of the Blessed Angela, most human, perhaps, of all saints, and say farewell to St. Mary of the Angels. Above me all day, like a Religious prostrate in his brown habit, on his knees, bending towards Rome, Monte Subasio would tower, whose snows are in springtime the one hard field of light in all the valley of Spoleto; for it is a valley of infinite softness and space, and the gesture of the mountains is of a profound nobility. At eventide I would come to Foligno, where in S. Felicita Blessed Angela besought of St. Francis a little happiness after great sorrow till she heard Christ whisper, one breathless morning, 'I love thee more than any woman in the valley of Spoleto.' And I, too, would beseech of St. Francis a little happiness, in St. Mary's of the Angels; and what might I not find— yes, even one so in love with life as I—in a land that held such gifts? So I set out not without hope.

It was night when I came to Perugia. The hostelry was comfortable, the host kind and thoughtful, the sunset as ever had been a passion of sudden glory. In that vast country, for so it seems, far from any real city, it is those primitive and absolute movements in the sky—the sunset,

the sunrise, and high noon, the gathering of the clouds
over the hills, the terrible onslaught and march of the storm
the mystery and silence of cloudless sunshine—that move us
that are of importance to us, as they never can be in a city,
where they are obscured by the foulness of life, the unnatural-
ness of existence amid millions of petty details, insignificant
and mortal. But here in Umbria, where Perugino was, in
fact, merely a realist who, so far as landscape is concerned
at any rate, painted just what he saw, the sweet movements
of heaven are of a due importance, and thrust themselves
not roughly, but very surely and quietly nevertheless, upon
our notice, assuring us almost with music of the existence
of God and His angels, and the beauty and simplicity of
life.

Tired by my journey, for Florence is far from Perugia,
I fell asleep into the night that had a blessedness scarcely
to be found in the North—seeing that the floor of heaven
here seemed softer than a blue mantle on which lay a
scattered multitude of lilies—to dream of to-morrow, that
delight of the traveller, its gifts, its dust and heat, its shade
and pleasant shallow streams, its weariness and satisfaction.

Just at dawn I was awakened, and went out into that
virginal hour, having eaten a mouthful of golden-coloured
bread, very pleasant to the taste, and a little honey, which
I bought in the market-place. Behind me and before me
lay the beautiful valley clad in a mist that was rose-colour
and gold, and softer than the bloom upon the grapes. Many
cities seeming white and very pure lifted their towers into the

sky. Perugia herself was in the attitude of prayer; Assisi, a little grey, lay still asleep upon the skirts of Subasio; little Spello seemed to stretch her arms towards the sky; while Trevi on her hill kept sentinel, armed at all points, her housetops battlements, her wind-vanes bright swords. Only Spoleto under her monastery, holding the very precious dust of Filippo Lippi in her heart, seemed to be watching the dawn which presently swept over her hills, covering them with a matchless glory. And it seemed to me in that hour that if the noblest day's journey in the world had to be chosen, it is by this way we should pass, down this valley we should come, perhaps from Florence to Arezzo, past Cortona, the city of Signorelli, that still holds, though hidden, the dust of that great unfortunate man who built the tomb of St. Francis and hid his body for six hundred years; past Lake Thrasymene where St. Francis kept his fast, and Perugia where Perugino learned the nobility of perfect space, and Assisi and Foligno and Spoleto, whose mighty fortress harboured Lucrezia Borgia, and Terni with her waterfalls, and so over the mountains to Narni, till from afar suddenly the classical form of Monte Soracte rises out of the Campagna, and at last after passing the vineyards of Monte Rotondo, at a little village called Castel Giubileo, far, oh! far away, we might see the dome of S. Pietro rise like the immense hope of the world, inexpressible and as yet unbroken, into heaven, blue and white like the sky itself. The supreme nobility of this Latin landscape, the cradle of our civilisation, moves us as no other sight perhaps in the world can do. This is the land of our second birth, and still beyond the remotest of horizons she holds for us most of that which is very precious.

. . . .

Those cypresses beside the Tiber, that villa over the valley, the sound of the bells that came to us lying under the olives—do you remember, little Princess, do you remember? or have you forgotten everything now that I am so far away?

Ah, no! you cannot forget that day when we, two pilgrims from a less lovely world, came to Assisi; and, seeing our simplicity, the Brother told us all his stories. That day at least you will not forget, for did it not seem to us that we had met St. Francis himself in the rose-garden beside St. Mary of the Angels, and when we had thanked him did he not hang his medals round our necks for remembrance—one for you and one for me; and since we secretly wished it, I think he blessed us? How tired you were when, for our delight, we had tried to see Giotto's work in that dark lower church glowing with precious frescoes; how delightful and cool you found the quiet Campo Santo; how happy we were over our bread and wine! Do you think I can forget your laughter, or the shadow of the swaying cypress that every now and then passed over your hair as a cloud passes over the sun, or the folds of your dress, or the gesture of your hands? Those old dead saints into whose dreams we came for a little moment, how long and long will it be before they hear your laughter again? And I, who was so happy with you in the byways and olive-gardens of Umbria, how shall I visit them again now you are far away? No; I shall not dare to visit them again without you. I shall wait, and since you are now so busy making others happy, I have reminded myself of all those things you have perhaps forgotten, that I may bring them to your remembrance and place them under the benediction of your hands.

Indeed, if we had world enough and time, for a little moment we might be content with remembrance. But Italy is changing—already how many thousands have looked with indifference on that which we found so precious; how many thousands, think you, Princess, have laughed at the stories we took for true? It is an army that passes.

But amid all the mediocrity of life from which it is so difficult to escape, am I not compelled to pardon and to cease to ask: O Life, why have you disappointed me?—since you have blown in the sweetest blossoms and passed me lightly, lightly in my dreams?

Do you remember, little Princess, do you remember!

May 21, 1904.

IMPRESSIONS OF THE CITIES OF UMBRIA

A

I

PERUGIA

AS you come to Perugia from Florence and Terontola, past the mystical lake of Trasimeno, where, on an island surrounded by whispering rushes that seem ever to be commanding silence, St. Francis spent the Lent of which the author of the *Fioretti* tells us, you might think the city that reveals herself so fantastically, first on the right hand and then on the left between the low Umbrian Hills, only a great fortress, the castle of some belated tyrant. On a nearer view there is something of a great dignity in her isolation on her hill-top, which is, after all, not the last low spur of the indestructible Apennine but the deposits, age after age, of the Tiber flowing towards Rome and the sea. And even as long and long ago the Tiber left her, so that now even after the fiercest storms or the deepest snows she hears nothing of his terrible song, so at last the world too has fallen away from her, leaving her alone on her beautiful hill, surrounded only by elemental things—the sun, the moon, the stars, and the unchanging mountains. More than a mile away the railway slinks towards Rome and the sea, fearful of her aspect, since it may never approach her, and has only dared to come so far by devious ways, and with many hesitations. She is so proud on her mountain, over-topping the soft green hills of her Umbria, for within her immense horizon no other city, ruddy or white, is like to her. Her brows are still pale in the morning, and golden with the setting sun; the sky is still above her serene and beautiful; her eyes, which are perhaps tired with waiting for the sunrise, may still rest themselves on her own green fields and many gardens of olives. It is only at evening some-times that you may surprise a kind of fear in her eyes, when suddenly above the Vesper bells at sunset she hears the electric tram, that has so lately been thrust upon her, rush without ceremony or weariness up her hillside, and with clanging iron and all the noise of modernity hurry through her ancient Corso, past the Palazzo Municipio, which in its beautiful old age it threatens to destroy, and has already brutally shaken; past the Duomo, which it ignores, into the Piazza Danti, whence it has already expelled the beautiful bronze statue of Pope Julius III. But after all, this modern contrivance, with its network of wires, its noise, and its convenience, is the one modern thing that has invaded her. The great beautiful oxen still stand patiently in her market-place, or draw the plough over her fields; her sons still sow broadcast, over the land they tread with their bare feet, the corn and the maize; the priest still blesses her fields; the tiny cross of bamboo with a branch of olive, silver in the wind, still marks her fields as the gifts of God to her who still remembers Him. In her cathedral the wedding-ring of the Blessed Virgin, mystic, wonderful, is safe in its many caskets. Her beautiful miracle-picture of Madonnina draws its crowd of pilgrims, and she herself, the queen of hill cities, is still beautiful within and without her Etruscan walls, on which Rome and the Middle Age and the Renaissance have not forgotten to leave their marks as beautiful and as indestructible. Her streets are even yet named nobly—Via della Cupa, Via della Conca, Via dei Priori, Via di San Francesco, Via delle Stalle. She has not stooped to flatter the new Royal House, as Rome and Florence and Naples have done. Her gates, many and splendid, have too in their very names a suggestion of her inviolable beauty—Porta Eburnea, Porta Augusta, Porta Sant' Angelo, Porta Sole, Porta Marzia. Within her palaces is some of the sweetest work of Perugino, and Bonfigli, and Fiorenzo di Lorenzo; and her prospect is of a thousand hills and valleys. Far, oh, far away to the north and west, lie the bare mountains above Siena; while to the south the hills are crowned with famous and lovely cities—Assisi, Spello, Trevi, Spoleto; and, like a rosy flower in the green valley of Spoleto, you see Foligno, the strange city of Blessed Angela; while beyond, Monte Subasio looks towards Rome with the city of St. Francis kneeling on its skirts, a religious, in the homely brown habit, vowed to God. Like a lily at her right hand towers St. Mary of the Angels, delicate with the colour of the day— white, or almost rosy, or sombre, under her sky. And far away to the west rise the mountains above Orvieto and little Todi on her hill, and, all between, the sweet Umbrian plain and the valley of the Tiber. And though in early morning this exquisite landscape is delicate and fragile and half-hidden in mist, at sunset it has something of the 'large- ness of the evening earth,' and a majesty of silence and repose, that is as it were suggested by the beautiful gesture of the mountains. It is above all this perfection, absolute queen from horizon to horizon, that Perugia stands, ever at attention on her hills, terrible of aspect with all her beauty, and with great angry eyes as of old searching out her enemies.

Of Etruscan origin, being indeed one of the principal cities of that strange, unknown people, we know nothing of Perugia till she submitted herself to Rome in B.C. 309. That is but the first of numberless surrenders—to the Popes, to many tyrants, to her own terrible sons, to the brutality of the mob, to Italy, and the modern world. The hand of the

Emperor Augustus has rested on her throat as certainly as that of the latest tyrant, Baglioni or Pope.   It was Augustus who in B.C. 38 rebuilt the city, which one of the citizens, Caius Macedonicus, in order to save her from the great emperor, burnt to the ground, so that she is now Augusta Perugia, and Perusia Etrusca no longer.   Yet, in spite of capitulation and outward obedience, she has ever nursed in her soul a fierce spirit of liberty, which has made her story one of the bloodiest in the history of Italy.

It was in the sixth century that Justinian, desiring to drive the Goths out of Italy, sent the general Constantine to Umbria, a vastly larger country then than now.   Constantine seems to have made Perugia his headquarters, and to have been left unmolested till, in the year 545, Totila, that terrible and magnificent figure, appeared, and having obtained possession of Assisi, prepared to drive Constantine from Perugia; but he found her, as ever, not easy of conquest; to be overcome rather by treachery than by fighting.   The siege which followed is said to have lasted for seven years, but at last Perugia fell before the fury of the Goth, 'upheld to the last by a new power, namely, that of her faith.'   It was the first of her patron saints, S. Ercolano, who upheld her, and, as it were, in those early years of terror and fight, formed her character there in the midst of mystical Italy, making her for ever after not unmindful of those mysterious powers which in all ages men have been anxious to win to their cause, since it would seem to be fatal to permit them to be unfriendly.   So to the starving city S. Ercolano, its bishop, comes with wise counsels; and as in ancient Rome, so in Perugia, in spite of the scarcity, food is thrown from the walls, and the Goths discouraged.   Bonfigli has painted the story with all his simplicity and sweetness in the Cappella dei Priori, now Sala Numero Due of the Pinacoteca.   It would seem that an ox having been fed with what corn remained to the city was thrown over the walls, when the Goths, finding it, supposed the Perugians to have so much to eat that they fed even their beasts with corn. 'But by chance,' says Ciatti, whose history of the city is full of an old-world sweetness, 'But by chance a young priest spoke from the walls with some Goths, and all unknowing revealed the terror and death reigning in the city.' And so the stratagem of the good bishop failed; yet on that day Perugia fell not without honour, and in all her future has never forgotten S. Ercolano, who was martyred in her cause, seeing she chose him for her patron saint.

In 592 Perugia, on her high hill, became a Lombard duchy, but was soon restored to the Byzantine Empire. Through all that mysterious Middle Age she grew stronger and more fierce. Her invaders were many, she suffered many violations. In the year 726 we find her, together with many another Italian city, siding with the Pope against the Emperor Leo III., the Iconoclast, when he published his edict against images in churches. It was about this time that Rome became practically independent under the Popes, and it will be in the memory of the reader that the controversy with Leo led to the separation of the Greek and Latin Churches in 729; to be united again at the Council of Lyons in 1274, only to be separated finally in 1277. Certainly, during those years of fierce and brutal energy, Perugia owed much to the Papacy. Thus, in 744, when King Rachis of the Lombards besieged Perugia, Pope Zacharias came to plead with him not unsuccessfully, and it is certainly true to the spirit of that romantic age that the king became a monk after listening to the Pope, retiring to the Benedictine monastery of Monte Cassino.

A time of some confusion follows. As ever in Italy, the aim of the statesmen was the balance of power, at that time between the Emperor and the Pope, as later between the great cities and provinces. By this means a certain communal liberty was attained.

In the year 800, however, Charlemagne having invaded Italy in 774, overcome the Lombards, and been crowned as Emperor of the West by Pope Leo III., Perugia came under the dominion of the Pope as a gift from the Emperor. From this time Perugia remained under the Papacy save for a short period in 1375, when, the Pope being in Avignon, a Republic was declared. The history of the city during those years is one of continual warfare with her neighbours—Assisi, Siena, Arezzo, Città di Castello, Gubbio, Foligno, Spoleto. In 1358 Perugia won her greatest victory over Siena. Having succeeded in defeating almost all her rivals she laid upon them heavy burdens: thus Foligno was forbidden to rebuild her walls, Città della Pieve was compelled to provide bricks to pave her streets, Arezzo to yield her marble to decorate the cathedral of San Lorenzo. Yet in spite of her fierceness, her strength, and her pride, she was ever unable to master herself, falling always a prey to her own passions, consuming her energy not in wars with her rivals alone, but also in massacre and havoc among her own citizens. Thus she wasted herself, turning her fierceness against herself at last till her streets ran with blood, her cathedral was defiled, her greatest sons assassinated, and she herself a mere beautiful bastion on a bleak hillside.

To describe the quarrels of the Baglioni and Oddi would serve no useful purpose. Their names are known for every kind of brutality and murder to every traveller in Italy from the sketch of Perugia which the late J. A. Symonds published in his *Sketches in Italy*. Matarazzo too, to whom of course Mr. Symonds was indebted, in a masterpiece of simple narrative—if indeed that naïve chronicle be the work of the distinguished humanist—is full of the dramatic story of their hatred, their glory, and their despair. I am content to refer the reader to those pages. It is, however, worthy of notice that it was during the years of internal revolution, when every sort of crime was rampant, when murder and destruction went barefaced up and down the streets, that Perugino and Fiorenzo di Lorenzo were painting their quiet and lovely pictures of the birth and death of Christ, while the young Raphael was at work in the studio of his master Perugino. It has been said that in the St. George of the Louvre, and perhaps in the horseman trampling upon Heliodorus in the *stanze* of the Vatican, we have a picture of Astorre Baglioni, that terrible and yet beautiful figure, now immortal since Raphael's eyes once rested upon him. It was to one of these figures—terrible, and yet not without a certain beauty too—that Perugia owed the opportunity of a new, and not altogether unnecessary, despotism. In 1535, Ridolfo Baglioni having murdered the Pope's Legate, Paul III. determined to send troops to drive Ridolfo out of Perugia. In this he was successful, and became himself ruler of the city. But in 1538 the Perugians revolted, the Pope having raised the price of salt. Paul III. promptly defeated them, and two years later laid the foundation, upon a ruined palace of the Baglioni, of the Rocca Paolina, which bore the legend 'ad coercendam Perusinorum audaciam. Thus began a rule in Perugia strong and steadfast and despotic, which, save for the incident of Napoleon, was not to pass away till our own time, when, on the 14th September 1860, the city was taken by the troops of Victor Emmanuel, and became an integral part of United Italy.

So the splendour and the terror of the past interwoven with the thunder of innumerable banners has sunk into the mediocrity of to-day, when even silence is denied her lest she should recollect herself and remember her victories. Beauty such as once belonged to Florence or Venice or Rome was perhaps never hers. She was a scarped crag of the moun-

tains, burnt with fire, beaten by the wind, splendid with the
sun. Even her cathedral was as relentless as a fortress, at
least in appearance. But the destroying centuries have
perhaps lent it something of their tolerance, giving the
clinkered brick the surface and the colour almost of a precious stone. It is not beauty but strength and passion that
you find in its brown walls that have been splashed with
blood and washed with wine. Inside there is scarcely beauty
at all, only silence and space and a softer and more sombre
light than is usual in an Italian church. And yet in its
homely, country aspect it might attract where a more
splendid church would leave you cold, but that its painted
stucco pillars, fantastic and incredible, seem to impress upon
you the fact that Perugino was right: religion, even in
mystical Italy, was for the mass of the people a kind of
sentimental emotion entirely without intellectuality, ready
at any moment to fall into sensual or frenzied desire, as
with the Battuti, the Flagellants, who from Perugia and
Assisi spread over Italy in the fourteenth century. And it
is not altogether strange that this people for whom Perugino
painted—often, we may think, with such contempt—held as
their most precious possession the wedding or betrothal ring
of the Blessed Virgin. It is kept under many locks in many
caskets in the little chapel to the left of the west door of
the Duomo, and may be seen five times during the year: to
wit, on March the 19th, which is the Festa dello Sposalizio,
on March the 25th, which is Our Lady's Day, on the second
Sunday in July, on July the 30th, and on August the 2nd.
Made from some agate stone, it is popularly believed to
change colour according to the hearts of those who look on
it. It was brought to Perugia in 1472 by Fra Vinterio di
Magonza, who had 'piously' stolen it from the Franciscans at
Chiusi. In this chapel too till 1797, when Napoleon took it
to France, whence it has never returned, hung the Sposalizio,

once supposed to be by Perugino, but by later criticism given to Lo Spagna.[1] A copy now fills the place of the original picture.

On the other side of the church is the Chapel of S. Bernardino, which belonged to the merchants' guild. A Deposition by Baroccio is over the altar; the window, perhaps the best in the church, is of the sixteenth century.

A very delightful picture, attributed to Manni, of Madonna, hangs over the little altar against the third pillar on the right. It is the famous Madonna delle Grazie, the most splendid miracle-picture in Umbria. With hands raised she seems to deprecate our prayers and to bless us. Innumerable trifles, silver hearts, and invisible thankfulness surround the altar of a 'miracle' picture in which even the unbending Protestant cannot but find at least a miracle of beauty. It is to this altar that the mother always brings her child, to lay him for a moment at the feet of Madonna after his christening in the Baptistery close by. Apart from these wonders there is but little to be seen in the cathedral. A fine altarpiece, however, in the winter choir, by Luca Signorelli, is one of the noblest pictures in Perugia : Madonna sits with her Child between St. John Baptist, S. Onofrio, S. Lorenzo, and S. Ercolano, while beneath are two beautiful angels, one of whom tunes his lute.

Outside the cathedral are the Piazza Municipio and the Piazza Danti. In the latter, the bronze statue of Pope Julius III., by Vincenzo Danti, used to stand, but it has now been moved to the steps of the cathedral facing the Piazza Municipio, where it is entirely out of place, in order to make room for the new electric tramway which ought never to have been brought up the Corso at all. This vile modern

[1] See *The Study and Criticism of Italian Art*, vol. ii., by Bernhard Berenson.

contrivance has almost spoiled Perugia, and has turned it from a city of silence to a pandemonium. It has also done, and is still doing, grave injury to the Palazzo Pubblico.

Close to the statue of Pope Julius, where it now stands against the cathedral wall, is the little pulpit from which S. Bernardino of Siena used to preach so passionately. It was while preaching here that it is said he heard his favourite bell, called Viola, which hung in the Campanile of the Convent of S. Francesco al Prato, now a ruin, fall to the ground, and, stopping his sermon, said to the people, 'My children, Viola is fallen, but she is not hurt.' But S. Bernardino with all his eloquence preached in vain. The people wept to hear him, burnt their books and pictures and finery on the stones beside the beautiful fountain, and then in a few days cheerfully cut each other's throats in the very place where they had listened to the good saint, and even in the Duomo itself. And was it not here, too, that the dead body of the beautiful Astorre Baglioni lay in state during two days, together with that of his murderer and cousin, Grifonetto?

The beautiful fountain which stands in the midst of the square was built in 1277 from designs by a Perugian artist, Fra Bevignate, a Silvestrian. The lovely statuettes and bas-reliefs which adorn it were designed by Niccolò Pisano, and sculptured by his son Giovanni.

The splendid and picturesque palace, the Palazzo Pubblico, which closes the Piazza opposite the cathedral, is one of the finest Gothic buildings in all Italy, and is the glory of Perugia. Built at the end of the twelfth century by Giacomo di Servadio and Giovanni di Benvenuto of Perugia, it was finished in the fifteenth century. The great entrance in the Corso is still guarded by S. Ercolano, S. Costanzo, and St. Louis of Toulouse, the three patron saints of Perugia. St. Louis of Toulouse was the great-grandson of St. Louis of France. He was therefore the brother of Robert, King of Naples, who beat the Ghibellines at Genoa. It was on this occasion that the Perugians chose St. Louis for one of their patrons. Thus we find also over the great door of their Palazzo Pubblico the two lions of the Guelfs, together with the griffins of Perugia. On the side of the Palazzo, towards the Duomo, are the lean lion of the Guelf cause again, in bronze, and the griffin of Perugia, while beneath is the Scala della Vaccara, a very beautiful flight of steps lately restored perhaps to its original design.

You enter the Palazzo Pubblico by the great entrance in the Corso; here all the business of Perugia would seem to be conducted. Groups of men stand talking, talking, and even their uncouth dialect cannot spoil the majesty of the Latin tongue. It is a picturesque sight, these bronzed *contadini* in their sheepskins and their great furred coats doing their business in the beautiful old portico of their Municipio. Though all things pass away, in Italy at least there is always left the shadow of former greatness—some suggestion on a fortunate day of all the tragedy of the centuries, in a great ruined gateway or the cold broken limbs of a forgotten god.

The churches of Perugia are many, and for the most part of little interest. S. Pietro dei Cassinesi, whose beautiful tower can be seen from the Piazza della Prefettura, is really the only church in the city which has not been emptied of its treasures. S. Pietro, it is said, enjoys this privilege because the monks befriended the army of Vittorio Emanuele in 1860, when that king took the city. As the traveller walks to S. Pietro down the Via Marzia and the Via Floramonti he will pass down the steps of S. Ercolano, and come upon that tiny octagonal Gothic church, built against the Etruscan walls in 1200 in the place where Totila is said to have martyred S. Ercolano himself. Beyond the beauty of its architecture there is nothing of interest in the church. Passing down the Via Cavour, you come on the left to the gaunt unfinished church of S. Domenico. The strange broken tower is beautiful from the Piazza della Prefettura, especially at night, when its wounds are hidden and it remembers perhaps its many prayers. Giovanni Pisano is said to have made designs for the church, which was begun early in the fourteenth century; but in the innumerable wars of that period the church he built was destroyed, and so in the middle of the seventeenth century it was rebuilt from the designs of Carlo Maderno. The interior is terrible in its dilapidated mediocrity. In the left transept is a fine tomb of Pope Benedict XI., 1303, by Giovanni Pisano. The Pope lies behind curtains which two angels are drawing close. The two spiral columns which support the canopy were inlaid with mosaic—stolen, it is said, by the soldiers of Napoleon; beautiful figures of children are sculptured on the pillars. This lovely Gothic tomb is one of the most interesting things in Perugia. The fourth chapel, too, on the south side, has an altar with some terra-cotta statues and other decorations by Agostino Ducci. The gaunt tower was lowered by Paul III. since it interrupted his view from the Rocca, and indeed overlooked the fortress.

You pass now on the way to S. Pietro under the Porta Romana, built by Agostino Ducci in 1476, and come upon the first Cathedral of Perugia, the monastic Church of S. Pietro dei Cassinesi, the most interesting church left in the city. It was built in 963 by S. Pietro Vincioli, of the Benedictine Order of Monte Cassino, but was redecorated in the fifteenth century. The beautiful courtyard and monastery, now secularised and turned into an agricultural school, have perhaps spoiled the original façade of the church, but in the quietness and loneliness which seem to have fallen upon it, it retains much of the spirit of its founder, the Benedictine

monk of that lonely monastery in Southern Italy. Only
three monks remain to guard the church, and as you pass
with one of them between the many columns of marble and
stone, taken so long ago from the temple of Venus which
stood where now a temple of Christ stands—how soon to be
quite spoiled like that of the goddess!—it is as though Time
himself had with a certain irony allowed you to look for a
moment on his mysterious vengeance, his destructive justice.
Humanism, the belief that 'nothing which has ever interested
living men and women can wholly lose its vitality—no
language they have spoken, nor oracle beside which they have
hushed their voices; no dream which has once been entertained by actual human minds, nothing about which they
have ever been passionate or expended time and zeal,' seems
to have come to pass under our very eyes at last, and to
suggest to us a tolerance even for those who have destroyed—
yes, here in Perugia, too—so much that was fair. How if,
after all, these soldiers from the North were but the unconscious agents of a profound Humanism, to which the dead
seem as passionate, as insistent, as the living, in whose hearts
even to-day Paganism is not more uncertain than Christianity,
since the saints are only gods whose spirits have awakened,
withering their beauty and their comeliness in a world that
has seen a star?

Well, it is not such thoughts, be sure, you will hear from
the kindly monks of S. Pietro. The church is a basilica
with nave and aisles and small transepts. Benedetto da
Montepulciano made the roof, which is gaudy and not worthy
of notice; and for the most part the pictures are feeble and
bad.

Over the high altar of S. Pietro dei Cassinesi Perugino's
Assumption used to stand, but it is gone to the North to-
gether with Raphael's 'Ansidei' Madonna, now in the National
Gallery, which used to hang in S. Fiorenzo, and the Sposa-

lizio by Lo Spagna, which was in the Cappella del S. Anello in the cathedral. The monks tell you that the choir stalls are decorated from Raphael's designs; it is hard to believe it. The view from the gallery at the end of the choir is very lovely, embracing as it does the whole valley of Spoleto. In the north aisle is a Pietà by Bonfigli, of a curious beauty; and a lovely altar-piece by Mino da Fiesole, over which is a circular Madonna and Child by Pintoricchio, now ruined. The sacristy holds five panels by Perugino of SS. Scholastica, Ercolano, Pietro Vincioli, the founder of the monastery, Costanzo, and Mauro, which are part of Perugino's Resurrection, now in Lyons. These lovely panels and the Bonfigli are surely sufficient excuse for a visit to S. Pietro. But in reality it is the quiet church itself that attracts us most. Built on the last spur of the hills it overlooks the immense valley of the Tiber, and seems to command silence. Beyond, the vineyards and the olives sweep away to St. Mary of the Angels and the numberless cities, ruddy and white, of the valley of Spoleto; while across the unshadowed fields where the sun marches in glory and splendour, S. Pietro speaks to S. Francesco, and S. Francesco to S. Feliciano, and S. Feliciano to S. Maria Assunta, and so on to Rome where, over the sadness of the Campagna, S. Pietro broods on the fortunes of the world and the death of gods.

It is in quite another part of the city that you find the only other church of any artistic interest—the Oratory of S. Bernardino, and that is but a shell like S. Ercolano. Passing under the Municipio, down the picturesque and almost mediæval Via dei Priori, where one turns back many times to see the roofs piled up into heaven and the arches of many a shadowy street; after passing the Torre degli Scirri, a thirteenth-century tower left alone of all those belonging to the private families of the city; past more than one church, too, of little or no interest, you come out at last into the Piazza di San Francesco, where stands in ruined splendoúr the façade of S. Bernardino, perhaps the master-piece of Agostino Ducci the Florentine. Built in 1461 by the magistrates of Perugia in gratitude to S. Bernardino for his efforts for peace and brotherly love among a people so disposed the other way, it is certainly one of the most charming of the coloured architectural works of Italy. Above is God the Father in glory, with two kneeling angels and eight cherubim; beneath, two griffins; and there in a flaming *mandorla*, surrounded by angels, is S. Bernardino, together with scenes in relief from the saint's life, one of which represents him preaching at Aquila while a star shines over him at midday. Many angels and virtues and arabesques, exquisite in their perfect style and beauty, finish the work.

S. Bernardino of Siena, whom this splendid monument commemorates, is one of the most pathetic figures of the fifteenth century. He was a true disciple of St. Francis. Born at Massa in 1380 of a noble family of Siena, he was an orphan before he was seven years old. He seems to have been brought up by his aunt Diana. The usual rather dis-agreeable stories are told of his childhood—stories common to all the saints, so that you wonder, hearing them, that those who in their earliest years were so commonplace and pious attained to such strength and sweetness in age. At eleven years old he was sent to Siena to school, where even then he seems to have attracted people by reason of a certain dignity in him. Yet he did not escape from the touch of the brutality of his day, though he shamed that man who would have injured him. At the age of seventeen, after a study of civil and canon law, he enrolled himself in the confraternity of Our Lady in the hospital of S. Maria della Scala to serve the sick; and it was here, after some years of discipline in the sorrows of the world, that he too heard

B

the implacable voice calling him to the difficult way of service.   Service for man, for this our world, it is the inspiration of S. Bernardino's life as it was of the lives of St. Francis and St. Catherine of Genoa.   In the year 1400 a frightful pestilence, that had already wasted many another city of Italy, fell on Siena.   These pestilences were no uncommon thing in that age of brilliant genius and bloodshed. It was from such a plague that Boccaccio, in the *Decameron*, withdraws his knights and ladies in order that they may live and tell many lovely tales full of piteous and laughing words.   But for S. Bernardino there was no such escape. He had heard some voice, and seen the dying and the dead too often to look perhaps at the sun again without a kind of shame.   So, together with twelve young men, he served the sick, expecting heaven.   During four months he seems to have managed the hospital with great skill, and to have shown a practical ability not rare in the lives of the saints. For it is the mistake of much popular criticism to think of the saints as dreamers almost incapable of action.   The lives of St. Francis, St. Catherine of Siena, St. Teresa, and St. Dominic seem to have been forgotten, or remembered only for a certain mysticism which, of course, the mass of men fails to understand.   But these great saints were in reality as great in action as in thought; they accomplished many marvellous things—as St. Catherine the return of the Pope to Rome from Avignon, or St. Teresa the reconstruction of an entire Order.

And so shortly we find S. Bernardino, having done much for Siena, retiring to a little house without the city, where the walls of his garden shut out the world.   It was after this that he took the habit of the Order of St. Francis at a convent of Observants not far from the city.   He made his profession, September 8, 1404, on his birthday, which was the birthday also of Madonna Mary, whom he served so eagerly.   In

ragged garments he went through the streets while the crowd
laughed at him, and, seeing one whom they knew to be of
noble family in the same condition with themselves, threw
stones at him; while his friends, in shame at the figure he
cut, pressed him to return with them. But he had heard the
very voice of Christ whispering in the sunshine and the heat:
'My son, behold Me hanging upon the cross: if thou lovest
Me and art desirous to imitate Me, thou also must be fastened
to thy cross; thou also must follow Me, and surely thou shalt
find Me.' Gradually he came to understand his true vocation as the orator of God. He too practised an art, the art
of preaching and affecting the hearts of men, the secret of
which he, as St. John of the Cross, that insatiable Spaniard,
found was just an ardent love. For a single word spoken by
love was, he knew, more powerful than any eloquence, the
profound longing of the heart speaking to the heart with a
kind of irresistible sincerity. And those who heard him
loved him.

In all that terrible age of slaughter and pestilence, and the
awakening of the destructive intelligence of man, he was
really a sort of peacemaker, pleading—at times not unsuccessfully—for love between men, seeing that He whom he served
had spent so much love for them. So the word of God that
he heard in the valleys silent and fair, or in the beautiful
streets of the immaculate city, or in dreams and dawns while
men slept, pale and lovely as the days that pass so quietly
over little children, became for him a consuming fire, a
flaming and lovely sword, a swift and terrible hammer,
breaking the hardest rocks. And he was a very flame, consuming all that was not passion. Dullness of heart—it was
his proclaimed enemy. One seems to hear him crying down
the centuries from the passionate streets, now dying or dead,
of Perugia or Siena: 'O ye sons of men, how long will ye
be dull of heart!' The name of Jesus was to him as mar-

vellous as the name of our beloved, for when it was whispered to him, or he dared to utter it, a thousand little flames shook within him and he became almost beside himself. For this cause Pope Martin V. sent for him more than once to examine him, but dismissed him with a blessing, offering him also in 1427 the Bishopric of Siena, as did Pope Eugenius III. that of Ferrara, and later that of Urbino—all of which honours he refused, since his diocese was the world, his parish Italy. Being at Ancona and hearing that Perugia was in arms against herself, he did not hesitate to hasten thither and proclaim that God had sent him 'as His angel' to proclaim peace on earth to men of good will. Nor was he unsuccessful; for they 'forgave one another, desiring to live in peace and to pass to the•Right Hand.' Later, from that little pulpit on the wall of S. Lorenzo, he watched Perugia at his bidding burn her books, the false hair of the women, the beautiful pictures, full of desire and life, of the great lords. His influence, at least for a time, over the hearts of these fierce, strong men can scarcely be exaggerated; he ruled Perugia for a moment by love, being himself a very flame of love. In 1438 he was appointed vicar-general of the Observants in Italy, and during the five years he held that office set about a reformation. He then returned to Siena, and being on the road, ever preaching, came to Aquila in the Abruzzi, where he was taken ill of fever, dying on the 20th May 1444, He was buried there in that little far city, and was canonised by Nicholas V. in 1450. Thus ended a life as necessary, as typical of that strange fifteenth century, as that of any painter or tyrant. His art was Love, as theirs was Beauty or Power, nor was he less strict in his service. Perugia at least would be less passionate without him, for amid all the splendour and beauty, the blood and the pestilence, the passion of his century, there in the dust and dirt we find the lilies of his love.

It is difficult to tear oneself away from thoughts of S. Bernardino while looking at the beautiful monument that the Perugians built in memory of him. Close by is the ruined church of S. Francesco, where he lodged on his visits to Perugia, and where hung his favourite bell 'Viola.' Some ancient frescoes of the school of Giotto are all that remain of beauty to the old church.

Not far from S. Bernardino, towards the Via dei Priori, is the little church of S. Agata, memorable only for its doorway, which is the sole remnant of Lombard work in the city.

The little church of S. Martino, easily reached from the Piazza di San Francesco by the Via della Siepe, Via del Poggio, Via Francolina, Via Armonica, and Via Verzaro, has a beautiful altar-piece by Manni and a Crucifixion of the school of Perugino. Thence to the Via Appia is but a step. This picturesque street is one of the most curious in the city. Passing down it you come into the Piazza Ansidei on the right, and thus into the Via Vecchia, at the bottom of which is the magnificent Arch of Augustus, the lower part of which is undoubtedly Etruscan. Passing thence up the Corso Garibaldi, and turning to the right just before you come to the Porta Sant' Angelo, you find the church of S. Angelo, a little round Romanesque building of the earlier part of the thirteenth century. It stands on the supposed site of a Temple of Venus, whence were taken the pillars for S. Pietro. Behind the high altar is a great stone, itself an altar to Marcus Aurelius, while the curious fresco La Madonna del Verde is certainly one of the earliest in Perugia. The lovely gate Porta Sant' Angelo is well worth seeing, with its Ghibelline battlements; it was part of a castle of Fortebraccio. It is here that St. Francis and St. Dominic are said to have met on their way to Pope Honorius, then in Perugia.

In the convent of S. Agnese, till lately only open to women, but now, by special permission of the Pope, open to all, there are three frescoes attributed to Perugino. The delightful garden of the nuns, full of old-world flowers and herbs, is perhaps as charming as the frescoes. It is horrible to think that in a short time those poor old women, utterly ignorant of the ways of the world, will be turned into the streets. But modern Italy has no pity for Religious; and so with the rest those harmless souls, with their wondering, frightened eyes and confiding, loving ways, must be beggared to satisfy the lust for spoil of the new monarchy. It is the least admirable characteristic of a government which is certainly not beloved.

Through many delightful byways you may wander round the walls of Perugia, coming upon Etruscan boulders or Roman brick and stone, or later additions of the destroying centuries. And go where you will, always you will find something to delight you, something that is too simple or too beautiful for any land but this. For here is Italia Mystica, full of lovely and magical cities and the byways of the Saints.

II

ASSISI

I

ASSISI is the city of St. Francis. It is impossible to think of anything but his simple and lovely life within the walls of what is really a great shrunken village, lean and emaciated with years and the ecstasies of the spiritual life. The little town has itself become a Religious, and has attained to a profound annihilation in God. Up and down its silent streets wander divine expectancies, a little sad and pessimistic, and yet beautiful withal, because long and long ago Jesus of Nazareth seemed to have returned to His earth. One finds oneself alone with the twelfth and thirteenth centuries and all that they have bequeathed and stored for us within the walls of this softly coloured city, warm with divine love, ruddy with the pale coloured life of Subasio, from whose side she has, as it were, been hewn, with only so simple a rearrangement of the stones as will allow of life, while one contemplates the story of Jesus of Nazareth or St. Francis of Assisi. Hallowed by the tears and the footsteps, sorrowful and bleeding, of many thousands of pilgrims, she has grown lovely under their love, beautiful in some exquisite Christian manner with the sorrows that the world has laid at her feet for hundreds of years now; a simple country virgin, very pure and innocent, who has had but one lover, Christ her Lord. Rome, the insatiable mistress of innumerable Gods and Kings, and Dreams and Tyrants and Liberty, who, years and years ago before Assisi was born, dreamed of the

strange divine figure of Christ, and desired Him, leading
Him and His dream away as captives and laying at His feet
the empire of the world, when, after more than a thousand
years, she saw Him arise again still unchanged, still the lover
of Love, humble and untouched by beauty in this quiet
country place, she came to Him, well, almost as a suppliant,
conquered by His simplicity, finding in just that something
indestructible, something that would support her in her profoundest tragedy; so that the Pope, amid all the uncouth and
yet Roman splendour of courts and courtly ways, sees St.
Francis upholding the Church which is about to fall, and
again later sees him, well, as another Son of God, with divine
and simple love radiant in his face, and the strange wounds
that the world has inflicted upon him, gaping insistent in his
hands, his feet, his side. It was indeed a vision of the Son
of God that Rome, dreaming in the chamber of the Bridegroom, beheld suddenly in that mysterious century, and
awaking found him gone, wandering in country places as of
old, divine love himself, simple and lonely as a star shining
over Assisi. And to-day, as always, there is nothing, can be
nothing in Assisi but just that. Goethe, the pioneer as it
were of the modern world, beautiful as a god, content with
nothing save beauty—visible, tangible beauty, for the most
part—coming to Assisi from Rome, in some unaccountable
way, blinded perhaps by the splendour and the strength of
Rome and Roman thoughts, missed it all : the very spirit of
the divine village, its ever-living beauty, its humanism ; preferring the beautiful little Temple of Minerva, which is still
divine but with quite another kind of beauty. Well, that was
perhaps one of the limitations of his genius, northern as it
was, choosing rather the far-fetched greatness, the eloquent
renown of the Rose of Rome than the Lily of Love, white and
immaculate in the fields, that was beautiful after all, chiefly
for country people, shepherds, and goatherds, or the labourers

in the vineyards who had never seen the crimson majesty of the immortal city, splendid with swords. He perhaps, being of the North, feared the mysticism so likely to conquer even so converted a barbarian as himself, and in that great refusal we see perhaps the first suggestion of his limitations.

As you come to Assisi from Perugia along that old and fair way down the hillsides pleasant with olives, into the immense valley of Spoleto, just before the little village of Ponte S. Giovanni, you come upon the immense tombs of the Volumnii, an Etruscan Necropolis of about 150 B.C. It suggests at once to the traveller the depth of antiquity around him, seeing that almost by chance as it were he has come upon the dust of men of whom we know nothing, or next to nothing, whose very language we cannot read, whose legend we cannot decipher. They too had their heroes and their gods, tragic in their deaths, immortal in the beauty of men's thoughts concerning them. Tall Troy, whose topless towers crash through the centuries, had gates for them, before which we too have waited for a glimpse of Helen whose beauty launched the beautiful ships, whose love shattered the world. Was it not here that Troilus died, and Hector in his despair left his perfect wife never to return? Iphigenia, the daughter of Agamemnon with the shoulders of ivory, is almost sacrificed, and Charon waits with his boat just touching the sands of life; and the human sacrifice that in all ages has fascinated the minds of men is found here too, the victim held down by the hair upon the altar, the priest as ever the slayer, ready with his weapon. Well, even so long ago men, it seems, were entranced by just life; as now, so of old, we appeased the gods, we went forth to battle, we loved, we laughed, and were in despair.

As you drive over the beautiful plain towards Assisi, in the footsteps of many armies, it is such thoughts that entice you from the sweet monotony of the way. And suddenly and in a moment, if you are fortunate, you are involved in the simple splendour of some procession between the fields— Madonna in all her robes carried before an adoring people, while the fields and the vines, the corn and the olives quicken before her gracious coming, and the chant of the boys, the immortal words of the priest, persuade you that as always men go forth until the evening and think of the wind and are subject to the sun and watch the clouds; sowing and reaping because the light is sweet and morning a pleasant thing, and time and chance happen to all. And gradually you understand that it was in this place that St. Francis was born and lived and died; that his footsteps have silenced the tramping of Cæsar's armies; that his gentle feet have bled along this very way. No splendour that came after—the pale, bloodless face, beautiful with the tragedy of sin, terrible with ambition, weary for sleep, of Cesare Borgia, or the carnival armies, Gothic, wonderful, of Charles VIII. of France, or any majesty or renown, has ever been strong enough to rase out his remembrance or to crush the flowers that lifted their heads in the summer days to catch the wind of his coat. And almost before you are aware St. Mary of the Angels stands before you, like a tall and perfect lily, waiting to give you something of the fragrance she has kept through all the centuries. For in all the valley of Spoleto there is none like to her. Standing as she does in the midst of the plain the sun kisses her with the soft kisses of the hills, transfiguring her with his glory. She guards a holy place, the Porziuncola and the cell where St. Francis died. It is said that the little chapel over which the great church has arisen was built by four unknown pilgrims, so that they might place in safety a relic of the tomb of the Blessed Virgin which they had brought from

Jerusalem. It has also been said that on the night of September 26, 1182, in which St. Francis was born, the angels' songs were heard here as on the birthday of Christ in the fields near Bethlehem. So legends grow in an old mysterious land where saints have walked; and especially here in Assisi, because in everything the legend of St. Francis must conform to the legend of Christ. But however it may have been with those pilgrims of the fourth century, St. Benedict, in the earlier part of the sixth, finding the place in decay and almost abandoned, rebuilt it for the monks of his Order, and called it Porziuncola—the little portion, because it was so small among the Benedictine foundations. And so when St. Francis came he also found the place in ruin, and having repaired S. Damiano, rebuilt this little church also, and begged the Benedictine abbot of Monte Subasio to give it to him, the which he did on condition that it should always be the mother-house of the Franciscan Order. Well, as you find the place to-day, rough and rude enough to prove the legend true, if you were inclined to doubt it, it is, I think, perhaps the most touching place in all Italy in its simplicity and littleness. The sumptuous and huge church which covers it is lost sight of beside so small a thing, and you find yourself won almost against your will by its sweet country face that has seen St. Francis singing the Office, and indeed been built by him and heard his voice and felt his tears and watched him die. As I came on one of the unforgettable and lovely days of my life—itself perhaps the loveliest—to St. Mary of the Angels from Perugia, the sun shone all the way, and the flowers were breaking in waves of blue and white and gold over the valley, for it was May. A friar, speaking my dear mother tongue to a pilgrim who would hardly let him go, came smiling towards me, and with the simpleness and kindness common in Italy, led me round the sacred church. To him it was a work of infinite pleasure, he assured me,

and yet I cannot but think that it must often have been
tedious. Almost all his world that he showed with such
eager courtesy was fairyland to so many of his guests.
'They do not understand, they do not understand,' was his
excuse for them. Well, to me at least, it seemed difficult to
misunderstand so expressive a place. Under the great dome
of St. Mary's stands the Porziuncola, a modern fresco of
no merit at all over the little west entrance; a fresco by
Perugino, robbed of all its sweetness by restoration and
disaster, in the like position at the east end. A fresco of
Fiorenzo di Lorenzo used to be on the wall here, but it has
been sold.

You may hear Mass in the Porziuncola very simply at ten
o'clock every morning, and surely in that dim and fragrant
chapel there could be no more fitting mystery. Over an
altar to the left of the nave and to the left of the chapel
of the Blessed Sacrament is a beautiful work in the terra-
cotta of the della Robbia. In the midst Madonna is crowned,
while to the left St. Francis receives the stigmata, to the
right St. Jerome in a vision sees Christ on the Cross.
Beneath are a lovely Annunciation, a Nativity, and Adoration of the Magi. The friar then leads you back across the
nave of the great church to the tiny room in which St.
Francis died. Outside there is a panel painted with a
portrait of St. Francis by Giunta Pisano. The panel is said
to have been part of the bier on which he was carried to
S. Chiara. On the altar, very dim and withdrawn till the
friar lights a taper, is a lovely statue of St. Francis by
Luca della Robbia. It is one of the most beautiful things
in Assisi—the sweet emaciated face, the spare but exquisite
hands, the profound expressiveness of the work, hold you
all day beyond even the frescoes at S. Francesco. One is
slow to look at the frescoes, by Lo Spagna, of the twelve
disciples of St. Francis that cover the walls of this tiny

cell, for the face of the Saint haunts one. In truth, it must have been so that Christ appeared when He was exceeding sorrowful ; it might stand for a statue of Man, seeing that it expresses certainly that which has captured the world. The friar shows you also the cord which the saint wore round his habit stained with blood. But even the pilgrim cannot turn to this from the perfection and beauty of the statue without reluctance. No nobler statue did Luca ever make in that humble way of his, interested as he always was in the simpler and less splendid things, even in his material, which, for the most part, was neither marble nor stone but just earth, from which he contrived infinite beauty.

I passed out of the cell where St. Francis died into the sumptuous modern sacristy with something of a shock, to find the walls panelled in woodwork, carved curiously, of the sixteenth century. There I found a lovely half-length Christ by Perugino, perhaps a genuine work of his; and yet it is, I venture to think, doubtful. There is a little chapel on the right where is an early picture of St. Francis, attributed to Giunta Pisano. It is said to have been painted on a plank of the saint's bed.

And so we came into the rose garden ; it is, perhaps, something of a disappointment. It may well be we had expected too much, but it is railed in so securely and it is so small that St. Francis must have had much ado to roll in it at all. No doubt pious hands must be kept from pious theft. One remembers the story of the wedding-ring at Perugia—and yet, and yet. . . . 'Well,' said the friar, 'this is Saint Francis's Rose Garden. One night he was tempted, oh, tempted of the devil, and so he came into this little garden, which was full of briars ; there he rolled among the thorns, but they suddenly burst into flower, and always they grow without thorns now. If we take them away either they die,' he said sorrowfully, 'or they grow with thorns. Either they die or they grow with thorns,' he repeated sorrowfully. And in answer to some question, 'they blossom in June and are red. It was in January that this miracle happened,' he continued softly, 'and his angel led him to the altar of Porziuncola and he saw Madonna and the angels, and Christ on His Throne in Heaven.'

But it is the Cappella delle Rose, which St. Bonaventura built over a cave where St. Francis would spend much time in prayer, that is really of great interest. There in the tiny sanctuary are the frescoes of a pupil of Perugino or Pintoricchio, Tiberio d'Assisi, which show something of the oversweetness of those masters—Perugino's sentimentality, Pintoricchio's delight in pretty faces—and yet they seem in place in this tiny chapel which is, after all, a sanctuary of sentiment. For around St. Francis, that little poor man of Assisi, the world—Catholic, Protestant, Agnostic, or what you will—has gushed now for many years. But the world does not understand him. His profoundly mystical soul, simple only in love and the limitations of his experience, has entranced the Protestant chiefly because he has come to think of Christ as a kind of adorable Free-thinker, and of St. Francis as a forerunner of Martin Luther. In my short study of his life, in another part of this book, I have tried to correct such misplaced enthusiasm, and to show St. Francis as the loyal son of the Catholic Church, which he ever looked upon as his Mother and his Father. Concerned for the most part as he was with the reality of the spiritual life and with poverty, nothing would have disgusted him more than the enthusiastic sentimentality of those who, without understanding either him or his faith, come to worship him. Fountains of scent, oceans of unmeaning sentimental tears begin to surround his legend ; a brutal excitement, a feeble consternation infest even the quiet spot where he lived and died; while a Protestant Frenchman has made his fame out of this saint of the Catholic Church, certainly to the satisfaction of the innumerable women who, with sighs, with outpouring of unsatisfied dreams, stay at Assisi or Perugia for a few days, on their way to and from Rome and Florence. Yes, St. Francis has conquered the world, but his victory would have made him weep.

II

The way from St. Mary of the Angels to Assisi is a pleasant way if you go by the byways through the vineyards and olive gardens. It is hot and dusty by the road, but the two miles which separate the great church from the city are charming, with their mighty views up the valley of Spoleto and back towards Perugia and down the valley of the Tiber. Piled up on itself, as it were, the little town glows in the sunlight almost like some precious rosy stone. You are attracted from the first by its homely face, its old-world simplicity, its placid brows. Many beggars haunt you with their frightful troubles; you are dazzled by their agonies, their importunity, their simple faith in their own miseries as their saviours. The sun almost persuades you that you have wandered into the forgotten centuries; the hum of the summer, the voices of the beggars, the dust and the light seem like a dream. It is out of all this that you come quite suddenly into the cool darkness of the lower church of S. Francesco. It seems more like a fortress than a church as you climb the hill, built as it is on arches of stone against the hillside; but as you enter you seem to have wandered back into the North with its twilight churches, where the sun never shines and they worship God in semi-darkness. And, indeed, it is not till evening that the level light of the setting sun throws a glory over the splendour that in the morning is rather felt than seen. S. Francesco is the mighty and splendid tomb of the little poor man, who should have been buried in the lee of some wood where birds sing, and the earth is carpeted in spring with primroses. Built by Frate Elias in memory and honour of his master, it will in reality ever remain his own monument, on which the masters of the Roman school, Pietro Cavallini and his pupils, Giotto and his pupils, and Simone Martini did not hesitate to lavish their genius. Originally, it would appear, nothing more than a nave, choir, and small transepts—indeed, very like to the upper church as we see it to-day—gradually, during the thirteenth and fourteenth centuries, the chapels were added, while Giotto himself is said to have built the Campanile. The great monastery beside the church was built, too, in the thirteenth century; it was secularised in 1866, and but few friars remain to guard the very precious memories of the Order. The church, however, is in the hands of the Conventuals of the Franciscan Order, and not, as St. Mary of the Angels, in the hands of the Friars Minor.

There is a wealth of precious work in the church—frescoes of Pietro Cavallini, untouched save by the hand of Time; magnificent Giottos, and frescoes of his school; Simone Martinis of surpassing loveliness, and it may be an Ottaviano Nelli. It is here, perhaps, better than anywhere else in Italy, that the beginnings of Italian Art can be studied. It is the irony of fate that the darkness which infests the church should make a sight of all the splendour so difficult. I shall content myself here with writing of the more important things without attempting to speak of everything in the church. There is a number of tombs quite uninteresting to the ordinary traveller, such as that of the Queen of Cyprus, who died in Assisi in 1240. It will be sufficient to notice the frescoes, not adequately, but as adequately as is possible, in a book concerned after all with other things beside Assisi.

To the left of the entrance is a Madonna with St. Francis and St. Anthony Abbot and some Bishop, by Ottaviano Nelli, whose beautiful work at Gubbio is so much better than anything else we have from his hand. He is supposed to have taught Gentile da Fabriano, and certainly, according to Vasari, that painter worked at Gubbio in his youth. But while Gentile's work is always, or nearly always, strong and lovely, Ottaviano's only once, in the Madonna del Belvidere at Gubbio, attains perfect beauty and expression, for the rest it remains in a sort of helplessness, often lovely enough certainly, but a little nerveless and provincial.

At the end of the vestibule, opposite the great doors, is the Albornoz Chapel. Cardinal Gil Alvarez Carillo di Albornoz was related to the royal houses of Léon and Aragon: he was born at Cuenca. While still a young man he was made Archbishop of Toledo by Alfonso XI. of Castile, whose life he is said to have saved at Tarifa in battle with the Moors in 1340. After the siege of Algeciras, which he conducted successfully, he was made knight. Pedro el Cruel hated him because he rebuked him for his licentious life, and on this account he fled to the Pope at Avignon. Clement VI. it was, a learned man, who made him Cardinal. In 1355 the Pope sent him to Italy as his General, to prepare for the return of the Holy See. Albornoz, certainly one of the most terrible captains Italy has ever seen, little by little swept the Patrimony and Romagna clean of those condottieri and bandits who in the absence of the Papacy had fallen on the country like a pestilence. Albornoz seems to have loved St. Francis. He founded this chapel not long after he was made cardinal, and dying in 1367 was buried here in that year. The frescoes which Vasari tells us are by Buffalmacco, but which certain later critics have given to Pace da Faenza, are

C

not in the Giottesque tradition, and indeed in many ways are but third-rate works : they represent the story of St. Catherine of Alexandria, while under the arch we may see the consecration of Albornoz, and opposite St. Louis between his bishops. Third-rate though they be, in the Marriage of St. Catherine, where at the supreme moment she seems to faint with awe and love, an idea of much force and beauty has found almost perfect expression.

As you pass into the nave of the great church the darkness is deeper. The first chapel on the left, S. Martino, has been painted in fresco by Simone Martini with scenes from the life of S. Martino. Simone Martini was born probably in Siena in 1283. He was the pupil of Duccio, and not, so far as his work tells us, much influenced by Giotto—certainly not his pupil. Far more in sympathy with the intentions, as yet unexpressed, of Umbrian art than with those of Florence, already pointed out by Giotto, he at least felt and, indeed, expressed very beautifully the splendour and magnificence of life, the sheer loveliness of our world. For painting, as such, for its problems and difficulties, unlike Giotto, he had no care. He has been called 'the most lovable of all the Italian artists before the Renaissance,' and, indeed, looking on the strange beauty of his work here, in the Cappella di San Martino, who can doubt it? He is so much sweeter than Giotto ; has, indeed, a sense of beauty subtler than, though not so profound as his. Is there anything in all pre-Renaissance art more exquisite than these frescoes where St. Martin divides his cloak with a beggar, and later, as he lies asleep, has a vision of Christ wearing that very cloak? And best of all, perhaps, that wonderful piece of work in which we see the young St. Martin girded with the sword and all the accoutrements of knighthood, his hands clasped in prayer. The gaiety of all that—for even to-day in Italy religion is not without a sense of joy quite other than that

sombre and unctuous pleasantness we have caught from the
Germans—the beauty of the young men who look on, the
splendour and magnificence of the emperor, the loveliness
of the thought, the perfection of the craft! A great painter,
you might almost feel inclined to say till you think of the
impassioned work of Giotto, and all it meant to Italy, and
means to us. And yet Simone Martini is a great painter,
though scarcely an original painter as Giotto is. He was
content to carry out the ideas of his master Duccio, by
whom he seems always to have been overshadowed. There
is nothing of the immense vitality of the Florentine. When
his young men stretch out their arms, as in this fresco, you
do not feel as though they might embrace you, as you do
with Giotto over and over again. To him life was a kind
of picture, a little unreal but wonderfully decorative and very
beautiful, in which nothing so indiscreet as movement, the
very significance of life itself, must ever come.[1] It might be
said that he was the most beautiful illustrator of the Book
of Life in all the pre-Renaissance, but the whole vitality and
reality of life were in the text. One looks on these frescoes
always with new joy, but never with the profound exulta-
tion with which one gazes at Giotto's work here and elsewhere. St. Martin, in the upper end of the frescoes, is
ordained and retires to Albenga; he preaches in some city,
possibly Chartres; he restores a child to life, and at last
dies. In all this work, too detailed to describe, one finds the
same sense of entrancing beauty. And so when in 1344
Simone Martini came to die, he had at any rate saved thus
much for us from all the visions of his life. Content with
beauty, and with beauty only, life came to him always as

[1] Professor Langton Douglas reminds me of Simone's much repainted
equestrian portrait of Guidoriccio da Fogliano. 'No knight of the
Renaissance,' he truly says, 'save Colleoni and Gattemalata moves
more surely and irresistibly towards his enemy.'

a perfect mistress—a little fantastic, a little unreal, but with grace, with charm, with joy; he has told us of her—well after all, as he had been taught to do.

Passing down the nave we come on the right to the pulpit, certainly one of the loveliest things in the church. Beneath it Madonna Iacoba de' Frangipani was buried in 1239 ; you may still read the epitaph : *Hic iacet Iacoba sancta nobilisque romana.* This noble Roman [1] lady was with St. Francis when he died. It was in her house he had stayed when in Rome, and she was one of his most eager disciples. Above the pulpit is an extremely lovely fresco, by Pietro Lorenzetti or another, of the Coronation of the Blessed Virgin.

Opposite the Cappella di San Martino is the Chapel of the Blessed Sacrament; fortunately, the frescoes attributed to Dono Doni are of no artistic interest. The next chapel on this side is that of St. Antony of Padua, which also contains nothing to keep the traveller. The next chapel, however, that of S. Maria Maddalena, which you enter by way of the south transept, is intensely interesting. It contains frescoes, by a pupil of Giotto, representing the legend of St. Mary Magdalen and St. Mary of Egypt. One may see here the condition of painting about the time of Giotto's death. The roof is painted with figures of Christ, Lazarus, St. Mary Magdalen, and St. Mary of Egypt. Below we find the Raising of Lazarus, and Christ in the house of Simon, where St. Mary anointed His feet, the *Noli me tangere*, and St. Mary miraculously coming to Marseilles, where, the legend says, she and Lazarus and Martha founded a church. In the lunettes are the Communion, Zosimus giving St. Mary of Egypt his clothes, and St. Mary Magdalen carried to heaven. Attributed to Buffalmacco, these frescoes are undoubtedly the work of a careful disciple of Giotto. Who he was I know not. But they are unmistakably Giottesque

[1] See pages 300-303.

the finest of the series, and the nearest to Giotto's own work, being the *Noli me tangere*. Under the arch towards the nave are some marvellously lovely figures of saints. How different is this humble yet enthusiastic work from the exquisite eloquence of Simone Martini!

Coming now to the high altar, around which are the beautiful works of Giotto himself, we are face to face with the most important paintings in the church. In the tomb below the altar, in the rock of the mountain itself, hidden there for six hundred years, lies the body of St. Francis; while above Giotto has told, with a sincerity and a genius never perhaps equalled, the story of the Poverello's triumph. This spot is really the centre of Assisi; it is in itself almost the reason for the existence of the city. Very difficult to see because of the darkness and the anxiety of the friars that one should not tread upon the steps of the altar over the tomb of the saint, the light—such as it is—is, I think, best in the afternoon, when the sun streams through the great windows of the choir. It is, however, extremely disappointing that these, among the noblest works of Giotto, should be so invisible. To the west you see the Mystical Marriage of St. Francis with Lady Poverty. Christ Himself marries them; while Poverty, in tatters, stands among the flowers and thorns. On her left is Charity, who gives her a burning heart; on her right Faith hands her a ring. Of the crowd which watches this most strange wedding, part is scornful, but part is full of understanding. At the feet of Poverty a dog barks, a boy pelts her with stones, and even a child thrusts at her with a stick. A kind of fear seems to possess the crowd, and it is for this cause they hate her. Among the crowd itself many kind or malicious, simple or worldly actions may be found; the whole picture is, as it were, an action. Above, many angels await the end of this mystical wedding.

To the south you see Chastity praying in a strong tower; some knight is receiving baptism before putting on his armour; while Penance drives away a demon, St. Francis receives certain novices. A winged figure dressed as a monk drives away a woman who seems to symbolise Desire, for she is blindfolded, and her feet are talons, while she is girt with human hearts, and her head is crowned with roses. Behind all comes Death.

To the north you see Obedience betwixt Prudence and Humility. Behind is a vision of Christ on the Cross, while before a friar kneels, holding a yoke upon which Obedience lays her hand, while with a gesture she commands silence.

To the east you see St. Francis in Glory in the robe of the deacon, the dalmatic, seated on a throne surrounded by angels.

These, the mature works of Giotto and his pupils, surrounded as they are in S. Francesco by the work of his predecessors and of his immediate followers, are of deep interest. Moreover, we may compare them with his own perfect work in the south transept and his early work in the Upper Church. In looking at them we may see the development of a great style—a style that dominated Italian art, and to a large extent insisted upon its adherence. While showing, as in all his work, an emancipation from the Byzantine manner, he is still a complete mystic, or, at least, immersed in allegory. He is not yet so much concerned with the expression of life as with the expression of thought. The desire for beauty, almost for its own sake, so exquisitely expressed in the Sienese painters, Duccio and Simone Martini, is by no means passionate with him. His people, his angels, his saints are seldom altogether lovely, only they have character, thoughtfulness, and, above all, life, in a way quite new—miraculously new, in a world concerned for the most part with lesser things. He was, perhaps, the first Naturalist—by which I do not mean that he was a Realist minutely copying Nature in every fragment of anatomy, but that, though he knows infinitely less than Michelangelo, I do not find much difference in their power of rendering the action of a limb, the turn of the head, for instance; not so much difference, at any rate, as there is between Giotto and his predecessors. Even his drapery is naturalistic, it actually clothes living people. It is not there for its own sake only, beneath it life betrays itself. And though it is probably impossible to exaggerate Giotto's influence on his art, he is, as these frescoes show so well, a profound mystic, a student of Dante, or, at least, influenced by his thought. These strange and scornful little figures in the foreground of his fresco, the Marriage of St. Francis with Lady Poverty, are not living figures but symbols, and though their gestures are very life to his subtle mind in a time that was still wrapped in dreams from which he almost alone in the world was awakening, that by no means robs them of their symbolism. Was it from him that Botticelli, certainly as mystical, in an age so enthusiastic towards naturalism as that of the Renaissance, learned to take the Centaur quite simply as a symbol for Discord? Greater, more fundamental, than all his contemporaries, and than most of his successors, in his apprehension of life, as a decorative artist he is the equal, at least, of any man of his country. His genius dawned like a star on a world ignorant of its own perfection and completeness. He would seem to have achieved in a moment the antique point of view, almost, all that was worth having, that the world had lost, during the terrible centuries of the Middle Age; all that was essential, at least, in that old art; and thus, sooner or later, to have assured us of our very selves, of the history of painting, of the direction and progress of Art.

Turning now to the south transept we come upon more of

Giotto's work.[1] These frescoes cover both the eastern and the western walls and vaults. Above, on the west, we see the Birth of Christ, the Visitation, the Adoration of the Magi, the Presentation in the Temple, and the Crucifixion. On the east, Giotto has painted the Flight into Egypt, the Massacre of the Innocents, Christ in the Temple, Christ led home by his parents, a miracle of the resurrection of a child of the Spirri family, St. Francis by the side of a skeleton representing Death, and, over a door, a half-figure of the Saviour. Looking on these frescoes, we see perhaps more easily than in the works in the vaults over the high altar, the extraordinary breadth of Giotto's genius—its curiosity, its profound poetry, its impassioned and simple energy and wisdom. And yet, if we compare these frescoes with that early picture of the Madonna and Child, which has been given to Cimabue, we become aware that, after all, something has been lost. How lovely that fresco of the Madonna and Child is, how sacred and noble, and how surely it marks for us the change from the Byzantine manner, to the manner of Giotto. Yes, there is a more tremendous interval between them than between Giotto and the School of Athens in the Vatican, or the frescoes of the Sistine Chapel.

Beside that great fresco given to Cimabue, and close beside the entrance into the Cappella di S. Maria Maddalena, Simone Martini has painted the half figures of certain Franciscans : St. Francis himself, St. Louis of Toulouse, S. Chiara, or perhaps S. Agnese her sister.

The chapel of S. Niccolò, which closes the south transept, and that of S. Giovanni Battista which closes the north transept, are the two earliest chapels built in S. Francesco. Vasari tells us, and no documents remain to help us to con-

[1] See Crowe and Cavalcaselle, *History of Painting in Italy*, edited by Langton Douglas and S. Arthur Strong (Murray, 1903), vol. ii. p. 37 and note.

tradict him, that the architect was Agnolo of Siena, who
about 1310 built these chapels for the two prelates of the
Orsini house, Gian Gaetano and Napoleone. The frescoes in
the Chapel of S. Niccolò, attributed to Giottino,[1] tell us the
story of the life of St. Nicholas. Fine as these works are, full of
life and action, they seem to me less splendid than the frescoes
on the outside of the entrance arch. They represent the
death of a child, and his resurrection by St. Francis, one of
the finest compositions in the church, while above is a truly
marvellous fresco of the Annunciation, which some have
given to Puccio Capanna. Whoever may have painted
these frescoes, and it matters little enough, they are among
the most remarkable things in the church.

We now turn to the north transept. The vault is painted
with the story of the Passion by Giotto.[2] For long attributed to Puccio Capanna, it is now no longer possible to
doubt that Giotto was the author of them. Under these
frescoes on the left wall is perhaps the greatest treasure of
the church, that fresco by Pietro Lorenzetti of the Madonna
and Child between St. Francis and S. Giovanni Battista.
Here at last it might seem the art of Siena has really expressed itself in a sudden ecstacy of beauty that is really a
vision fading on the wall. Above it Pietro Cavallini, as it
is said, but as seems more likely Pietro Lorenzetti, has
painted the Crucifixion. You may see his work again in
the Chapel of St. John Baptist which closes this transept,
where over the altar he has tried to repeat, but in a less fortunate moment, that vision of Madonna between St. Francis
and St. John Baptist. The picture that stands close to it

---

[1] Mr. Langton Douglas (Crowe and Cavalcaselle, *op. cit.* vol. ii.
p. 199, note 6*) regards the authorship of these frescoes as an unsolved
problem. Whoever painted them was, I think, a very close follower
of Giotto.

[2] See Crowe and Cavalcaselle, *op. cit.* vol. ii. p. 147.

over the altar, Madonna enthroned between SS. Elizabeth, Francis, Catherine, Louis, Clare, and Anthony of Pudua, is one of the best works of the too much despised La Spagna.

The sacristy, which is entered from the transept, is full of wonders, the Blessing of Brother Leo, for instance, written by St. Francis himself, an early portrait of the Poverello, and many gifts and relics.

The Upper Church, entered from the outer sacristy, is a temple of colour and light. Of the same form as the Lower Church, save that it has no chapels, it gives us an idea of space and beauty such as we never receive in the Lower Church, where the low roof and the twilight mask the frescoes, the chapels, the colour on wall and ceiling, and even the very church itself, in the sombre, mysterious night of the catacombs. But in the Upper Church all is changed; it seems to glow like some perfect jewel, and almost to illumine itself rather than to receive light from the sun shining over the world outside. And it is here are preserved some of the most precious frescoes in Italy. Pietro Cavallini and his school have painted the roof with at least a perfect understanding of the decorative value of colour and design. We find Cavallini's work to-day in S. Maria in Trastevere, where in the Tribune certain mosaics by him, mentioned by Ghiberti, may still be seen. And lately frescoes of the Last Judgment, given to him by the newer criticism,[1] have been discovered in S. Cecilia in Trastevere. A pupil in the Roman school, that school which under the Cosmati attained to so great a position in Rome, Cavallini and his pupils seem to owe very little to Byzantine influence, but to have learned almost all they knew from works of classical antiquity. Their chief claim upon our notice, after the exquisite quality of their own work, is that they purged Giotto's work of the Byzantine tradition which was para-

---

[1] See Crowe and Cavalcaselle, *op. cit.* vol. i. p. 91.

mount in Florence and Siena, and showed him the true
source of all art, that marvellous antiquity which seemed to
have disappeared so completely. Their work here in the
Upper Church had an immense influence on Italian art.
Over the choir, the four Evangelists, with their symbols and
the Angel who should bring all things to their remembrance,
speak to the four quarters of the world. Then in the nave
we find Christ in benediction, the Blessed Virgin, St. John
Baptist, and St. Francis. And in the vault at the west end,
the four Doctors of the Catholic Church—St. Gregory with
the Dove, St. Ambrose, St. Jerome, and St. Augustine. In
the upper parts of the walls are painted scenes from the history of the world and the life of Christ; utterly ruined, in a
state of almost complete destruction, they are yet enough to
prove to us the power of that Roman school which died so
early and which has been so utterly forgotten. Even yet,
we may see the strange influence of antiquity in those genii
lurking so delightfully among the fruit and flowers; are
they not the ancient world itself almost, in its lightness, its
gaiety, its natural and yet fanciful beauty? It is here that
we may see the human form, not in its perfection, but perfectly apprehended, nevertheless, through the dimness of the
Christian centuries; not to reappear again till an Umbrian
painter, a man so much greater than his fame, Luca Signorelli, suddenly confronts us with it, in all its splendour, in
The Blessed Virgin holding Her Divine Son in Her Lap in
the Uffizi, where the shepherds are surely the dear gods of
Greece dispossessed on that musical night. In the four
Doctors of the Church, in the last vault towards the west
end of the nave, we find this painter of the Roman school at
his strongest. It is very obviously, it seems to me, the work
of a man who was thinking in mosaic rather than in fresco—
the immense dignity of the figures, and especially of the fur-
niture, being really the inspiration of an artist in the more

durable material. But after all, for us at least, slaves for the most part to our own æstheticisms, it is in the decorative value of these frescoes that we shall find our deepest delight. They are perfect, at least as decoration, and the colour has grown magical with age. The same painter is supposed to have painted the walls in their upper parts, of which, however, almost nothing remains but a lovely and ruined suggestion of precious colours on the damp walls. The influence upon Giotto of these works must have been very great. Working, he and his pupils, on the long spaces below these once majestic works, he could not have escaped their authority. Day by day as he worked on his frescoes of the Life of St. Francis, which it may well be are among his earliest works, these frescoes of an earlier master in all their beauty no doubt told him many a secret, confirming him in the way he desired to go, correcting his enthusiasm, and suggesting something of the exquisite dignity which we find in all his work. And though there might seem to be little enough left of the work of Giotto in the spoiled and over-painted frescoes we see to-day, how magnificent is the gesture of Pietro Bernadone in the fresco where St. Francis has been taken before the Bishop only to renounce his father for ever; how naturally, in another fresco—that of the death of the Lord of Celano—the saint rises in haste from the table where he is sitting; how lovely are those angels who bear him to heaven, clothed in light, in the ruined picture of his death. Well, in all this there is doubtless something of the teaching of the older painter learned with a new spirit that was all Giotto's own, that for some time, at any rate, he kept with him in his grave, but that was eventually to inform all Tuscan art. These frescoes by the young Giotto, repainted though they may be, are still fulfilled with a certain majestic beauty. In their simplicity and naturalness they are of the centre of the movement that was soon to excite all Italy to enthusiasm. Earlier than his work in the Lower Church, they precede it as dawn antici- pates noon, and they remain among the most precious things in Italy, strewn though she is with the triumphs of the world.

Before leaving S. Francesco, it is delightful to pass down the dark nave of the Lower Church, through the Capella di S. Antonio, to spend an hour in the cloistered Campo Santo, where the tall cypresses, like flameless tapers, tower over the dead. It is a place divided from the world, as certain days are from the rest of life, by an inviolable and sacred silence. One hour I spent there, snatched from the rest of life like a lily from the fingers of death, seems to me now, in the wastes of the years, the most· precious of my life. Slowly in the soft air the cypresses sway under the sky, and in that little island of once, noiseless with the footsteps of the dead, all that is really precious in the world seems to have come to me, graciously, silently obliterating everything else. Scarcely anything of sorrow is there in that tiny graveyard, and the brutal sentimentality of such a place of death, so vulgar and common with indifference in the North, is not to be found there. Oblivion has washed itself of iniquity in the summers of the earth, and those who once went up and down with so much charm and dignity and simple goodness, forgotten though they be, do not resent an intrusion made for love, meditation, or refreshment. Waiting there for a great thing, which never comes perhaps, though it may be we there caught a glimpse of it for the first time, we seem to hear the years trampling over Assisi, with hushed feet, their wings furled, while the many armies pass by and the Popes and the Emperors quarrel or are friends, the North flows and ebbs again, the Saints grasp at heaven, and ever the Umbrian summer is as lovely, and men and women are loving in the world, and the sun shines, then as now. It is in some such vague dream as this that one loses oneself in a place so noise-less as to echo even our thoughts.

It is really after many nights and days spent in her desolate piazzas, her tawny palaces, and her silent, cool churches, that Assisi becomes for us something real, something more visible than the life of her saint. How many beauties she has! That little chapel for instance, Cappella dei Pellegrini, all that is now left[1] of the Ospedale founded in 1431. Some of its frescoes they have carried away to the Museo Civico, but those in the chapel still remain, as does the chapel itself, a little shadowy place in the wide grass-grown street. Over the doorway under the eaves is a much damaged work of Matteo da Gualdo, the Eternal Father among the Cherubim.[2] Within, above the altar, the same master has painted, the Annunciation, the Madonna with her little Son between S. Giacomo and S. Antonio to whom the chapel is dedicated. The walls were painted by Pier Antonio da Foligno, called il Mezzastris, about 1482; on the right is the story of St. James of Compostella, and on the left that of St. Anthony Abbot. Above in the vault are the four Doctors of the Church, or, as some think S. Leo III., S. Isidore of Seville, St. Augustine, and S. Bonaventura, by the same master.

Then there is the little Tempio di Minerva, close to the Palazzo Municipio: at first certainly it might seem to be but the fabric of a vision. Thence one passes perhaps up the precipitous ways to the Duomo of S. Rufino, whose façade is a vision of beauty, and at whose font St. Francis and the Emperor Frederic II. were baptised. There, too, is all that now remains of a very beautiful triptych by Niccolò da

---

[1] The Hospital of the Pilgrims was demolished in 1885.

[2] For all that concerns these frescoes consult Giuseppe Canonico Elisei, *Ill. St.-Or. della chiesa dei Pellegrini in Assisi.* Tip. Metastasio, Assisi, 1896.

the hair shirt, pitiful enough to-day, they too, like all relics, long ago should have obtained the satisfaction of oblivion. The tiny chapels in their simplicity, founded as they are on the bare rock, bring back to us perhaps, as nothing else can, the humility of the great saint. Even to pass through the doors it is necessary to stoop, and one is but divided from Nature by the greater silence. Just outside is the forest, a wooded cleft in the hillside, cool and dark, and full of a kind of mystery. One comes back to Assisi after a day on that mighty hillside as to a new world. Its warmth, its colour, its fantastic beauty seem more friendly, more homely than before. San Francesco is less dark, and all the people of the city have friendly faces, for outside in the woods and the forests, on the hills and in the cold tiny corridors of that strange refuge our own souls confronted us with be-seeching eyes, begging perhaps for a new tyranny, a new love, and the years devoured us; and we—how should we satisfy them ?

III

SPELLO

SPELLO is so near to Assisi, and the way thither is so
pleasant, that all save those who are desperate with
hurry should walk or drive thither from the city of St. Francis.
There is but little to be seen : a few Roman remains, an amphitheatre, a triumphal arch in ruin, a gateway, Porta Veneris,
over which lean the heads of two men and a woman ; and,
save for a sculpture here and there, that is all that is left of
the Roman Hispellum. It was not, however, to find Roman
things that I came to Spello on her little hill, but to see
the work of the great and exquisite sentimentalist, Pintoricchio. Nowhere save in Siena can you see him so well
as in this small clambering city, where in 1501—the year in
which Perugino was painting in the Cambio—he was busy
with his dainty superficial dreams in the Duomo, S. Maria
Maggiore. A painter who delighted in beauty, you might be
tempted to say as you look on his charming and exquisite
work to-day in the Baglioni Chapel there, in the Duomo.
Nor, after all, would you be wrong. Beauty, conceived as he
conceived it, was his conscious aim. I do not know in all
his work a woman who is not surpassing pretty. He pleases
us by the lightness of his touch, the daintiness of his perfect
handling, the nicety of his finish. Almost a painter of *genre*,
but of a cheerfulness never found in the North, he is so
much greater in the Sistine Chapel than anywhere else that
we are always startled to find so much promise, after all,

D

merely talent. He seems to have been so susceptible to influence that in the company of great men he becomes almost one of them, just as when left to himself, or with the subtle and scornful Perugino, he becomes—well, just a painter of 'out of doors,' a great 'space composer,' as Mr. Berenson has said, so much less great than his master.

The Duomo in its small piazza is not a very interesting building. The western façade is simple, and some Romanesque designs of animals and vines and flowers, together with reliefs, are on the doorway. In a simple and more country fashion they suggest the great Romanesque bestiaries at Spoleto. In the Cappella del Sacramento, however, we find the frescoes we have come to see: on the left the Annunciation, in front of us the Nativity, and on the right Christ among the Doctors. The best of these is, to my mind, the Annunciation. For once Pintoricchio seems to have been possessed, really captured, by the beauty of the vision of Mary. She, that beautiful maid who has become the loveliest of all our loves, winnowed by the dreams of men, persuaded by their prayers, wearied but still listening to our devotion, is still in the dawn of her simplicity, reading some simple and entrancing book, when suddenly, before she can turn the page, God has sent His messenger, a kind of splendid knight, to tell her of her destiny. So it is in the midst of her day-dreams that she is interrupted, and having overheard, as it were, the love of the Rose of Sharon, is suddenly confronted with Love himself, whose Mother, in a less happy way than in the old Greek world, but with a new tenderness and refinement, she, a white maid, scarcely wakened to life as yet, is to be. There is nothing here of the profound melancholy of Botticelli, whose Madonnas looked, it might seem, for some more human affection, nor of the profound and subtle joy of Leonardo's Virgins. Here is the story as it has been told to us in our childhood, not

actually as it came to us then, but as we remember it now
when we are old, seizing the superficial beauty of all that,
and unable to comprehend its sheer loveliness and perfection
since it has become too simple for us. In the Nativity
Pintoricchio is less fine, is indeed what we have come to
regard him—a mere pupil of Perugino, without that master's
magical spaciousness and splendour of proportion. It is the
same with the Christ among the Doctors, and yet the picture
strikes one with a kind of thoughtfulness. This man might
surely have been a great painter had he been brought up in
the thoughtful Florentine tradition. He is without strength:
Umbria with her light and space and gentle landscapes, soft
hills and sweet plains full of sunshine, was too enervating for a
personality susceptible to every influence, so sensitive was it.
In contact with Rome he achieved a kind of greatness, in
contact with the valley of St. Francis and mystical Italy he
attained only to a reticent sentimentality; understanding
the achievement of Perugino, and yet unable to express himself through the same medium of perfect spaciousness and
light, he gave away his heart to the beauty of some girl who
haunts all his pictures. Her hair is gathered across her ears
and falls behind her, her forehead is beautiful and delicate,
she has dove's eyes, and her ears are a little pointed. Her
body is a lily of the field, and her hands are small and veined,
and softer than the tendrils of the vine. At first we turn
away our eyes from her lest we should love her as he did,
but little by little we weary of her, for she looks forth on
the morning fair as the moon, and her light and loveliness
are borrowed. ·Little by little we see that she is not beautiful; it is the sun or the sky or the air that has given her
something that she herself will never possess. Surrounded
by these, inspired by their splendour, we suffer her, though
we be wearied with her pretty beauty, and soon we are able
to forget her altogether in the delight of another and

infinitely greater master who led her away and transformed
her with his genius and love, and from many a canvas she
looks at us, an immortal soul shining in her eyes.

One wanders to the Gothic church of S. Andrea, where
is a large altar-piece by Pintoricchio of Madonna and Saints,
painted in 1508; the same qualities meet us in this work,
only a little more superficial in its exquisite pictorial prettiness, as in the frescoes in the Duomo.   In the Municipio is a
fine picture by Niccolò da Foligno taken from the Convento
di Vallegloria, a Crucifixion where beside our Lord stand
Madonna and St. John the Divine, and a Bishop, while at the
foot of the Cross St. Francis kneels.   It is certainly one of
the loveliest of all Niccolò's works.

It is delightful to walk to S. Girolamo under the olives,
with its early frescoes by Pintoricchio, where it is so cool
in the glittering shade, and look down the valley of Spoleto,
that ever since we left Perugia has been opening before us.
It was here, as I sat reading on a May afternoon, that I saw
a poor man sowing his seed in his tiny field, broadcast, with
a primitive and splendid gesture, as in the early world.   And
having made an end of his work, in a corner of the field he
knelt and prayed to God.   Thus in old Umbria they scatter
their seed and their prayers, and are sure of a miracle.   It
was for such a cause that St. Francis lived and made his
Canticle of the Sun; and St. Angela heard Christ speak by
the wayside; and Blessed Columba wandered in sadness
through many cities.   And I, who go up and down over the
world thinking of pictures and the little difference 'twixt
this and this, what am I beside such a man as that?   Has
it made glad my heart, that nothing can happen or stir in
the fields without God's approbation?   Have I understood
that God is my friend who holds all chances, all awakening,
and the being of all things, fast in His hands?   Have I
begged nothing of man before first reminding myself of

God ? Ah, but my peasant had understood the simplicity of life as I have never done, for he is one with the absolute things of Nature. The corn which he sowed he knows lived and died, and, if God will, shall live again, grow and be green, washed with the rain, swept by the wind, dried with the sun, and golden in the summer heat. In the cool nights under the stars it is watched over by some divinity; then reaped with labour and joy, and all for him a sinner. Happy in his fields, how shall I attain to his simplicity in the noisy and trumpery cities where I shall not see the sky ?

IV

FOLIGNO AND MONTEFALCO

FOLIGNO, in the broad valley of Spoleto, is known to the world as the city of the Blessed Angela, or as the town of a few towers that hovers in the background of Raphael's picture, Madonna di Foligno. A busy enough place on a market-day, seeing that to-day as ever it is the meeting-place of the roads from Arezzo, Perugia, and the north, and from Ancona and the Adriatic, for Rome, it has not changed much, since the beginning of the sixteenth century when Raphael put it into his picture. The inns are somewhat poor, and the place itself of no great interest to the traveller, save that in its primitive prosperity it is perhaps alive, while Spello and Assisi are dead or dying, concerned only with things long ago. But Foligno is of a certain commercial importance and a military station. It is not, however, these things that will bring the traveller here on his way from Assisi to Spoleto, but perhaps a desire to see the church where Blessed Angela heard the preacher and confessed her sins, or it may be the strange frescoes of Ottaviano Nelli and Niccolò da Foligno, who was born here.

Going from the Piazza della Fiera into the Via Cavour, where on the right one passes the inn, the Albergo della Posta, a rather delightful hostelry, in no great while one comes to the Piazza Vittorio Emanuele, for Foligno is nothing if not modern. On the far side of this Piazza rises the Palazzo Trinci, the dwelling-place of a race which Symonds tells us was subject to the usual vicissitudes that dogged the steps of the great families of mediæval Italy. 'All that can be affirmed with accuracy,' he writes, 'is that in the Middle Ages, while Spello and Bevagna declined into the inferiority of dependent burghs, Foligno grew in power and became the chief commune of this part of Umbria. It was famous, during the last centuries of struggle between the Italian burghers and their native despots, for its peculiar ferocity in civil strife. Some of the bloodiest pages in mediæval Italian history are those which relate the vicissitudes of the Trinci family, the exhaustion of Foligno by internal discord, and its final submission to the Papal power.' The Trinci family, it would seem, was practically ruler of Foligno during the whole of the fourteenth century, and until in the early part of the fifteenth century the Pope expelled the house. Siding with the Church as they did in the struggle of Guelph and Ghibelline, it seems that they always had their power from the Pope, so that when in 1439 they quarrelled with Eugenius IV. they fell never to rise again. It was, however, in 1424 that they employed Ottaviano Nelli of Gubbio to paint their chapel for them, attaining thereby an immortality, at least among us travellers, that none of their other deeds would have given them. The chapel is built on the upper floor of the palace, and is painted in fresco with the History of the Blessed Virgin. On the roof Ottaviano has told the story in brief of St. Joachim and St. Anne, the mother and father of Mary.

For, as it happened, they loved one another and were wedded, but they had no child. For this cause they made their offerings in the Temple, and, being childless, they were suspected of some evil and turned adrift from the Temple where they served. St. Joachim in his wretchedness went into the desert, and there, after many years, an angel found him and told him to go to the Golden Gate of the Temple, nothing doubting, to meet St. Anne; and in truth it all happened as the angel said, and soon a child was born to them, the Blessed Virgin herself—Rosa Mystica, Lilium Convallium. Soon Mary herself is presented in the Temple, and marries Joseph, whose rod alone among those many others blossomed, and she too hears the message of the angel and Christ is born, and the great Kings come from the East to worship Him. He is crucified and ascends into heaven. The Apostles, as was most fitting, come to the Blessed Virgin before they go into all the world, as the Prince of Life had said. Suddenly they are recalled and see that most sweet Rose droop a little, and pass into the heaven of her Son.

Thus Ottaviano Nelli has painted almost the history of the birth of Christianity on these walls, where in the spring sunshine his work still tells us of one of the most curious souls in all Italy. Nor is he concerned only with that early age, for as though to suggest something of the years that were even then passing, he has painted St. John Baptist, St. Antony, St. Dominic, and St. Francis, certainly four of the greatest names even yet in Christian history. There is little, if any, æsthetic delight in these rude paintings, but as I think a very strange revelation of a soul as ecstatic as that of Jacopo da Todi. Here is a man who is simply outside the history of art. He does not partake of its progress; is, indeed, utterly indifferent to it. But on some day of sunshine after rain he has dreamed a dream or heard a voice or seen a vision, as St. Francis did, as Blessed Angela did, as St. Catherine did, and henceforth he is, as it were, indifferent to the world, intent as he must ever be on the sweet and strange experience that met him by the way. He is not in love with beauty at all, but is anxious to tell us his own dream, which was not so gentle a thing as those visions of Fra Angelico, whose contemporary he was, but something ruder, stronger, perhaps, and certainly less initiated, less of a compromise with the beauty of the world. 'A marsh growth,' Mr. Berenson has said, and indeed strange and

wonderful things come from a marsh. But it is, I think, as
the brother of God's fool that I at any rate have come to
think of him, uncouth as he is, without an elementary sense
of beauty, save that he had noted the colour on the hills,
perhaps, and found a kind of satisfaction in it; a painter
possessed, one who has seen a vision, and is dumb therefor;
but for him the great thing was to have seen that vision,
and for us that he has tried to tell us of it.

The Cathedral of S. Feliciano, on the eastern side of the
Piazza, is an entirely modernised building. S. Feliciano, to
whom it is dedicated, was à bishop, it is said, of this city in
the third century. But it is not for him that we come to it
to-day, without fresco, or painting,[1] or sculpture as it is; à
modern church, full of the horrible modern decorations that
deface the churches of the Catholic Faith all over the world.
It is for Blessed Angela's sake we come and meditate for a
moment amid all that modernity. For was it not on the
morning after her prayer to St. Francis for guidance, that
'she found a friar, a true chaplain of Christ, preaching
in the Church of S. Feliciano, to whom she made a full confession in bitterness, shame, and grief; receiving, still with
those after sobs shaking her like a weary child, his absolution.' It was from this point that Blessed Angela set out upon
her slow and wonderful journey towards purification, and
was for many years 'full of grief and without consolation.'
And it is of her we think as we pass to the old desecrated
Church of the Annunziata, where is a ruined work of
Perugino—the Baptism of Christ. To get to it we must pass
through the shop of a carpenter, which, to the traveller who
is something of a symbolist, will surely not be displeasing.

But it is perhaps in the Church of S. Niccolò, where Niccolò
da Foligno, the pupil of Benozzo Gozzoli of Florence, has
painted his magnificent altar-piece, that you will find your

---

[1] Yet Niccolò has left here a Crucifixion rather strange than beautiful, but not unworthy of him.

real excuse for having come to so strange a place as Foligno at all. Of Niccolò I speak elsewhere, but something may, perhaps, be said of this immense altar-piece in which he expresses himself so eagerly. In the central panel the Blessed Virgin and St. Joseph adore the Bambino. The figure of Mary, so strong and beautiful, seems to me to be Niccolò's best piece of work ; behind, not far away, the shepherds, impatient to see that Saviour who is Christ the Lord, run towards Bethlehem ; far and far away the three kings journey through a strange landscape to find the place where the Child lay. Above, Niccolò has painted, not without a real strength, the Resurrection, while at the sides are St. John Baptist, St. Nicholas, and St. Sebastian, with two others, and St. Nicholas of Tolentino, St. Jerome, St. John Evangelist, and St. Michael, with two others. The poor Coronation, in a side-chapel, is unworthy of this impassioned painter, but the triptych is, I think, his masterpiece, and worthy of patient study.

From S. Niccolò we pass again down the Via della Scuola, and turning to the right find the Piazza Giordano Bruno (did I not say well when I said Foligno was nothing if not modern ?), wherein are the two churches, S. Domenico and S. Maria infra Portas. The latter is a very ancient building, containing many antique frescoes utterly ruined. Many curious legends surround it with a kind of fascination which attracts one as much as the obvious beauty of the place. Once, so we are told, it was a temple of Diana ; and then again, that St. Peter celebrated Mass there in the little chapel on the right. However this may be, it is worthy of a visit chiefly because of its picturesque doorway, I suppose ; though, indeed, I found the church itself delightful.

So the traveller passes through Foligno, for the most part without enthusiasm ; and yet for me, I protest, it holds memories of summer days, when in the heat and dust I have found her churches cool, and her pictures at least free from the trail of the tourist and the vulgarity that the camera has thrust upon so many masterpieces. Moreover, when it is too hot in the valley one may go to Montefalco so easily, and find there coolness and silence. The road to Montefalco is beautiful with views of the ever-changing valley and the mountains; and the little city herself, high on her hill, is like a flaming torch thrust into the sky at noon. Her unfrequented streets seem still to shine with the beautiful footsteps of the saints; her aspect is that of some mystical hermit whose face is flushed with some marvellous sweet thought of God, whose eyes search heaven for His advent. Only a lesser witness than Assisi to the great Saint of Umbria, she seems to look across the wide valley to Assisi as a daughter towards her mother. It is not Giotto who has clothed her with his own inexpressible glory while telling the legend of St. Francis, but Benozzo Gozzoli, the pupil of Fra Angelico, who with his simple realism and delightful sense of the loveliness of such natural things as flowers and animals, has painted for her the same immortal story—not in vain, for his influence is found again and again in such men as Bonfigli, Niccolò da Foligno, whose work one has learned to care for in Foligno, and in Fiorenzo di Lorenzo. Nor, as it seems to me, did Pintoricchio wholly escape his charm; much of his delight in those natural beauties which crowd his pictures is, it may well be, owing to the work of this Tuscan painter. It is in the little Church of S. Francesco— desecrated now and used as a picture-gallery—in what was once the choir, that we find the frescoes of the life of St. Francis, painted in the middle of the fifteenth century by Benozzo Gozzoli. It is here for the first time almost we come upon that growth, that progress towards some half-apprehended ideal, which every legend seems to possess. St. Francis was a man so like to Christ as almost to be

mistaken for Him; it is therefore certain that he too, like to
the Prince of Life, was born in a stable. And even as old
Simeon and Anna had prophesied of Christ, so a pilgrim tells
of St. Francis, and a poor man spreads his coat for the saint
to tread on. Thus gradually in the minds of men St.
Francis became, even in lesser things, a kind of imitation of
Jesus of Nazareth. The first words of the *Fioretti* are a
proof of this, for it is there written that 'At first, needs
must we consider how the glorious Saint Francis in all the
acts of his life was conformed unto Christ the Blessed One:
how even as Christ in the beginning of His preaching chose
twelve Apostles to contemn all earthly things, to follow Him
in poverty and other virtues, so St. Francis in the beginning
chose out for the founding of the Order twelve companions,
possessors of the deepest poverty.' Thus in the very beginning of the legend we see how men's minds were impressed
by the strange and beautiful likeness of the Poverello to the
Saviour of the World. It is only strange to us of a material,
unimaginative age, that those who loved him should have
assured themselves of the fact that he too was born in a
stable, and was recognised by the old who had seen visions.
The frescoes continue the life of the saint almost as in the
upper church at Assisi, where the work of Giotto was doubtless known to Benozzo Gozzoli. They are particularly interesting as the early work of a man who, brought by Fra
Angelico to Rome and Orvieto—where, as here, his work is
really an imitation of his master—was later to develop a very
lovely kind of originality, as in the frescoes in the Riccardi
Chapel, or at S. Gimignano, or in his masterpieces at Pisa,
where he painted from 1469 to 1487. Here in Montefalco
he is the pupil of Fra Angelico, and almost nothing else. But
in that humility, the attitude of the scholar to one who was
so worthy of his allegiance, it may well be, we find his work
really greater than when he had, as it were, forsaken his

dreams of Christ for the beauty of the world. Of far more importance, it seems to me, in Umbrian than in Florentine art —where he is really a mediocrity—he was, in Central Italy certainly, the means of awakening much thought and energy in painting. It was Mr. Ruskin who called Ghirlandajo a goldsmith, and the same accusation might with even more justice be brought against Benozzo Gozzoli. Born near to Florence in 1420, he was, as indeed were other artists, apprenticed to some metal-worker, and even helped Ghiberti to forge the gates of Paradise. In his early work, however, under the influence of Angelico, he, having had a glimpse of heaven, turning to the earth found it every whit as fair. And it is at this moment, I think, while still under the spell of the Frate that he is valuable to us, rather than in his far more popular frescoes in the Riccardi Chapel. He tells the story of St. Francis here in Montefalco like a romance almost, in which the spirit of adventure, the call of the road, the magical persistence of to-morrow blend very happily with the lovely life of the little poor man. Looking on these frescoes, how tawdry seems the splendour of the journey of the three kings in Florence, how superficial the gorgeous works at Pisa! Here his work is so uninitiated, so boyish, as it were, as almost to disarm criticism, and in that very freshness, without ulterior ideas about art, he comes nearer by a very great way than Giotto to realising for us the spiritual beauty of St. Francis's life. Certainly for me he realises that spiritual beauty, and strives to make us realise it as no other painter of the Franciscan legend whose work I have seen has been able to do; and so, though for no other cause yet for this, Montefalco is worth the trouble of a visit. There is more of his work, sadly ruined now, in the chapels of the north aisle, of which the angels still keep something of their former beauty, and tell us not a little of his pupil Bonfigli. Perugino has left us a remembrance of his genius close to the west door—a lovely fresco of the Adoration of the Shepherds, whose landscape, with that wide Umbrian sky so full of light and space, tells us more of Italia Mystica than any picture I remember. For with Perugino there is at least this much saved from the wreck of time—to wit, his marvellous apprehension of space, of serene light, and the spiritual effect of just that. It is as though he had contrived to seize the poetry of a clear, serene sky and ample landscape, and to place in that apprehension all his treasure, so that in spite of his sentimentality and insincerity and scornfulness he is a great spiritual poet, composing out of just light and space wonderful dreams.

One of the best frescoes by Benozzo Gozzoli is in the monastic church of S. Fortunato, outside the city on the road to Spoleto, that terrible road on which the sun is so pitiless. That quiet master Tiberio d'Assisi, too, has painted there with all his charming serenity the story of St. Francis and the roses; and, indeed, the chapel where his frescoes dwell is the Chapel of the Rosary, a cool and lovely place in which to think of all the departed beauty of life and of the world. Shall we ever again, as in old days, love beauty and simple ways as they used to here in Italy, as we did ourselves long and long ago? I know not; but in England, so far away over the sea and the mountains, I am sure they dream very different dreams from these so delicately suggested to us in this cool church. There St. Francis is either a legend without any reality, a piece of exquisite but antiquated poetry, or a kind of rebel; while for us in Italy is he not alive? shall we not meet him, it may be, on the way, or in the hottest part of the road, or praying in the woods or the hills, or succouring some desperate poor man in the city? Is he really gone for ever, he of whom we were so sure—as Christ went, as all the saints have gone—leaving us so alone, never to return? It may well be ; and as one looks on his desecrated churches and dismantled convents, how can we dream it otherwise ? And yet, and yet, I am sure I shall see him, though not now ; I shall find him, though not here, the stars he looked on, are they not mine ? and the mountains that he loved I love too. In the byways I still hear him singing those French songs that he loved ; and Poverty is she less fair, or Obedience less to be desired, or Chastity so common, that every man has possessed her since the days when he went barefoot ? Ah, no ! As the sunset touches the hills at last, he will come back to us, and love us, and be good to us as of old. Be sure, though all men die, he is not dead. Though our dearest are forgotten like spilt wine, and we labour in that earth which is laden with our dead, we cannot watch the birds, or see bright fire, or hear the faint notes of a song across the valley, or hope for the spreading roses, or think of love, or care for the soft earth, or the tender sky, or the sound of waters without remembering him ; for he was part of all these things, joyfully feeling their secret life that we feel too, but seeing something beside in all the immortal beauty that we have forgotten, of which he will return to remind us.

V

TREVI AND THE TEMPLE OF CLITUMNUS

THE way from Foligno to Trevi takes us at once almost into Virgil's country, the valley of the Clitumnus. If the night is spent at Montefalco—not so daring an adventure as it seems—you may drive to Trevi by a way as pleasant as any in the world, following the river as it flows, and crossing both river and railway to climb up to Trevi. But the way by S. Martino is beautiful exceedingly, and the torrents after the rain only add to the charm of the road. All travellers have wondered at Trevi since she perched herself on the top of her precipitous hill, and though few of them visited her on her lonely height, she impressed her memory upon them even from a distance. 'I am so very tired and sleepy,' writes one of the most charming travellers that ever followed where the road led—to wit, Nathaniel Hawthorne—'I am so very tired and sleepy that I mean to mention nothing else to-night [did he not keep one of the most delightful note-books in the world?] except the city of Trevi, which, on the approach from Spoleto, seems so completely to cover a high-peaked hill from its pyramidal tip to its base. It was the strangest situation in which to build a town, where I suppose no horse can climb, and whence no inhabitant would think of descending into the world after the approach of age should begin to stiffen his joints. Looking back on this most picturesque of towns (which the road, of course, did not enter, as evidently no road could) I

64

saw that the highest part of the hill was quite covered with a crown of edifices, terminating in a church tower; while a part of the northern side was apparently too steep for building, and a cataract of houses flowed down the western and southern slopes. There seemed to be palaces, churches, everything that a city should have; but my eyes are heavy and I can write no more about them, only that I suppose the summit of the hill was artificially tenured, so as to prevent its crumbling down, and to enable it to support the platform of edifices which crowns it.'

We may perhaps remember for our comfort that Hawthorne was 'so very tired and sleepy,' since he uses so hateful, so vile a word as ' edifice ' twice in a short passage. Well, I was tired too when I came to Trevi at sunset, and the inn was poor even for an Umbrian albergo. But I was tired, and forgot the poverty of my room in the relief of being able to sleep; and indeed the bed was soft and clean, things common in Italy even in the poorest places.

There is nothing but a fine Perugino and the strange situation of the place itself to bring one to Trevi. Half-way down the hill, in the church of La Madonna delle Lagrime, is a magnificent picture, the Adoration of the Magi, set in a beautiful landscape, which it is said Perugino painted when he was seventy-five years old. Having seen this, there is really nothing else to keep you. A few pictures by Lo Spagna, a Madonna by Tiberio d'Assisi, and nothing more. But in one of the Lo Spagnas, the Entombment in La Madonna delle Lagrime, we see a copy of Raphael's picture in Rome very much in the same manner as Mr. Berenson has taught us to see a copy of Raphael's Sposalizio in the picture at Caen. It will perhaps interest the traveller to consider this.

But this is Virgil's country, and it is surely of him we should think when we first set foot in it. Could it have been

E

of any other city, think you, that he sang, than Trebia of old,
when in the second Georgic he writes—

> ' Adde tot egregias urbes, operumque laborem,
> Tot congesta manu praeruptis oppida saxis,
> Fluminaque antiquos subterlabentia muros.'

Ah, those rivers flowing beneath ancient walls! Was not
one of them the Clitumnus? For see, only a little earlier he
names her—

> ' Haec loca non tauri spirantes naribus ignem
> Invertere satis inmanis dentibus hydri ;
> Nec galeis densisque virum seges horruit hastis :
> Sed gravidae fruges et Bacchi Massicus humor
> Implevere ; tenent oleae armentaque laeta.
> Hinc bellator equus campo sese arduus infert ;
> Hinc albi, Clitumne, greges, et maxima taurus
> Victima, saepe tuo perfusi flumine sacro,
> Romanos ad templa deum duxere triumphos.'

The white, the snowy flocks of Clitumnus, where are they
now? And the bull that bathed in the sacred stream before
it was led the chiefest victim to the temples of the gods, the
triumphs of Rome; and these temples, are they quite gone
from our world? Let us see.

As you set out for Spoleto, if you are wise enough to go
by road—it is but twelve miles—when you have passed a
third of the way you come to a tiny temple high over the
stream, which here among the trees and the grass has its source.
And it is the temple of the river god that you look on, in all
its little splendour of silence and ruin. At least, I hope it is;
but some speak of a Christian building and will not listen to
Pliny. But however that may be, it is a place too beautiful
for any to pass by. I confess that, following the advice of the
younger Pliny, I bathed there, and found, as he had said,
the water as cold as snow. But in vain, in vain, I looked for
the god Clitumnus and could not find him, though Pliny said

that he was there, 'not naked but adorned with the toga.' And then in the shade, within sound of the beautiful river, I read again in Virgil. Is it not thus one might desire to spend endless days? But for us travellers who go on foot the sun is ever something of a god; imperious as he is he commands our days. He was slanting down the sky, reminding me that Spoleto was still far and I alone, and night would follow him. So I set out at last with regret; and later I came to S. Giacomo in Poseta, where I saw some of the finest Lo Spagnas in Italy, especially a Coronation of the Blessed Virgin. Later, as night fell, I came to the gates of Spoleto.

VI

SPOLETO

SPOLETO is a beautiful city of rose colour set on a high hill. Her silent, maze-like streets assured me at least of a primitive inn fully sufficient for a poor man, and of an almost entire absence of that mighty army of martyrs who are led about Italy by Baedeker. I came to her in an evil mood, hating my fellow-men, and especially the tourist, as I have said; I left her after a long time refreshed and rested, at peace with all men, having understood her beauty and her joy, and indeed it is in a kind of sudden and overwhelming joy that her towers pierce far up into the sky—those rosy towers that at dawn and midday and sunset are musical with soft bells, and that fade away into the night from rose colour to violet and deep purple under a sky of innumerable stars. Behind her rise higher and higher forests of primæval ilex, the sacred tree of the Latin race, shrouding her, as it were, in a mantle most rare of darkest green. Over her head, far away above the forests, a Franciscan convent soars like a brown bird floating on the wind, whose bells are not heard, but only seen to ring, or heard only in the most fortunate days when their sound is little more than the piping of those crested larks that sang St. Francis up to heaven. Joy, joyousness—it is the very mood of the city whose valleys are so soft and sweet. It was in one of these valleys, luminous beyond our northern dreams, that S. Angela of Foligno heard those breathless words of Christ: 'I love thee more than any woman in the valley of Spoleto.' So in the vineyards and the valleys of Umbria, of old, men and women talked with God, and indeed the whole land, even to the most superficial observer, seems blessed. Climb up to the great Roman aqueduct that spans the profound ravine which isolates Spoleto on her round hill, and at evening look across the valleys to the hills and the mountains; that luminous softness, a delicacy so magical that you had thought only the genius of Raphael or Perugino could imagine and express it, is just reality. With light, with fragile glory, with the wide and tender glance of the sky, every delicate form of hill and cloud and mountain is embraced. The hills are round and softer than the clouds almost. It is a landscape that is profoundly feminine in form, that has the very aspect of a young and exquisite woman moulded by God out of the earth He made. And it is amidst these perfect hills that Spoleto sings for joy.

Yet she too, like to Perugia and Assisi and all the cities of Umbria, has her terrible aspect. She too in her day has poured forth insolent armies, and, grimly crouched beneath her Fortezza, awaited the signal, holding her heart for fear. Even now in days of still sunshine—days so mysterious in Italy, that produced, doubtless, something of the mysticism of her countless saints—La Rocca, her fortress, holds still all the terror of the Middle Age, all the fierce and cruel joy of the Renaissance, that saw the streets of these cities, now so quiet, run with blood, that looked for sudden and fierce encounters at the street-corner in the sunshine or the moonlight, at the same time as it produced the soft work of Perugino and the curiously impersonal and dry paintings of Piero della Francesca. Still La Rocca watches for the foe, and does she not see him advancing surely down the valley of the Tiber? Already he occupies Perugia and Assisi, soon perhaps she too will be in his grip. For Modernity will make but little of ridding her of her precious possessions, her maze-like ways, her dreams, her quiet, and above all, her joy.

On first coming to her it is to the cathedral we climb, breathless, for her ways are steep and ruinous, to see the frescoes of one of the most delightful of the Florentine painters, Filippo Lippi. They are his masterpiece, and tell the story in brief of the Virgin Mary in her own cathedral, S. Maria Assunta. The chief fresco is that of the Coronation of the Virgin. Pale from the encounter with Death, in which but a moment ago she has proved victorious, tall and slight, Regina Angelorum is crowned, not by Christ her Son, but by God the Father, in a heaven delicate as the petals of the flags in the valleys full of corn, powdered with stars that seem to have risen just over the sea. The sun and the moon beneath her feet are lesser glories where she is. About her a company of angels sings and dances for joy since heaven is by so much richer than our earth. A few with a shy and timid grace, magically charming, hand her a few flowers from the highways or the woods of heaven, as though to ask her if they might be sweeter than the lilies she loved as a girl, or the wild flowers of Palestine. The rest of the frescoes—the Annunciation, in which she stands so surprised, so agitated, that she twists her fingers together and is not sure what to answer; the Nativity, a magnificent fresco, now but a shadow; and the Death of the Virgin, where Christ Himself with a tenderness, but with a tenderness and love, carries His Mother to heaven—are much over-painted, and by a lesser hand. And yet we catch some shadow of Filippo in them all, so that even in their ruin they are not the least among the precious things at Spoleto. In a quiet and sunny chapel of the great church, the dust of Filippo Lippi, that vagabond and joyous mortal, was laid by the jealous people of Spoleto in 1489. Lorenzo de' Medici, who seems to have loved him, tried in vain to secure his ashes so that they might lie in Florence. But Spoleto, proud and poor with but little that was very precious in her possession, would not have it so. You are rich and we are poor, she seems to have said; excuse us then if we keep the bones of this one great man, which you can well afford to leave in our keeping. Lorenzo would seem to have consented, perhaps a little reluctantly, contenting himself with building a noble tomb for the painter in S. Maria Assunta, and with composing a long Latin inscription.

The strangely adventurous life that came to an end here in Spoleto is very typical of certain aspects of the Renaissance : its profound passion for liberty, its experiment in romance and sentiment, its desire above everything for passion. And it is curious and not insignificant that it is not in the exciting and creative earth of Tuscany that Filippo Lippi, the fatal and erring son of the greatest of modern cities, is laid to rest, but among the quiet and blessed hills of Umbria, that mystical land that produced no great intelligence, only a spirit that to how large an extent has influenced the world.

It is, however, a mood the very opposite to this that overwhelms us in the Chiesa del Crocefisso, which has been built from the ruins of a Roman temple. To-day its façade guards the Campo Santo with its hard white crosses and beady flowers, and all the frippery of modern death. Magnificent pillars, Roman and Pagan, group themselves round the choir and chancel; and the nave is ennobled by the remains of the shafts, now ruinous, that once bore the weight of some splendid roof. Pagan prayers to Pagan gods, not dead but living in exile, perhaps in the ilex woods that crown the city and seem from here to envelope her in their sombre mantle, creep piteously into the warm sunshine that floods the church from the open door. They seem to knock at our hearts; and gazing at the feeble and terrible 'decorations' of the Christian altar loaded with hard and crude artificial flowers, and candlesticks covered with silver paper, the dirty hangings, the impotent and ugly obviousness, set there between the majestic pillars of an alien religion, it is rather of the nobility of that past, which is so present everywhere in Italy—of its beauty and its sufficiency, save in certain moments of profound feeling—that we think, than of its superstition and decay, in which it would sometimes appear it is so closely followed by its Christian successor. And yet that is perhaps over-emphasised. Who here in Spoleto can resist the touching appeal of that little ugly shrine that greets the traveller on his way to S. Paolo, that old thirteenth-century church? It is a picture of S. Maria Immacolata, and bears the marvellous and lovely legend: 'Et macula originalis non est in Te.' As I passed by at evening some children were decking the shrine with wild flowers, gathered on the Umbrian Hills. The hideous cage that guarded Our Lady, perhaps from the stones of the unbelievers, was starred with buttercups as lovely in their tender yellow as those which doubtless in old days sprang up beneath the white footsteps of Persephone as she crossed the rivers of Sicily on her way to Demeter, after her unwilling exile from our world. Will she not know and smile and understand, this Virgin that is the one goddess left to a sorrowful world? Be sure if she is not mindful of the flowers of the maidens and children, if in that Heaven where she is she does not smile to her Son upon His Throne of chrysoprase and jasper to see these, simple of heart, bringing the flowers of the field for her Festà—ah, then, Persephone never trod our world, nor was Demeter bereft and sorrowful; all, all, is a lie—the beautiful, austere gods, the terrible love of Christ, the very Fatherhood of God, since even these so simple of heart may deceive themselves on their lovely way to death.

The convent of S. Paolo is now used as a poorhouse round whose walls is pictured, not inappropriately perhaps, the Way of the Cross. In so peaceful a spot amid the cypresses and olives, those who have been a little defeated in a wonderful world contemplate the way to heaven. But whatever it may be that attracts us so strongly in Spoleto, she remains a very perfect city of light and joy. S. Pietro, that magnificent fragment of Romanesque architecture overlooking the ravine, is but another example of her simplicity and piety. Behind the church rises the wooded Monte Luco, and on a platform, reached by a series of antique steps, this church, perhaps the most striking Romanesque building in Italy, has stood for more than a thousand years. Its façade is sculptured in reliefs with moral fables, partly from the Bestiaries. Here the wolf feigns penitence in order to capture the lamb; the fox lies on his back, to all appearance dead, in order to seize the more surely the foolish doves. But it is only in this splendid and simple façade that the lover of beauty, for whom, after all, all architecture and painting and sculpture and literature really exist, will find delight; the church itself is but the mediocre whitewashed barn we grow so accustomed to in the south; with nothing really to recommend it, existing as it does without the mysticism and beauty of the Gothic building, or the sense of space and light to be found in the Romanesque and in the buildings of the Renaissance.

It was Holy Week when I came to Spoleto; a certain silence and wistful sadness, very touching in their simplicity, seemed to invest the city; the streets were very quiet, the churches sombre and mysterious. All day long I watched the processions, with their torches and innumerable tapers, wind along the hot roads; all night as I lay in my bed I seemed to hear the sombre chants that accompanied them up an endless Via Crucis. In reality it would seem Christ died this afternoon. It is true; now at last mankind is desolate. The tones of the Vexilla Regis seem to wave like long streamers from the church towers. Here, at any rate, we have heard the Bride, heart-broken and weeping, sigh to the world that is, it seems, spread out in its entirety at our feet :—

'O vos omnes qui transitis per viam, attendite et videte,
si est dolor sicut dolor meus.'

Then there is silence. Spoleto, with finger on her lip, awaits the dawn of Easter. At last it breaks, very cool and sweet and full of promises. An immense hope seems to have swept over the world. In the churches they sing again Alleluia, and I, with the whole city, go to the cathedral to greet the Christ, now risen from the tomb, in the Easter Mass. It is for me, at least, the world of true Romance—the real world of my dreams. At home Easter is so noisy, so icily jubilant, and only a little because Christ is risen from the dead—if indeed we remind ourselves at all of so old, so far-fetched a story. For the most part, in England, Easter is a festival of a short cessation from toil, in which brief moment it would be fatal to happiness to think of any sombre thing. But here in Umbria—the real Italia Mystica—the days of Holy Week and Easter seem endless.

Out of my window, as I write, I can see St. Mary of the Angels gleaming in the sunlight beneath the mass of Subasio. It is only the mountains that hide Orvieto from me, and even perhaps Rome herself. The coiling Tiber shines for miles on his way to the Eternal City and the sea, and innumerable roads wind over plain and mountain to half a hundred cities that the world has forgotten. I seem to see them all in the soft lucidity of evening, that is the most spacious part of the day in this land where, every evening, God paints for us those pictures which taught Perugino all he knew—his magnificent spaciousness, his sense of luminous light. Before the sunset Spoleto, like a tall and sweet maiden, kneels on her hill and seems to pray. Ever she has the attitude of prayer; and after dark when her little lights gleam far over the ravine, I seem to know that they burn before the shrines of many saints whose prayers she has desired, simple of heart as she is, kneeling at the head of her long valley under the soft sky.

VII

ON THE WAY TO NARNI

THROUGH the valleys of oak and ilex I set out on a
fair morning as ever was, before the sun was high, for
Terni and her falls, which, as it happened, I was never to
see; for I had scarcely gone five miles on my way when I
was overtaken by one of those sudden storms of wind and
hail and rain that are not uncommon in the valleys round
the Tiber. Is it not of such a tempest that Virgil has
warned us, so that we may note its coming?

> ' Continuo ventis surgentibus aut freta ponti
> Incipiunt agitata tumescere et aridus altis
> Montibus audiri fragor, aut resonantia longe
> Litora misceri et nemorum increbrescere murmur.

But I was heedless; and, taken with the beauty of the
way, I had not observed the signs infallible of the moon, or
the sudden swift flight of the stars sweeping over the sky.
Not till the murmur of the woods prevailed against the
whisper of the summer day did I understand that Nature
was awake and angered, her heart tumultuous with some
passionate remembrance, and she herself singing upon the
mountains. Through the valley under the storm I went
rejoicing; it was one of the great days of my life. I was
drenched with the rain, and the hailstones cut my face like
a whip, and the great wind embraced me. What cared I
for a wet skin? I was alone with the world, and I loved her.

The long white road hissed before me, and suddenly, as it seemed, under the fury of the storm, was overcome and no longer resisted the invincible rain, but was musical with a million fountains. All Nature sighed in the ecstasy of that embrace, and spoke in the song of the storm of the antique tragedies of the world. And I alone heard it all in the sacred groves of ilex in the old and beautiful valley, through which a little river ran hurrying before me.

It was raining still when I came to Terni; and being, as I have said, wet to the skin, I went to bed in the inn of my country while my host dried my clothes. And the next day and the next it rained, and so it happened that I did not see the famous falls of which Childe Harold wrote so well, but went on to Narni ignominiously by train.

I came to Narni in the evening, and immediately it was fine weather. So I knew I had done well, seeing that I had bowed to the will of some unpropitiated saint or forsaken god who had decreed that I should not see the Cascate delle Marmore.

The 'Angelo' at Narni is an inn of no great pretensions, but the host is a good host, and understands that for so magnificent a person as your lordship nothing is good enough. He is proud of his picturesque and antique city, but especially is he proud of his view, which is more wonderful than his tale, and the great Roman bridge, so magnificent a ruin, that strives in vain to grapple the shores of Nera. And, indeed, he is right; the Ponte di Augusto is one of the most beautiful ruins in the world, chiefly perhaps because it has been left alone with age and death. In its youth and prime it carried the Via Flaminia towards Rome; in its age it warns us of the desolate splendours that the Eternal City still guards. An outpost of the Campagna, it knows the gods are dead or dying in the loneliness of that mysterious desert which surrounds the

Capital of the World.   What need is there of any splendid
road to Rome, since the messengers of Christ pursued by
implacable victory came, not with beauty and delight, in
gilded chariots and with horses, but in rags with bleeding
feet?   Should it bear on its back the brutal and barbaric
armies of the Goth? or make the way smooth for the
strange bedecked columns, gay with harlots and with silk,
of Charles VIII. on his way to Naples, there to find no
kingdom but an immortal pestilence?   The great days of
Latin triumph come no more.   It is the moment of trumpery
cities with bridges of iron, foul and unbeautiful.   The
Bridge of Augustus watches the traveller pass by on another
way to Rome unheeding, remembering only splendid days.
But still one arch is perfect, waiting for the return of the
armies of Cæsar, which so many ages ago went out to
conquer the world.

They have triumphed; when will they return to avenge
the spoliation of their City and the death of their immortal
gods?   Is it for that return this Bridge of Augustus is
waiting, not quite ruined, not altogether destroyed, through
the' ignoble centuries?   Ah! do you not often wonder that
the gods do not return to avenge themselves; that they
are not enraged at the wounds we have made in their
indestructible temples; that they suffer us to deface their
beautiful statues, to steal their pillars, and to forget them
altogether, or believe them dead?   Looking on this bridge,
that like a beautiful broken bow lies useless beside the
stream, can you doubt of their return, since all the contrivance of man since they left us has failed to produce a
thing so beautiful and so strong?

There is but little to be seen in Narni itself.   The Duomo
is now chiefly a building of the sixteenth century; it holds
a few old marbles, a curious screen, nothing more.

In the Palazzo Municipio there are also some old sculptures, together with a fresco by Lo Spagna of 'St. Francis receiving the Stigmata,' and a fine work of Ghirlandajo, 'The Coronation of the Blessed Virgin.'

But it is not for these things I came to Narni, but to see the road to Rome, that used to march with so much confidence and pride over that broken bridge, beside which, as in the days of Augustus, so to-day, the irony of the gods has permitted still to flow

'Sulfurea Nar albus aqua fontesque Velini.'

VIII

TODI

IT was one night at Narni, a night of many nights, when I had assured myself often enough that it was too hot to go to Rome, that I decided to make a long journey by road to Orvieto, where I had agreed with myself that I wished to be. I made up my mind to this far departure from the railway the more readily, since I should thus see Todi, a little city very awkwardly situated for the tourist, but nothing so bad for the traveller. I had been told that without its gates I should find the most beautiful church in the world. It is true that he who brought me this news added, that I at least should think so; but it was the last reservation in the world to encourage me to give up my journey, since it appeared that he knew of my love for Romanesque and Renaissance buildings and told me accordingly of one of the finest in Italy. Todi was, moreover, the city of the ever-famous Jacopone, who made the most lovely of songs, *Stabat Mater Speciosa.*

The way was a pleasant way, as all ways are, be sure, in Umbria, and it was hot. I slept an hour at S. Gemini in a kind of barn among the hay, and travelled by good luck on a great country wine-cart as far as a place whose name I have forgotten—it was but a handful of houses; and at sunset, by the help of a great Lord who courteously gave me a seat in a most splendid and strange coach, I was not far from Todi, where I came at last out of the immense darkness of the Umbrian night. I was alone in the valley; night came so swiftly that she had caught me still on the road. After a time I came to a parting of the ways, of which one seemed to climb uphill, the other to go straight on. And I sat down by the roadside. The great cypress under which I found myself was moaning in the wind that came gently through the darkness, filled with the odour of some flower. Suddenly I looked up. Aloft, on what seemed to be a mighty hill, a single light showed me that there lay the city I had come so far to see. A single bell tolled the hour; somewhere, it seemed far away, a woman began to sing for a moment, then there was silence.

Softly behind me a man came out of the darkness that was a little desolate. When he saw me sitting by the roadside, he stopped and looked at me for some time. Presently he spoke.

'The Signore desires to go up to the city?' he said, not without a certain kindness.

Yes, that was the Signore's wish.

Well, then, he would carry the Signore's knapsack, since it was a great distance and steep—but steep.

So we set off, he a little in advance. A noise of running water was the only thing audible, but presently that too died away, and we were in the great silence of night upon the hills. Overhead heaven was precious with stars, and the great snow-capped Apennines across the valley, miles and miles away, seemed like the immaculate memorials of angels slain in the fight with Lucifer thousands of years ago. Sometimes, as we came to a turning of the way that wound ever upwards, we rested for a moment beside what at first seemed to be a rough shelter of heaped-up stones, for the hill is stony, but which I found was an old station of the Via Crucis—this very road which we were climbing so laboriously —now in ruin, its frescoes almost obliterated, its crucifix gone for ever. Soon everything but night and a sense of the

F

immense space everywhere round us, in which the stars hung like many lovely lamps, fell away from me. We seemed utterly alone. A kind of terror at the depth of the silence seized me; and I am sure my companion, who still kept a little ahead of me as though to show the way, was a little fearful too—his eyes were so wide and bright, and he stepped so carefully and softly. At last the weight of the loneliness, the unbreakable silence, became unbearable, and it was almost with a cry of relief that I came quite suddenly to the gate of the city and so to the inn, which was in darkness. My companion set down my bag and pulled the bell for me, and then, when I had paid him what he desired, disappeared into the darkness.

Todi is one of the most ancient cities in Umbria; it boasts of a foundation older than that of Rome. Its walls are certainly in part Etruscan, patched by the Romans, and destroyed by the Middle Age and Renaissance, that have left their mark, how splendidly, on this little city built on so precipitous a hill. In its day, surely, it was a place of some renown and greatness, seeing that there is so much ruined splendour even now within its walls. And I for one find it to-day one of the greatest surprises in Umbria. No one goes there. It is far from the beaten track, thirty miles from Orvieto, which is itself a silent, forgotten city, passed almost always by the hurried tourist eager for Rome or some famous city of Tuscany. Perugia whom the tourists have violated, with her two great hotels, is more than thirty miles to the north of Todi, who on her terrible hill has, after all, but little to offer them. But for us who are not in a hurry Todi holds much—a great and beautiful Piazza, more than one very lovely church, and Silence. You hear no train, even in the stillest night; no tram rushes past your windows to remind you of the horrible new world that has only time for action, that has forgotten to think. Ah! it is not happy, that great modern world from which I have fled away, and it desires happiness so eagerly, and is not perhaps altogether un-deserving of it, since it has been unhappy so long. And why? Has it not driven Beauty away to such eagle-nests as this? And it is here, indeed, we find her in tears, but free upon the mountains. Not chained in the galleries of the cities of the people, where even the most brutal and the most base may gaze upon her and defile her with their thoughts, but free in her own world, which we are stealing from her, under the soft unsullied sky, among simple people who live with her and are glad because she is there. It is good to live in such places, however simple they may be; it is good to live with men who have never understood the slavery that our own contrivances are thrusting upon us, to look a little at the stars and to feel the heat of the sun.

In that beautiful Piazza between the Duomo and the Palazzo Municipio at Todi what thoughts will not adventure, even to us, from the beautiful indestructible centuries. It is in such solitude we begin to understand those things which the world has been content to forget so disastrously. Here, surrounded by a garden, vast and interminable, under the shadow of the laurels and the roses, I have watched the giant cypresses, each solitary as a god, count the innumerable hours; and I have understood something of the profound joy of that troubadour of God, who beheld as it were in a vision one of the most beautiful and terrible tragedies of the world, and carved it there in immortal verse. Looking back now on those fortunate days, when from the cool shade at sunset I looked down on burning Umbria and many smoulder-ing cities, I know that even those tearless sorrows that dry up the roots of life, those brutal disappointments that can never be erased from the memory, may be made into a kind of beauty, into an almost perfect music in the midst of so beautiful a city that is dead.

It is perhaps as you stand in the Piazza before the Palazzo Municipio that you begin to feel how beautiful a city Todi really is. To the north the cathedral, beautiful by reason of its proportions and its simplicity, brings you a kind of joy. It is a Romanesque church of great beauty, with a façade of later work. A fine stairway leads up to the three doors, 'each surmounted by a wheel,' which are somewhat elaborate; they are of the fifteenth century. But the main part of the church is of the eleventh century; and beautiful as it is as seen from the Piazza, it is from the east that it appears to best advantage, when all that you can see is eleventh century work. The variety of the ornament is extraordinary; this is noticeable especially in the windows and the columns which support the arcade. The interior is less lovely, but even there the beauty of the proportion of the building makes itself felt, and you forget the later additions and alterations in the severity of the original design. The choir is of the fourteenth century, and covers a crypt where are certain paintings of little interest by Lo Spagna. You feel always that the church would have been lovelier with less ornament. The fourteenth and fifteenth centuries have really spoiled a building that must once have been of far greater beauty than to-day.

The Palazzo Municipio, which for want of a better name passes as Gothic architecture, shuts in the east side of the Piazza. The windows are beautiful, and the staircase finer than the one at Perugia. There is a small Pinacoteca on the ground floor, where you may find a picture or two by Lo Spagna; among them a Coronation of the Virgin painted in 1511. The Renaissance palace on the south side of the Piazza—its name escapes me—is beautiful too; indeed the whole Piazza is lovely, and never sufficiently to be praised.

The two churches of S. Ilario and S. Fortunato, built in the thirteenth century (the one in 1249, the other in 1292) are also worthy of praise. The façade of S. Ilario restored, but not so brutally as usual, is very fine. But it is to S. Fortunato that we return again and again. This magnificent Romanesque church has a flight of steps like to the cathedral, which leads to three doors. Only the middle one is pointed, however, the others being round; while in the late façade of the cathedral there are three pointed doors. The façade here, however, would seem to be also of the fifteenth century, as is without doubt the vaulting.

In the Dominican church of S. Maria in Camuccia, there is a number of frescoes; one of a Virgin della Misericordia, and several of the Virgin and Child. They are, as I think, worth study, being of some antiquity, though restored in parts possibly in the fifteenth century.

But, after all, it is to the great church of S. Maria della Consolazione that the traveller will turn with the greatest eagerness. Built as many have supposed by Bramante, but given now to Sangallo, it is one of the most lovely if not the loveliest of Renaissance churches in Italy — that is to say, in the world. Here at last we have a really fine realisation of the Renaissance ideal in architecture. Not a perfect realisation of it by any means, but the best we possess. It is well to remember, in looking on this church, what S. Pietro might have been but for the so-called Reformation and all the evil it worked for Art. The idea of Bramante, it will be remembered, was to build a church in the shape of a Greek cross under a dome. It was an effect of light and space he aimed at, light and space confined, and therefore not confined, within a perfectly proportioned building. Well, the Reformation came, and spoiled all that. Rome remembered the pilgrims from the North, and considering how important it was that such as they should be impressed, decided to build that long nave which to-day makes of Peter's—well, not a beautiful church, but one into which you can pack eighty thousand people. Coming into S. Maria della Consolazione we realise for the first time perhaps what we have lost. It is not a church; it is a magical space in heaven between the sun and moon, and the light is level and beautiful. It is strange this effect of space—absolute space, flight almost, in what is really so small a building. And it is right that this ideal should have been achieved, if anywhere then in Umbria, where the beauty of the whole country is really that sense of lightness, of light and spacious air. It is the secret that Umbria has striven to confide to the world through many painters: through Piero della Francesca, through Perugino, and at last through the sweet and quiet genius of Raphael. These men composed with space as a musician composes with sound, and indeed the effect is very like. You seem suddenly to have stepped out of our world into a pure and clear sunlight, not terrifying by its infinity, but enfolding us with security and a kind of perfection. You gaze only upwards. That dome borne on the wings of clouds on clouds of angels, soars in its beauty and its perfection like a splendid and irresistible thought in the mind of man. There is no uncertainty, no dimness, no tricks of shadow, no self-accusation, no deceit, no fear, no shame at all, but the clear light of the sky that is the most lovely and precious thing in the world. And it is thus, clothed in joyful and beautiful thoughts, that man has chosen at last to meet his God. You think there is no mysticism in that, no mystery? Ah! you do not know the mystical power—strange and more wonderful than the spirit of the forests of the North, or of the cathedrals of the Gaul and the Goth—to be found in the unappeasable sunlight of a still, hot day. That Silence is more profound than the whispering depths of the most ancient forest, or the echoing intricate splendours, the dim unseen vaultings of the great mad churches of the North. If in the already worshipped Sun there be mystery, or in the unpierced Heaven there be angels, though we may not see; if in silence surrounded by light and the immense loneliness of space, God wanders so that I may find Him always near, then that Latin genius, which has taught us all the Arts as a mother teaches her children, and to which we owe everything that is precious in the world, has not made this unthinkable failure in architecture of which we accuse her so easily, but has comprehended there too more than she has ever been able to lead us so far as to apprehend; and we in our gloomy, miserable lands, living like wild beasts in our forests in the most splendid days, dragged away like the brutes to make a holiday more strange in Rome, a spectacle more terrible, preferring even now darkness before light, barbarous and sad in our trumpery cities, must acknowledge at last with what grace we may the indestructible, untiring genius of Latin blood, that with us, lost in our fog, it has become the fashion to scoff at and to despise.

IX

ORVIETO

THE way to Orvieto, that city of convents and monasteries, on her bastioned hill of pale and tawny tufa, is difficult. Not many seek her out in her silence and her solitude; she is so strange and sorrowful in the midst of that barren landscape, burnt by the sun, wasted by the wind, cleansed by the rain, gay only with forgotten garlands. She is the city of a miracle, herself the greatest miracle of all. Through her streets pass and repass, haggard and fantastical, the beautiful or brutal dreams of the Middle Age. Still she wanders, as it were, in a mystical desert, and every morning sees that faint mirage of the heavenly city, and every evening watches Christ's blood flame in the firmament. Her brows are still bound with sacred gold, her crown is still splendid with jewels, still in her heart of hearts she guards the Eucharist; but her life is so languid that the grass grows in her streets, she is so silent that you might think her without inhabitants. In all that melancholy valley, she alone, high on her rock, is splendid and beautiful like a star fallen on the mountains.

But it is not to the impatient traveller that this city of great silences, and the immense intervals of meditation, will reveal her secret; but to him who, having spent sufficient time in the silence of her Cathedral, has cleansed his heart so that he may understand her story. You might almost say that within her walls is contained the whole

Christian *mythos*, beginning with Genesis and ending with the Coronation of the Blessed Virgin ; the centre, the climax, the supreme mystery of the whole being the tremendous secret of the Doctrine of the Blessed Sacrament. And it is not in the Cathedral alone that Orvieto declares to us that Christianity has conquered a reluctant world, for in herself she is a monument of that victory. In the Piazza del Duomo there are four buildings beside the Duomo that are inevitably connected with the Church, and so with Christ. The oldest the Palace of the Bishop, stands beyond the cathedral, and though begun in 977 and enlarged by Adrian IV. in 1151, it is now mainly a building of the sixteenth century. We then turn to the Palace of the Popes—Palazzo Soliano, that with the decay of religion has been turned into a museum— built by Boniface VIII. in the end of the thirteenth century. Beside this palace rises the Ospedale, built in the end of the twelfth century, and opposite the cathedral itself we find the Opera del Duomo, built in the fourteenth century, a magnificent piece of work. Thus for Orvieto, at least, half her life was laid up in heaven, where also her treasure was. For it was to a miracle that she owed not only her beauty but her true being, there on her great rock over her melancholy valley—a very miracle herself, famous and holding gifts. And even as she owed her splendour to the blood of Christ, so she seems to have desired the blood of man ; staining her streets with that mystical and shameful river in the month of August 1312, and at other times, when civil war reigned in the streets and many hundreds of citizens perished. And, whether under the Monaldeschi or the Popes, or the Neapolitan king, always her streets ran with blood—it is as it were the very symbol of herself.

The miracle of Bolsena, which the cathedral of Orvieto was built to commemorate, happened in this wise. Raphael with his profound and scholarly insight has painted it, as it is supposed, opposite to the 'School of Athens' in the Vatican. A certain German priest—even then it might seem that the Teutonic intelligence was less trained, less sure of its own limitations than the Latin mind—had presumed to doubt in the little town of Orvieto the doctrine of the Real Presence of Our Lord in the Blessed Sacrament. Utterly tired and weary of his doubts, disturbed by his uncertainty, he set out for Rome, so that there, in the capital of his religion he might decide at last or be persuaded. For it began to appear plain to him that if this which he dared to doubt were indeed untrue, then other things, that he had scarcely thought of as yet, might be untrue also. It was, therefore, we may well believe, in a certain sadness of heart that he set out for Rome, and 'resting one day on the shores of the beautiful lake of Bolsena, he, at the request of the villagers, celebrated a Mass for them in the church of Santa Cristina, which is with us even to this day.' And although Santa Cristina is rejected by all authority, she has her lovers in the sweet Umbrian country who will never forget her; and perhaps for their love she brought these things to pass, being in heaven at the time. For it happened that as our German doubter (Raphael says he was but a lad) elevated the Host, more than ever troubled in his mind concerning the doctrine that none of those simple folk in the church there thought of doubting for a moment, he saw drops of red blood upon the Corporal, 'each stain severally assuming the form of a human head with features like the "Volto Santo," a portrait of our Saviour.' Oh, wonderful! What shame in his heart, what anger at his doubts, what love, what certainty, what gladness! Overcome by fear and reverence, he, sinner that he was, dared not consume the Holy Species; but with eagerness, with love, reserved the Body of Our Lord, and travelling in haste to Orvieto, where the Pope then was, he, not without shame, confessed to him not only the miracle, but his doubts also. The Bishop of Orvieto at the command of the Pope hastened to Bolsena, and brought from the altar of Santa Cristina the Sacred Host and the Blessed Corporal. The Pope himself—Urban IV. it was—passed with all his clergy, with joy, with music, in procession to meet him, who indeed bore Christ along with him.

Thus was instituted the magnificent festival of Corpus Christi, whose office St. Thomas Aquinas, the angelical doctor, composed. The Sacred Host rests to-day in the Cappella del Corporale in the Cathedral, surrounded by the magnificent frescoes of Ugolino di Prete d'Ilario, that tell the story to the world. As you descend to-day through the vineyards to Bolsena, perhaps past the town of Bagnorea, the birthplace of the author of *The Nightingale of the Passion of our Lord*, and *The Journey of the Soul to God*, known to us as S. Buonaventura, something of that ancient mystery seems still to invest the little city with a languid and fantastic beauty, a silence so profound, a light, a sunshine, so subtle. Forlorn upon her lake, over that pale green water, there came to her at dawn—perhaps in the very hour which freed us from eternal sleep—a whisper of that winged mystery which has confounded the world. For if Christ's life was a miracle of mystical years, numbering thirty-three, His Resurrection was, as it were, the triumphant solution of that miracle into a law and commonplace for the world; and His presence in such absolute, simple, and elementary things as bread and wine, changing their simplicity into His subtile life, His perfect beauty, is a piece of profound poetry strange enough to be believed, too beautiful to be untrue, in keeping with the belief of the whole world, which has already apprehended during countless millenniums the God hidden in the vine, the divine nature of bread, of life. And, indeed, this country—volcanic, tawny, and ardent, strewn with strange rocks of basalt in the mysterious shapes of temples of hundreds of forgotten religions—here a quincunx, there a triangle or circle—was created for the manifestation of some divine thing which we cannot understand. Doubtless the miracle of the Volto Santo was not the first that happened here. Cristina, saint and martyr, though without the Roman Calendar, had seen angels hovering over that pallid lake, and had talked with them, and they had clothed her at last in a wonderful white garment, as she was almost sinking in its waters with a great stone tied round her neck by her murderers. And yet, as ever happens in the lives of the saints, so disappointingly, so dishearteningly, though God Himself interfere for any virgin or golden lad, of all of them not one but in the end died the victim of his foes. It is but for a moment that heaven interposes betwixt the saints and death; in the end martyrdom, only delayed by the menace of God, has its way with them, and they pass out the victorious victims of the impotence or the unwillingness of heaven, of the brutality of man. So it was with Cristina. Three times the angels saved her, only to let her perish at last by a far more horrible death than drowning. So have the gods ever defended those who loved them.

Thus in simple days miracles happened and men believed, and chased the devil down the vistas of his own damnable doubts. To us valiant shopkeepers who believe in science, who dispute about the reality of matter, all that is doubtless but a fairy tale at best; some of us even may be so strict as to call that miracle of Bolsena and the convenient German priest, a lie—yet I can but hope they are few. Truth or lie, or what you will, it has built the Cathedral of Orvieto; nor is there anything more marvellous upon earth. Fra Angelico did not hesitate to spend his genius on her walls. Signorelli, who is so much greater than his fame, in 1499 began to paint the vaulting and the walls; and amid all the magnificence and richness of the work around one, it is again and again to his work that the traveller will return—always with joy.

The Duomo as it stands to-day is in form of a Latin cross, consisting of a long and broad nave, with two aisles divided from the nave by pillars, two large chapels to the north and south of what would be the transepts in a Gothic church, and a kind of square chancel. The artist who designed this strange building, so glorious without, so sombre within, is unknown. You have heard a whisper of Arnolfo di Cambio and of some unknown master of the Roman school, and yet it seems impossible that Arnolfo should have had any hand in it. The Cathedral, which was originally without the two transept chapels, is Romanesque in style, probably built in imitation of S. Maria Maggiore in Rome, that great Latin church which was, after all, the cradle of Christianity. It is really a matter of indifference who was the architect, for the church of Orvieto is not a beautiful church—it is ill constructed; soon after it was built it was decided to add a transept, and the two chapels to north and south were glued on, as it were, to the older building. The church, badly built in the first place, and terrible wounded by this addition, began to fall to pieces.

It was in 1310 that Lorenzo del Maitano was brought from Siena to buttress the gaping walls of the Duomo, to restore the fabric in many particulars, and to design and to build the façade; and it is, so far as the building is concerned, with this façade that we concern ourselves to-day. It is in itself one of the most extraordinary works of art in Italy, while the church is a mere building, and as such almost entirely without interest. 'Imagine,' says d'Annunzio, 'imagine a rock in the midst of a melancholy valley, and on the top of the rock a city so deathly silent as to give the impression of being uninhabited—every window closed, grass growing in the dusty grey streets. A Capuchin friar crosses the Piazza, a priest descends from a closed carriage in front of an hospital, all in

.

black, with a decrepit old servant to open the door; here a tower against the white, rain-sodden clouds, there a clock slowly striking the hour, and suddenly, at the end of a street, a miracle—the Duomo.'

And it is really as a kind of miracle—an exquisite painted frontispiece to the church of a miracle—that we look on the façade to-day flaming in the sunshine. It is a kind of precious marble, carved and subtly contrived and set with gems. Jewelled with a cunning and profound knowledge beyond the art of the goldsmith, it shines to-day almost like a casket, since it is not till later we discover it is only a single wall, only a façade after all, with no real relation to the rest of the church, which might have been finished in various other ways no more incongruous than this. In this want of any inevitable relation to the church itself, the façade of the cathedral here at Orvieto is like to that of the Duomo at Siena, only perhaps a little less strange, a little more in place, and it may well be that it is owing to French influence, just then beginning to count for something in Italy, that the façade is sculptured and has three gables.

The question of French influence in Italian work is an interesting one, as yet only lightly touched upon by historians of Art, but as it seems to me of no little importance to us since we find it in the work even of such a Realist, such a profound student of Nature, as Donatello. Lorenzo del Maitano made many drawings for the façade, of which two, certainly, are preserved in the Opera del Duomo to-day. Here in Orvieto, however, French influence is to be found in the gradual substitution of three gables for the one of the earlier drawing. It is well to remind ourselves, as we look on this marvellous façade, that it was the work of Sienese artists of the beginning and middle of the fourteenth century, and to remember too that the façade of the cathedral at Siena was not begun at that time. The Sienese sculptors were for the most part pupils of the school of Giovanni Pisano,[1] they were therefore practised in the art of sculpturing bas-relief. Mr. Langton Douglas has proved almost beyond a doubt, in a very able and delightful paper[2] on the cathedral of Orvieto, that the work in bas-relief on the pilasters and façade is from the hands of Maitano and his pupils. He believes that the reliefs were completed in 1321, since it was in that year, nine years before his death, that Maitano set up the *fabbrica* of mosaic.

'The reliefs on the pilasters of the façade of Orvieto Cathedral,' he says, 'were executed in the period 1310 to 1321, in part by Lorenzo del Maitano, in part under his supervision. They belong to the golden age of the art of Siena: to the age of Duccio and Simone Martini, to the age of Pietro and Ambrozio Lorenzetti, to the age of the architects of the great unfinished cathedral. Maitano was an artistic kinsman of Simone. Like Simone he owed a great deal to the influence of Giovanni Pisano. Like Simone he was a great designer. He had, too, something of that painter's marvellous grace of line, something of his devotion to an hieratic sumptuousness, something of his love of brilliant colour, as well as something of his extraordinary fineness— we might almost say fastidiousness—of technique. Excepting the works of Jacopo della Quercia, the reliefs of Orvieto were the greatest achievement of the Sienese school of sculpture.'

'The greatest achievement of the Sienese school of sculpture'; and when we remember the immense superiority of the Sienese school at that time, we shall not surely undervalue the splendour of this achievement. Among the most lovely things in Italy, certainly anywhere else they are unequalled. It is necessary to go back to the Greeks—yes, in

[1] See Fumi, *Il Duomo d'Orvieto e i suoi Restauri*, p. 92.
[2] See *Architectural Review*, June 1903, p. 203.

spite of the splendour of Chartres, and the Gothic and yet Classical sculptures of the North—to find their fellows. But as with all Sienese work, the pictures of Duccio and Simone Martini, so here we find a satisfaction with mere splendour and graciousness, a desire for beauty but not for life or strength. A little conventionally, one might say, these Sienese artists deal with their art, and yet after all, where, for more than two hundred years, will you find such a sense of form, such a delight in beauty and simplicity? What pathos in that figure of Adam who is dead or ever he had life, whom God approaches so eagerly, so graciously in the garden. The astonished angels wait, with how profound an agitation, for this new thing. And again, when that deep sleep fell upon our father, and God with blessing—for He does bless her—draws woman from his side, how he seems just to sleep as one weary after the pleasures of the day, for he is alive and dead no longer. Two angels hesitate in the garden among the trees, the one seeming to tell the other of all that had gone before, while Adam lay a marvellous shape of dust waiting the touch of the finger of God. As you look on this strange, pathetic figure of Man, the sublime dream of Michael Angelo comes to you as he painted it on the roof of the Sistine Chapel. For there Man, half alive, lies over the world and stretches out his finger—ah, languidly—to touch the finger of God; he is almost unconscious, still wrapped round by dreams, yet a touch of the finger-tips will suffice to awaken him to life itself, and all that God holds, woman and the future, in the fold of His garment.

The whole history of the Creation is expressed on this façade, sometimes with a kind of realism, sometimes with a kind of half-discovered symbolism. Thus Christ is the chief figure in the creation of the world, God the Father being represented by a hand, and the Holy Spirit by the Dove, with outspread wings hovering over the waters and the world, among the stars. And again what energy, what realism in that figure of Adam where he stands with Eve for a moment beneath the tree of knowledge, and God almost with a kind of severity forbids them to eat of that fruit. Eve listens with a certain meekness, an almost superficial and easy acquiescence. But Adam stands at his full height and looks God in the eyes as a beloved son, and really understands that this tree which he touches with his fingers bears the forbidden fruit. And so this poem in stone, not less than the perfect page of the English Bible, or Milton, tells the valiant tale of the tragedy of Man, and the Redemption of the world. And at last in those two reliefs of the Resurrection and of Hell, we find—well, a kind of understanding very different from that of an artist so close to that time as the painter of the Triumph of Death at Pisa. Maitano was, in his fashion, certainly Sienese, but still naturalistic, concerned with men and women rather than with stories or ideas. How the people crowd in the upper part of the Resurrection, how they press forward almost with passion towards the light, herded almost in the first dazzling ecstasy of that resurrection by their angels! And in the lower part how they struggle and thrust aside the stones of their graves! Many have already stepped half out before they have thrust away the lid of the tomb for ever.

In the relief of the Hell, a kind of brutal emotion, half hideous laughter, half despair and weeping, has swept over these poor people tortured by devils. Their fate has driven them mad. They no longer feel anything but a kind of stupid terror; while the Vine, that is Christ, loaded with fruit, sweeps upwards for ever beyond the gaze of their dull agonised eyes.

Well, it is to find such work as this that we have come to Orvieto; nor, so far as I know, will you find anything like it in all Italy.

G

But Maitano, that great artist, was not content to design the façade and to cover it with reliefs; he designed the mosaics also. 'He set up a *fabbrica* of mosaic in Orvieto in 1321,' says Mr. Langton Douglas, 'and the early mosaic pictures on the lower part of the façade were executed by him or under his supervision. This work was continued by his son Vitale, by Andrea Orcagna, and by other great artists. But of the early mosaics that adorned the façade not a vestige now remains. It was not until the year 1570, two hundred and sixty years after Maitano had begun the work, that the façade was completed. Only one important alteration was made in the original design, and that was the work of another Sienese, Antonio Federighi, in the middle of the fifteenth century. Already in 1417, more than thirty years before Federighi took office, proposals had been made for a change in the design. Finally in the year 1450 Isaia da Pisa had been commissioned to make a new design for the uppermost story of the façade. The design this artist provided was the cause of great controversy, not settled until after Federighi became *capo-maestro* in the year 1451. Federighi finally decided to raise the altitude of the central gable of the façade, by inserting a row of niches above the circular window similar to those Maitano had placed on each side of it. He also increased the height of the pinnacles which flanked the central gable. Thus he gave the façade a more imposing appearance than it would have presented had Maitano's final design been carried out. For the rest, the façade to-day differs in no very important particular from that designed in the fourteenth century.'

Thus we have, as practically the work of one mind, perhaps, the most glorious façade in Italy, one of the finest pieces of sculptured architecture in the world. Alas! it is only a frontispiece, of almost tragic beauty, to an inferior church

decorated with stripes of black and white marble. In spite
of the wonder of the tourist, the Duomo of Orvieto is not
beautiful, it is only strange. Bare and cold as it is, one has
not the profound sense of space and light as in the churches
of the Renaissance. No overwhelming sense of greatness and
beauty excites our tears, as in S. Maria Maggiore at Rome ;
there is no perfection, no life at all, only a kind of mediocrity,
a kind of sadness in an old battered church as ugly as old
age ravaged by disease, in one who can never have been
beautiful even in youth, but who desiring beauty above all
things has worn a lovely mask designed by a great artist,
behind which he hopes to hide his infirmities and the
wounds of the years. And so it is really only when we pass
through the western doors and see this great church from
the inside that we understand how ugly she is. And yet
even here too she has tried to redeem herself. In the left
aisle of the nave Gentile da Fabriano has painted a Madonna
and Child, spoiled now, and never perhaps one of his happiest
works. In the choir the naïve artists of the countryside have
painted the Life of the Blessed Virgin and the Advent of
Christ. They are not beautiful, these little rude acts of
faith that are hung on the walls with all the assurance of the
most pretentious votive offerings, but they serve to sanctify,
as it were to enliven that strange and barren interior. They
redeem the church from the sin of accidie, of overmuch
sadness, which has so terrible a place in Dante's Hell. And
in the Cappella del Corporale how magnificent is the casket
which holds the bloodstained Corporal, for which the chapel
was built. It is perhaps the finest example in Italy of
mediæval goldsmith's work—the work of an artist, Ugolino
di Maestro Vieri, the Sienese, when the very painters
were the pupils of such an one. And then how mysterious
and lovely is that Madonna by Lippo Memmi, another Sienese,
who with hands joined seems to pray for us and to receive our

prayers, while companies of angels guard her round about, and at her feet kneel—the people of Orvieto is it, or some religious society of which she was the Patroness? But it is in the Cappella Nuova, the Cappella della Madonna di S. Brizio, as it is now called, that we shall find the real treasure of the Duomo, rare beyond any casket carved with golden roses or the many miracles of the church. There in 1447 Fra Angelico has painted Our Lord and the Apostles, and Luca Signorelli has prophesied of Michelangelo with a greatness all his own. So much greater than his fame, this Umbrian from Cortona began to paint the vaulting and the walls in 1499. And amid all the beauty and richness of the façade and the loveliness of Fra Angelico, it is again and again to his work that the traveller will return—always with joy. Born at Cortona in 1440, Vasari declares that in his day his works were more esteemed than those of any other master. It is strange that they should have fallen into such neglect in our own. It is the human form that especially delights him, so that in the Uffizi we find a picture called, 'The Virgin Holding her Divine Son in her Lap,' in which the shepherds in the background are naked and unashamed, as in an elder age. It is, however, in the Cathedral at Orvieto that we find his best work. Says Vasari: 'I am not surprised that the works of Luca were always highly extolled by Michelangelo, or that for his divine work of the Last Judgment in the Sistine Chapel he should have *courteously availed himself to a certain extent* of the inventions of Signorelli, as for example, in the angels and demons, in the divisions of the heavens, and some other parts, wherein Michelangelo imitated the mode of treatment adopted by Luca as may be seen by every one.' In looking at his work here in Orvieto it is perhaps a question whether Michael borrowed to advantage. Nothing more extraordinarily thoughtful and subtle than the Anti-Christ is to be found in Michael's Last

Judgment. So like to Christ as indeed always to be mistaken for him from a distance, Anti-Christ has all the
beauty, all the cynical hatred of mankind, which listens to
him in adoration that, after Luca has suggested it to us,
we might expect. It is hardly necessary, one might say,
for the devil to whisper to him; in his heart all the cruelty
and villainy of the universe have been sown and have come
to flower. Opposite, the fresco of the Resurrection, with its
huge naked angels sounding their death-destroying trumpets,
decked with the banner of the Cross, crushes us beneath its
tremendous imaginative power. In his magnificent mind
the Resurrection took form, so that he was able, as it were,
to comprehend it and its humanity, and to show it to us
ere it had been resolved out of the confusion of the trumpets
into the order of the syllables of God. Visions as splendid
as those of Dante dawn upon him—the Punishment of the
Wicked, the Reward of the Blessed, and Paradise. Perhaps
Luca Signorelli alone of all great painters, not excepting the
author of the Triumph of Death at Pisa, has, as it were,
comprehended heaven and hell. I speak of him and his
work elsewhere in this book, and it is to that critical estimate
of his achievement that I must refer the reader. With his
tremendous thoughts as our companions we walk the streets
of Orvieto, ever finding it necessary to return again to the
Cappella della Madonna di S. Brizio, where among the poets
of Greece and Rome and Italy we see the tragedy of our
world, the pathetic drama of the soul of man.

In the Palazzo Soliano, a building of the thirteenth century, once the palace of the Popes, which stands to the
south of the Duomo, we find Luca himself and a picture of
S. Maria Maddalena, of no little interest; and it is here, too,
that we see that shrine by Ugolino, which he made to prove
his ability to the people of Orvieto before they entrusted him
with the casket of the Corporale. The city also is full of

curiosities, such as Etruscan remains, and charms, and the well of St. Patrick, built by Sangallo in 1527 for Clement VII., who, after the sack of Rome, had come to Orvieto for safety. In order to insure the supply of water in case of siege, he had this strange well made. It is like the Tower of Pisa, buried in the earth, save that there are two stairways, the one above the other. Looking down, one sees the water at the bottom like a perfect small jewel, across whose surface visions might well pass.

But after all, it is not in such mere curiosities as these that the charm of Orvieto lies, but in her very self, isolated in that barren world on her precipitous rock. Reached as she now is from the railway by a funicular lift, the traveller little understands how difficult she is to approach. But he who comes to her from the valley by that road which winds for miles up the hill towards her, may even yet understand that she was ever a city of refuge. And was it not, perhaps, with that idea consuming her, that she desired at last the very Body of Christ, so that she might be indestructible and impregnable for ever? She is even yet the city of miracle and mystery, pale and languid with thoughts of death. It is not for nothing that she alone in our world has opened her gates to welcome the very Christ. The whole city having received Him with joy, seems to have passed into the cathedral with Him, and even yet to be hanging on His words and kissing His feet and hands, and waiting for Him to tell her some new great thing. And so the grass grows in the streets, and the people are few, and the fountains have ceased because there is no one to rejoice in their music ; and the very city herself, with finger on her lips, pale and immaculate among the mountains, waits for the Voice as of many waters.

X

VITERBO

VITERBO, that ancient and forsaken city on the slope of
Monte Cimino, may easily be reached from Orvieto either
by road or by rail ; and by whichever way one comes to it one
is compelled to pass through the scarcely less interesting city
of Montefiascone, set on that ridge of hills which divides the
plain of Viterbo from the plain of Bolsena. The way by
rail from Orvieto leaves the main line at the little station of
Attigliano, where it is necessary to change carriages; thence
the train climbs westward through a wilderness of low hills,
turning suddenly to the south just after leaving Montefiascone. By road one follows the highway to Bolsena, but,
some two miles before reaching it, the way turns southward
at Osteria Biacio, climbing at last into Montefiascone just as
one comes into the Via Francigena, which leads to Viterbo
and Rome.

Montefiascone, set on the height of the ridge of hills above
the Lake of Bolsena, is one of the strangest and most beautiful
places in this desolate country that is so nearly a desert. Far
and far away to the north Monte Amiata rises in her loneliness
and her pride like some fabulous mountain all of blue and
silver, her horn that strange and beautiful *cima*, it may be
tipped with snow. In the plain, scarcely six miles away, lies
the lake, steel blue, and marvellously still, far more lovely as
seen from these hills than from its own shore, solitary and forsaken. Above one, on the hill top, stands the city of Monte-

fiascone, the dome of its great church seeming to throw its
shadow across the plain. 'Well may this height,' says Dennis,
in his *Cities of Etruria,* 'well may this height have been chosen
as the site of the national temple! It commands a magnificent and truly Etruscan panorama. The lake shines beneath it
in all its breadth and beauty, truly meriting the title of "the
great lake of Italy "—and though the towers and palaces of
Volsinii have long ceased to sparkle on its bosom, it still
mirrors the white cliffs of its twin islets, and the distant
snow-peaks of Amiata and Cetona. In every other direction
is one "intermingled pomp of vale and hill." In the east
rise the dark mountains of Umbria, and the long line of mist
at their foot marks the course of the Etruscan stream—'

> 'The noble river
> That rolls by the towers of Rome.'

'The giant Apennines of Sabina loom far off, dim through the
hazy noon; and the nearer Ciminian, dark with its once
dreaded forests, stretches its triple-crested mass across the
southern horizon. . . .'

Indeed, Montefiascone may well occupy the site of the
ancient Fanum Voltumnæ, the religious centre of the
Etruscan Confederation. To-day, however, it is one of the
most neglected cities in Italy. Its greatest treasure, if,
indeed, we except that famous wine which the Bishop of
Augsburg loved too well, is the Church of S. Flaviano,
which stands just outside the Roman gate. Built in the
eleventh century, and restored by Urban iv. in 1262, it
may almost be said to be two churches, for its enormous
triforium is so great that it has a high altar of its own as
well as a bishop's throne. Under the high altar, in the
lower church, S. Flaviano sleeps between the enormous
pillars, and there in the nave lies Johann Fugger, the
famous bishop, who being a great wine-bibber, and as some

say a great traveller, on this account sent his valet before
him with orders to taste the wine of all the cities on the
road, and where he found it good to write on the gate of the
city the word 'est.' On coming to Montefiascone, this flunkey
was so taken with the yellow wine of the place, that he wrote
not 'est' only, but 'est, est, est.' And his master, following,
agreed with him so well in his verdict, that he died of the
excess, 'desiring with his last breath that a barrel of this
delicious vintage might every year be spent on his grave ;
bequeathing a considerable legacy to the city on this condition.' Indeed, the conditions of the will were actually
carried out till a few years ago. The inscription on his
grave reads :—

> 'Est, est, est,
> Propter nimium est,
> Ioannes de Foucris,
> Dominus meus
> Mortuus est.'

Omar Khayyám's lines might seem more fitting :—

> 'Ah, with the Grape my fading Life provide,
> And wash the Body whence the Life has died,
> And lay me, shrouded in the living leaf,
> By some not unfrequented Garden-side.
>
> That ev'n my buried Ashes such a snare
> Of Vintage shall fling up into the air
> As not a True-believer passing by
> But shall be overtaken unaware.'

It is but eight miles from Montefiascone to Viterbo.

Of all the cities of Umbria, Viterbo is the most neglected
by the modern traveller, yet, save the very greatest, she is
perhaps most worthy of a visit. Long and long ago, when
the Via Francigena led our fathers to Rome, it was not so,
but then no one seems to have cared for the things of the
Middle Age, so that one did not stay, but passed on to
Rome. Later, when we began to care for Mediæval art, the

railway had already been built, and still we passed to Rome without a thought of Viterbo, for the railway passed by Orte. So Viterbo remained unknown, utterly abandoned by traveller and tourist. Standing, as it were, between these two periods, Hawthorne, though he visited her, writes thus concerning her : 'Viterbo is a large, disagreeable town built at the foot of a mountain, the peak of which is seen through the vista of some of the narrow streets. . . .' It is really all he has to say of a city which, rightly understood, is among the most interesting in Central Italy. For while she has nothing as famous as the Church of S. Francesco at Assisi, the Duomo of Orvieto, the Palace of Urbino, she still keeps the quarter of S. Pellegrino, now the poorest quarter of the city, but a museum, as it were, of the architecture of the Middle Age perhaps more perfect than anything to be found in Siena or Perugia or Assisi, frowning there still with a certain intolerance and disdain of the squalid and restless town that has slowly gathered about it, in the midst of which it is a stranger.

Some idea of the isolation of this quarter may be had most easily perhaps from one of the great towers of Viterbo, the Torre del Municipio for instance, whence this ecclesiastical fortress, for it is little else, seems grappled to the city by an iron bridge across the ravine between them. In the highest part of this island stands to-day the Duomo and the Bishop's palace, but long and long ago the fortress stood there, which was 'the cradle of Viterbo,' the whole place, little more than a walled village, was known as Il Castello di Viterbo, and was one of the last places that the Lombards occupied in Southern Umbria. The story goes, that when King Desiderius came through this region to besiege Pope Adrian, he spied out Viterbo, and was so struck by the natural strength of its position (for it was everywhere surrounded by precipices, and could only be reached by a bridge thrown over the valley by the Etruscans) that he encamped there. To his camp came the Papal Legate, who cursed him and his and excommunicated him. Terrified, perhaps, by the thunder of the Church, Desiderius hesitated and was lost. Soon he learned that Charlemagne had crossed the Alps, and with all speed he hastened back to his great capital of Pavia. But Charles was not to be denied, Pavia fell before him, and Desiderius ended his days in a French convent.

His army, however, the greater part of it at any rate, remained at Viterbo, and establishing itself in that strong place, formed a sort of military colony which was ready enough to mix with the local population, gradually strengthening it by marriage, with barbarian blood, and the forgotten instincts of a warlike people. Even to-day Signor Pinzi, the learned historian of Viterbo, professes to find many signs of the Lombard origin of both city and people.

It was, it seems, the quarrel of the 'investitures' that helped Viterbo to greatness. While the Popes excommunicated the Emperors, and the Emperors supported anti-popes, Viterbo, like every Italian city, concerned only with herself, gained a real if not a juridical freedom. It was then she built her walls; and having made herself safe, she at once began to threaten the safety of others. So wonderful was she in her own conceit, that Rome herself, now become a pope's eunuch, dreamed of envy. One Emperor gave her the title of city, and thus hoped to use her to humiliate Alexander III. Frederick Barbarossa, for it was he, made a solemn entry into the city, and as the representative of God on earth, the Lord paramount of the world, he blessed the people as he passed, extending his hand; and they replied by acclamations. Then Barbarossa went on to the siege, in which he was presently successful, and while his Germans pillaged the treasuries of St. Peter, the Viterbesi contented themselves with carrying off the bronze gates of St. Peter's Church, which they set up in their walls as a trophy. Thirty-three years later Rome avenged herself. Not content with one enemy, Viterbo had raised against herself the Senate as well as the Pope, and though the interdicts of the latter might do her no harm, the army of the former carried her walls, and would have wrecked the city but for Innocent III., who prevented it, seeing perhaps in Viterbo a future stronghold of the Papacy. Nevertheless she was compelled to restore the gates of St. Peter.

A little later, however, she was in worse dangers from Federigo II. With the help of the Ghibellines within her walls, he had drawn her into his alliance, overwhelming her meanwhile with favours. Then as evidence of his affection he proposed to furnish the Castello with a German garrison, and proposed to build there a palace where he and his court might lodge. These marks of his favour touched the Viterbesi; they promptly expelled the Ghibelline faction and besieged the Castello. Federigo seeing himself so well understood, wished to embrace her, and was repulsed. We hear of his sending all through Tuscany for men; his engines threatened the walls, a city of wood faced the city of stone. Yet the Veterbesi dared not despair, they knew what awaited them in case of defeat; Federigo's cruelty was as famous as his perfidy. So she a simple Commune of some sixty thousand souls faced the bastard heir of all the Cæsars, the master of Germany, and of the greater part of Italy, the King of Jerusalem; and the fight that even so might seem unequal and hard enough was more difficult still, for in the Castello there was a strong German garrison. It was Capocci who saved her. This great churchman and captain faced all dangers. He invented machines to break the machines of the Germans, and he mined even under the walls to the camp of the Emperor. Now when the hour of assault had sounded, the Germans, after a hard struggle, broke down the strength of their enemies, and were already

howling like wild beasts in the chase, when a terrible clamour
rose behind them; and looking backward it was seen that
the imperial camp was on fire.   Panic reigned supreme.
In vain Federigo tried to rally his men.   Then rang out the
great bell of Viterbo, sounding for the attack.   The day was
lost and won.

If in her fights with exterior foes Viterbo is but a pattern
of every city in Italy, she is not less their sister in her
struggle with herself.   Indeed, these were the most furious
quarrels of all.   From the twelfth century, the city was
divided into two camps with recognised chiefs, one side
being commanded by the Gatti, the other by Tignosi, and
around them the lesser nobles grouped themselves, following
them with their vassals and dependants.   The feuds seemed
to have come to a head in 1216, another fearful outbreak
followed in 1221, and still worse in 1223.   Of this dreadful
but marvellous period · something remains to us in the
quarter of San Pellegrino.   There among those dark towers,
pierced by a rare window, in those narrow ways plunging
down under arcades or suddenly turning aside and losing
themselves in a gloomy obscurity, about those stairways and
steep passages without end, behind doors that seem to have
been shut for the last time, to-day the poor live.   Here the
towers of the nobles were thickest.

In a tiny piazza in the midst of this decayed splendour,
these indestructible ashes, stands a humble church, while
beside it rises the palace of the Alessandri, the patched and
broken skeleton of what was once a feudal dwelling.   Its
story is a long drawn out tragedy, often brutal enough and
always disastrous.   The Alessandri were of the Gatti faction.
No quarrel was complete without them; they lived on the
brink of the grave.   None stirred in their house, not even
their servants, without arms.   Day and night, through
generation after generation, the oil was kept boiling in the
cauldrons, to be used at any moment from the tower.   One of

the Tignosi faction, Niccolò Cocco, swore to make an end of them. By what marvellous means I know not, he found his way with certain of his fellows into the palace. Once within it was a kind of shambles. Two Alessandri were wounded at the first collision. Amid the rush and skelter, over the shrieks of the women hiding in dark corners, or half stripped, cringing here or there for shelter, the cries of the sentries on the tower were all that reached the outside world. The friends of the Alessandri poured in, not one of the followers of Cocco escaped in that tumultuous and narrow fight. Well, that was only an episode, authentic as it happens, of the terror and hatred that old palace has seen.

But it is not alone in that marvellous quarter of S. Pellegrino that we are vividly reminded of the Middle Age. In the Piazza del Plebiscito two buildings of the thirteenth century remind us that here lived the captain of the people close to the old Palazzo del Comune, now the Palazzo Municipale. Turning thence again to the Duomo, we find the secret of the greatness and importance of Viterbo, of which alone to-day only the ruins are left. Near Rome as she was, she could not escape the influence of the tumults which almost daily shook the eternal city. It was necessary that he who ruled Rome should hold Viterbo also ; so the Popes were wont to sojourn here. Paschal III. was here as a prisoner of Henry V.; Adrian IV., the Englishman, fled hither for refuge; Innocent III. held a council here ; Alexander IV., chased from the Lateran by the Ghibellines, came here with his court and died in the Episcopal palace. Here, too, his successor was elected Urban IV. Then the Viterbesi built a new palace for the Vicegerent of God, but it was Clement IV. who took possession of it. He too died here, and in the great palace eleven Italian cardinals and thirteen foreigners entered the conclave to elect his successor. For many months they could find no one worthy to sit in the throne of Peter. So the Podestà of Viterbo, perhaps fearing a riot, threatened to coerce them.   He was immediately excommunicated, but the whole world was uneasy.   Even S. Buonaventura dared to suggest that the electors should be enclosed till a Pope was elected, and the advice was taken.   For on a certain day the cardinals were seized in their houses and taken to the great hall of the pontifical palace and locked therein.   Still they could not choose.   As a joke, one day the Cardinal Bishop of Porto said to his colleagues: 'Let us lift the roof, which prevents the Holy Spirit from descending to us.'   This saying was rumoured about the city, and, coming to the ears of the magistrates, they ordered the great hall to be uncovered, thus leaving the princes of the Church at the mercy of sun and rain.   In the midst of this dilemma and confusion Louis IX. and Charles of Anjou arrived in Viterbo at the head of the debris of the crusades.   But the cardinals were immovable; they departed without obtaining anything.   Not long after, however, the conclave appointed a commission of six cardinals to elect the Pope.   This commission chose Tebaldo Visconti, a mere archdeacon, then in the Holy Land.   He took the name of Gregory IX.

There are the tombs of two Popes in the Duomo, that of Alexander IV. and John XXI.   Here in this dark but splendid church Clement IV. excommunicated Conradin, when he came into Italy to dispute the Empire with Charles of Anjou. Surrounded by cardinals, prelates, and the whole ecclesiastical court, a torch burning in his hand, the Pope read the Bull, or, as some say, listened while it was read by a herald.   Then suddenly he stood up, cast the torch to the ground, and cried in a loud voice: 'Let him be excommunicate,' the clerks repeating the sentence after him.

It seems to have been in the Duomo, though some speak of S. Silvestro, that Henry d'Almaine, son of Richard, Earl of Cornwall, and nephew of Henry III. of England, was murdered by Guy de Montfort to avenge his father's death at Evesham.

Holinshed tells us that 'Henrie, the brother of this Edmund and son to the foresaid King of Alemaine, as he returned from Affrike, where he had been with Prince Edward, was slaine at Viterbo in Italy (whither he was come about business which he had to do with the Pope) by the hand of Guy de Montfort, the son of Simon de Montfort, Earl of Leicester, in revenge of the same Simon's death. The murther was committed afore the high altar as the same Henrie kneeled there to hear divine service.'

Dante finds the murderer in the seventh circle of Hell :—

> Poco più oltre 'l Centauro s'affisse
> Sovr' una gente, che 'n fino alla gola
> Parea, che di quel Bulicame uscisse,
> Mostrocci un' ombra dall' un canto sola,
> Dicendo, Colui fesse in grembo a Dio
> Lo cuor, che 'n su Tamigi ancor si cola.[1]

It seems that the English princes had been with King Charles of Anjou at the siege of Tunis. They had returned with the army to Sicily, abiding there, as Villani[2] tells us, 'some time to revive the sick and to be refreshed and to repair their fleet; and those kings and lords were held in much honour by Charles, King of Sicily; and afterwards they departed from Sicily, and King Charles with them, and came in the kingdom of Apulia, and by Calabria to Viterbo, where was the papal court without a Pope, and at Viterbo there tarried the said kings, Philip of France and Charles of Sicily, and Edward and Henry, his brothers, sons (sic) of the King of England. . . . Whilst the aforesaid lords were in Viterbo there came to pass a scandalous and abominable thing under the government of King Charles, for Henry . . . being in a church at Mass at the time when the sacrifice of the Body of Christ was being celebrated, Guy, Count of Montfort, who was vicar for King Charles in Tuscany, having no regard for reverence towards God, nor towards King

---

[1] *Inferno*, xii. 115.   [2] Villani, *Chronica Lib.*, vii. cap. 39.

Charles, his lord, stabbed and slew with his own hand the said Henry in revenge for Count Simon of Montfort, his father, slain, through his own fault, by the King of England. And of this it is well to preserve a notable record. . . . The court was greatly disturbed, giving much blame to King Charles, who ought not to have suffered this if he knew thereof, and if he did not know it he ought not to have let it go unavenged. But the said Count Guy, being provided with a company of men-at-arms on horse and on foot, was not content only with having done the said murder, for as much as a cavalier asked him what he had done and he replied : " J'ai fait ma vengeance," and that cavalier said, " Comment ? Votre père fut trainé." And immediately he returned to the church and took Henry by the hair, and, dead as he was, he dragged him vilely without the church ; and when he had done the said sacrilege and homicide, he departed from Viterbo and came safe and sound into Maremma to the lands of Conte Rosso, his father-in-law. By reason of the death of the said Henry, Edward . . . very wrathful and indignant against King Charles, departed from Viterbo and came with his followers through Tuscany, and abode in Florence, and knighted many citizens, giving them horses and all knightly accoutrements very nobly, and then he came into England and set the heart [of his cousin] in a golden cup upon a pillar at the end of London Bridge over the Thames to keep the English in mind of the outrage. For the which thing Edward, after he was king, was never friends with King Charles nor with his folk.'

In the Church of S. Francesco at the other end of the city are two more papal tombs, those of Clement IV. and Hadrian V. Beside them lies Pietro di Vico, Ghibelline and villain, robber and fornicator, blasphemer and sacrilegist, who, repenting on his death-bed, ordered that his body should be divided into seven parts and buried thus in S. Francesco in expiation of his sins.

The tomb of Clement IV. has as strange a history. This Frenchman was first buried as he had wished in S. Maria de Gradi of the Dominicans. It was then found that miracles were performed at his tomb. This brought both fame and money to the church. The canons of the Duomo began to grow jealous, and were supported in their jealousy by the whole of their quarter. The conclave, which anxiously enough watched the whole disgraceful quarrel, ordered that the body should be removed to a church in another quarter. However, one morning the body was discovered in the Duomo. Only a threat of excommunication was strong enough to force the canons to give it up. This was in 1275.

Everywhere in Viterbo we come upon fierce and cunning memories that one seems to think might easily awaken. She is a city of the Middle Age, and it is delightful that the one thing in her past that she still remembers should be not any hardly won battle but a victory of love, the love of S. Rosa, whose festival in September she keeps so religiously, and with so much enthusiasm. The whole province of Viterbo flocks into the city for love of S. Rosa. She was a Franciscan Tertiary, who died in 1252, famous only for her love of the poor and the disinherited. Yet even now, on the third of September, sixty men carry the great car, weighing three thousand chilogrammes, bearing her image, from the Porta Romana through the Piazza del Popolo to the Piazza di S. Rosa before her church. And whenever you come to the city, that church will be the first place your *vetturino* will take you to. Nor will he let you enter alone. He will leave his horse, and climbing the steps with you, kneel at the shrine, which guards the uncorrupt body of the little Saint. There you will be given roses, and for sure he will beg one of you. And, in truth, of all I saw in Viterbo, as it seemed to me, it was only these few fading roses that I cared to remember when I got back to Orvieto.

XI

CITTÀ DELLA PIEVE

I WENT from Orvieto to Città della Pieve for the sake of Perugino, who was born there in 1446. I stayed there more than three days, which was all the time I had, for its own sake. It is a little city, some miles from the railway, set on a hill sixteen hundred feet above sea-level.

The Peruginos which remain there are not the best works of the master. It would seem that for the most part they are the work of his pupils, or of his old age. But the city itself, with its views of the lakes of Trasimeno and Chiusi and the tawny valley, a veritable work by Piero della Francesca, southward towards Rome, the quiet peace of the place, the magnificent woods beneath it, are in themselves more valuable than the mediocre work of the great painter who was born there; for they remain for ever in the memory as a piece of the last forlorn beauty of mediæval Italy. It is surely the sun that redeems modern Italy from a sort of vulgarity, or the suspicion of a kind of hideous squalor. He clothes her with an imperial beauty, so that we look into her eyes even now as into the eyes of a queen. Her faint and fading beauty seems to us worth everything else in the world because the sun shines upon her—the sun which is the smile of God.

And so it is perhaps to the sun, who robes this little city, too, in a mantle of splendid colour all through the day, and at evening adorns her with bright fire, his fierce smouldering jewels, and the radiance of his face, that we owe the curious fascination of a place so poor, so desolate, and so forlorn.

The Oratory of S. Maria de' Bianchi holds the most considerable work attributed to Perugino that the little city can boast. It is an Adoration of the Magi in the well-known manner of the great Umbrian. Under a lofty shed, uplifted by four graceful pillars, Madonna sits with the Divine Child in her lap, while the three kings stand or kneel before Him. An immense number of figures moves across the picture. And the background is just one of the exquisite Umbrian spaces fulfilled with light, air and delicate hill, and a faint gesture of the mountains in the distance. Fantastic trees, through whose branches filters that limpid clear air, spring here and there from the nearer hills. A few delicate, wing-shaped clouds float lightly, magically, in the soft sky, from which an angel plunges, hinting, as it were, at benediction. And over all lies the profound peace of yesterday, the immaculate morning of the old world. Many and many a time has Perugino painted a scene like this, and almost always with the same secret understanding of space. He seems to say to us, 'Lift up your hearts,' and to have already anticipated the answer.

There are other pictures by Perugino, or his pupils, in the city, which it does not seem worth while to describe, because no description of a picture, however careful, however tactful, can really create in a reader's mind the very thing itself. And if you will not come to Città della Pieve, these pictures are not of so much importance that it will grieve you to miss them altogether; and if you come, why, you need no description from me.

But it is Città della Pieve herself that I would have you love, finding in her gates, Porta S. Agostino and Porta S. Francesco, a real and homely beauty. Her brows are bound with fading leaves, yellow and red, in the autumn of her life; it is only the sun who is still faithful to her in his profound impartiality towards good or evil, old or young; and he, looking into her face, finds her still beautiful with the adoration that he compels from the meanest and the simplest.

. . . .

It is but six and twenty miles from Città della Pieve to Perugia, through the valley and over the low hills; and returning by this route to the capital of Umbria, it is possible to see the beautiful picture of Perugino at Panicale, in the Church of S. Sebastiano, of the martyrdom of that saint. It is worth some trouble to see. At Chiusi, northwards from Città, there are innumerable Etruscan remains; but I did not go there, both because the weather was bad and because I wished to visit the Etruscan cities with some sort of plan; it was too hot to venture into the Maremma. And it seemed to me better to see Chiusi with those strange cities of death, than with the more mediæval towns to which I had confined myself. Besides Chiusi is in Tuscany, though only just across the frontier. The traveller, however, who is not likely to come this way again should see everything he possibly can, and not put off visiting a city for any reason whatsoever unless he be indifferent to it.

XII

GUBBIO

IT was one morning of early summer that I set out from Perugia by the Porta Augusta for Gubbio, across the mountains. The way was musical with streams, for there had been rain in the night, and the world was beautiful. Downhill into the valley of the Tiber I went, past the olives and the willows, whose leaves were dancing gravely in the wind, watching their own beauty in the shallows of the great river. Then, gradually, after I had crossed the Tiber, I came into a desolate land of mountains and bare hillsides, utterly forlorn and without the fellowship of trees or flowers. The wind was dismal and lonely, wandering over the moorland as though in search of companions. Now and again a shepherd clad in goatskins towered in silhouette against the furthest sky—a magnificent figure, simple and antique, keeping the world sweet; and sometimes a little group of trees, scarcely sufficient for a copse, whispered together as though in fear of the indestructible silence. Far and far away, the beautiful valleys of Umbria led me down innumerable vistas towards many a splendid city, famous and deserted, full even yet of lovely things—the profound, material dreams of the great artists, or the lives of the saints. And all day over all the splendour and the ruin, the uplifted Apennines towered in the sunlight, their brows white with snow that the sun transformed into glory.

Towards evening I came to a valley, and crossing it in the magical evening light, solemn and grave and quiet with a kind of immaculate peace, I entered Gubbio at sunset.

Gubbio is the dream of some mediæval miniaturist. Built on the lower slopes of Monte Calvo, the little city, now too small for its great old walls, rises in terraces one above another, where the cypresses behind and among the palaces and churches point their joined hands ever upwards in that long life which is an everlasting prayer. Behind the city Monte Calvo, arid and tawny, lifts its head into the soft sky and seems to cry to innumerable hills and valleys, and to the great, indifferent mountains, Repent! Repent! Repent! Over the city, crowning it so perfectly that it surely cannot have been placed there by chance, the beautiful Gothic Palazzo dei Consoli, forlorn and deserted, arises in ruin from some dream of the Middle Age. And indeed in that old time Gubbio was full of dreams. So old that it is impossible to decide the date of its foundation, or to account for its curious religions, it still possesses the remains of a Roman theatre in the immensity of that plain which has consumed so great a part of the old city. Utterly destroyed by Totila, it was again besieged in 1155 by Barbarossa when he had done with Spoleto. And it was then that its famous Bishop, S. Ubaldo, saved it from the hands of that strange and terrible General, who indeed was threatening to consume even the Papacy in his insatiable desire for Empire. In 1364, the people of Gubbio invited the Counts of Montefeltro, who had established their lordship over the town of Urbino, which ever after gave them their title, receiving investiture of it from the Popes in the thirteenth century, to expel from the city the tyrants Gabrielli. It was Antonio, Count of Montefeltro and of Urbino, who was called upon, not only by the people of Gubbio but by those of Cagli also, from which city he expelled the Ceccardi. Less than a hundred

years later we read of the magnificent welcome the city gave
to Borso, Marquis of Ferrara, who in March 1471, on his way
to Rome, spent four days at Gubbio and Urbino, with an
escort of 500 horsemen, 100 foot, and 150 mules.

'He was met at the frontier by the Count,' says Dennistoun, 'accompanied by the Lords of Faenza, Rimini, and
Pesaro, with a noble following, and conducted to the palace
of Gubbio, Federigo and his nephew, Ottaviano della Carda,
leading the palfrey of this proud parvenu.'

That palace of Gubbio, the Palazzo Ducale, is now, alas, a
ruin. It stands close to the cathedral, splendid even in its
decay—only the courtyard remains to remind us how beautiful it once was. Built perhaps by Francesco di Giorgio,
perhaps by Baccio Pontelli, or again by Luciano Laurano,
the architect of the palace at Urbino, it is described by
Sanzi as 'facing south-east and flanked by mountains on the
north, overlooking fertile valleys and smiling champaigns,
and excelling the attractions of Urbino in charming prospects
and pleasant pathways.' The initials of the two Montefeltrian
Dukes Federigo and Guidobaldo appear in the decoration,
and even the oak of the della Rovere family, which might
seem to suggest restoration, at the least, at a later date.

'Differing much,' says Signor Luigi Bonfatti, 'from the
architecture at Urbino, its courtyard is very fine, of the
mixed or composite style usual in that age. The windows,
doors, and chimneys have stone lintels, exquisitely chiselled
in low relief with masterly arabesque designs, those in the
interior being touched with gold. The ceilings, now partially
decayed, are all of wood in half-relief compartments with
heavy cornices, and roses coloured and gilded. The palace
was completed by Duke Guidobaldo, who commissioned the
cabinet or closet of superb *intarsia*, thirteen by six and a half
feet. This tiny room is nineteen feet high, but the inlaid
work goes only half-way up. It is of the finest patterns and

workmanship, including several emblematic representations of music, literature, physical science, geography, and war. On the cornice is an inscription now in part illegible.'[1]

When in 1518 the Dukedom of Urbino passed to Catherine de' Medici, then a child, and the Pope unceremoniously seized, almost like a highwayman, the territory of the Rovere, Gubbio, 'which had shown itself less devoted' to the interests of that family than Urbino *fidelissimo*, was made the capital of the Duchy. The della Rovere, however, got back their own; Francesca Maria was restored, and Urbino once more became one of the most glorious cities of the Renaissance. But the Papacy still desired to possess a province so near to Rome, so splendid and so famous. And at length, the last della Rovere, frightened by disease and priests and mountebanks, bequeathed to the Popes what they had so often tried to obtain by fraud. It is perhaps one of the most tragical histories of the world; that story of a strong and powerful race falling at last into the hands of priests and dreamers, and yielding very willingly at last, and almost with a sigh of relief, what its ancestors had lived and died to save. Thus Gubbio in 1631 came under the rule of Rome.

Gubbio, however, whose life would seem to have been so eventful in worldly affairs, is by no means insignificant in the history of Umbrian art. Oderigi da Gubbio, that contemporary of Giotto to whom Dante speaks in Purgatory, was the forerunner, it may well be, of the Umbrian school, so delightfully pictorial, so unreal in its criticism of life. 'O, diss' io lui, non se' tu Oderisi,' says Dante:

> 'Art not thou Oderis,' I cried,
> 'Of Gubbio, and that school the pride

---

[1] See also the *Memoirs of the Dukes of Urbino*, by James Dennistoun of Dennistoun, 1851, vol. i. p. 164.

Which they of Paris àll
The limner's mystery call ?'
'Brother, more bright the pages shine,
Bologna's Franco did design :
Now his is all the fame
'Less I some part may claim.

.   .   .   .

So Cimabue deemed the field
Of painting his, but now doth yield
To Giotto his renown,
And all obscure hath grown.' [1]

This legendary painter—for no work of his is actually
known to exist—was placed in Purgatory by Dante, it would
seem, on account of his pride and zeal in his art. The son
of a certain Guido of Gubbio, in 1268 he went to Bologna,
and Dennistoun suggests that he founded a school there, on
what authority I do not know.   Certainly he painted there,
'in fifteen days, no less than eighty-two miniatures, in good
azure blue, in an antiphonary, for which he was paid thirty
Bolognese soldi.' Vasari says that he met Giotto in Rome ;
however that may be, his pupil Guido Palmerucci, born about
1280, whose work may be found up and down Gubbio, more
or less ruined—in S. Maria dei Laici, in the Palazzo Com-
munale—was the master of Martino Nelli, whose son
Ottaviano was the greatest of the Gubbian painters. I speak
of Ottaviano Nelli elsewhere ; his works are not rare in
Umbria, nor are they without that decorative value for us
which, after all, is the chief delight of all primitive painting.

Martino Nelli, the father of Ottaviano, has left certain
fragments of frescoes in Gubbio, which are his rather by
tradition than by any direct evidence we possess.   But
Ottaviano may be seen in all his country splendour in
S. Maria Nuova, where he has painted over the first altar in
the south aisle Madonna with the Divine Child in her lap.

---

[1] Shadwell's *Dante*, Purgatory, xi. 79.

The Child lifts His hand in blessing the wife of .S. Pietro, as it is said, and the Donor presented by St. Antony, while He listens to an angel playing on a kind of violin. God the Father, surrounded by angels and cherubs, is in the act to crown Madonna, who gazes out of the picture with something of that indifference which we expect from Ottaviano. Behind her, angels lift a kind of canopy or curtain.

It is, as I think, in such a picture as this that we find the fading influence of a man evidently so great in his time as Oderigi. The whole picture is a huge miniature with much of the gaiety of colour to be found in those delightful works that enliven certain pages or corners of the great dull service-books. It is difficult to believe that, for these early painters, Art was more than 'an accidental play of sunlight and shadow for a few moments on the wall or floor'; that their naïve works scattered up and down Italy in the churches and museums are anything but such a space of fallen light, entirely pleasant if we are content to consider it as such, rather than as an attempt to realise life. No more than the Japanese did these early men grapple with life; their work is for the most part designed to carry out the decoration of a church, to symbolise a certain religious truth, rather than to bring it down to the level of everyday experience. It might seem that as soon as doubts of these religious truths began to disturb the minds of men they sought with great earnestness to realise them, succeeding only in proving them the more improbable. To a Fra Angelico heaven was of more value than the whole world; all that was lovely in the earth or the sky he, nothing doubting, laid up in heaven. But the great painters, Signorelli, Michelangelo, Raphael, and Leonardo, when they deal with a religious subject, either realise it for us so that we think of it no longer as supernatural but as a kind of fairy tale, or else as in Raphael's Madonnas content themselves a little sentimentally with the divinity of all Motherhood. As decoration, their work is to my mind inferior in beauty to that of the early men which was content with symbols. The Sistine Chapel fails as a chapel, it is a magnificent picture-gallery. Those languid or passionate figures thrust themselves upon us with terrifying insistence. Man is so omnipotent there that there is no room for God. But in the Upper Church at Assisi, or, better still, in that great golden Church of S. Marco at Venice, which is simply a vast mosaic, man is dwarfed beside the beautiful symbols of God, the expression of the Faith, the importance of just that, expressed with a profound understanding of decoration as such, so that God might have at the least a House Beautiful.

Among the pupils of Ottaviano at Gubbio may be mentioned Domenico di Cecchi, Bernardino di Nanni, and Giacomo di Bedi, whose works in S. Agostino are still fair upon the old walls.

It is in the Palazzo dei Consoli are preserved the famous Eugubian Tables found in 1444 in a subterranean vault, not far from the Roman theatre in the plain. Those tables, so old that it is possible they date from B.C. 200, are really the most interesting things in Gubbio. They contain possibly the rules of a College of Priests—the Fratres Atredii, as it is said—and are written in Etruscan and in Latin characters. The language is, however, Umbrian. M. Michel Bréal in *Les Tables Eugubines* has made an interesting study of them.

In the same building we find the small collection of pictures that the city has brought together. Apart from the Umbrian pictures, which are of interest chiefly to the student, there is but one picture of real beauty and importance—a Madonna and Child, by Fra Lippo Lippi of Florence. An example of the famous Gubbio ware of the sixteenth century glows like a great ruby in a cabinet in the gallery.

But it is not in such a museum as this that the mere

traveller will delight but in Gubbio itself, its picturesque old streets, and perhaps in its churches and fields; for Gubbio is a garden.

The Church of S. Agostino stands just outside the city by the Porta Romana. It is in the choir of this church that Ottaviano Nelli himself, perhaps, and certainly his pupils, have painted the story of St. Augustine's life. It is useless to recount again a life so well known as that of St. Augustine. Even the headstrong Protestant will recognise the various scenes in the life of one to whom he has appealed so vehemently. Lately other work of Ottaviano's has been brought to light here, a fresco of the Last Judgment among the rest. In S. Maria Piaggiola, close to the Porta Vittoria, you may also find a ruined picture of Madonna; and as in that picture by him in S. Maria Nuova, we feel that this man, whose work at Foligno one critic at least has found little better than 'a marsh growth,' had a real understanding of the convention that is the condition of art.

I missed the great Festa and Procession of the Ceri, which happens on the 15th of May. Mr. H. M. Bower in a book called *The Elevation and Procession of the Ceri at Gubbio*, has written with knowledge of this most ancient feast. The figures of S. Ubaldo, S. Giorgio, and S. Antonio on great pedestals, each lifted by more than forty men, are rushed through the little city. It is a festa of renown. All Umbria goes to see it and rejoice. Whether it be a remembrance of the benign reign of Ceres or a feast of Ceri—Tapers,—or, as Mr. Bower seems to suggest, a feast of the god Cerfus, whoever he may have been, I know not; it is one of those ancient and joyful things that are still left, as it were, in the corners of the world, which to miss is a misfortune.

XIII

MONTONE AND CITTÀ DI CASTELLO

IT was for the sake of Luca Signorelli that one summer day I set out very early in the morning by train for Città di Castello. The way is fair enough and, indeed, before long I came into the upper valley of the Tiber, just before Umbertide, where I stayed awhile, again for his sake, for in the church of S. Croce there is his picture of the Descent from the Cross. Old as he was when he painted it, he had lost none of his power, for I found it certainly one of the most beautiful and tender pictures of a scene he seems to have loved, since he has painted it so often. It is true that this work has been over painted, and in part, it seems, destroyed, for an old Crowe and Cavalcaselle tells us there was a lunette above containing a Pietà, but how splendid it is in spite of these misfortunes. They have just loosed the divine Body from the Cross, a rainbow coloured scarf of Umbria supports it, caught round the crutch of the Cross and held by one of the Apostles. Two others are mounted on ladders, and gently, slowly, they are trying to lower the Son of God that he may rest for three days in the earth he has loved. Other two of the Apostles hold the ladders, and at the foot of the Cross itself Madonna has swooned away ; two holy women look to her, while St. Mary Magdalene, half mad with tears, places her hand under the divine wounded feet, and grasping the Cross to save herself from falling, seems about to gather

our Lord into her arms almost as one might a child.   In
the foreground, on the right, St. John seems to be praying
for Madonna, and then suddenly into this picture, so solemn
and tragic, steals the beautiful and only half sorrowful figure
of a girl splendidly dressed, her hands clasped before her.
She seems just to have halted for a moment at the sight, and
to have lowered her eyes as Madonna, swaying like a lily, fell
softly to the ground.   Who is this figure that passes by ?

Not far away in the landscape they bury Christ in the
new tomb of Joseph.   And, indeed, though the whole picture
is full of tragedy, the world, that spacious world of Umbria,
is at Spring, all the trees have budded, and the fields are
golden in the sun, the sky is full of glory and very pure.
It is with a sort of surprise one passes from the tragedy of
that death of God to the pictures of the predella, yet to
a fifteenth century mind the transition was natural enough.
There, in the midst, Luca has painted the Discovery of the
True Cross, and on the left the March of Constantine, on
the right the Entry of Heraclius into Jerusalem.   Indeed,
as we look on the two last little pictures, it might seem that
the whole earth had suddenly arisen to march to the Holy
Sepulchre.

When from Umbertide I proposed to myself to go to Montone, a little lofty town some eight miles away in the mountains
to the north, it was for the sake of Bonfigli I set out, for,
as I was told, he had painted a Gonfalon for that very place,
a thing so splendid and lovely that to see it was worth all
the weariness of the way.   It was not, however, any work of
Bonfigli I saw, when just after Mass on Sunday morning I
entered the Church of S. Francesco.   Montone has many tradi-
tions, and was the birthplace of one of the greatest of the Condottieri, the founders of the Bracceschi clan, to which Niccolò
Piccinino belonged—Braccio Fortebraccio.   The mangificent

standard, which a place once so famous was able to command, was painted in 1482, if we may judge from its style, by some pupil of Fiorenzo di Lorenzo, certainly Bonfigli can have had no hand in it.   In the midst Madonnina stands like a flower, her arms spread a little wearily, supporting her cloak over the people of Montone and their city, above which she stands. Her hands, which St. Francis and St. Anthony of Padua seem about to kiss, are more delicate and fair than the petals of the lilies, and her body, clothed in a marvellous patterned cloak, as delicate as the calix of a flower, rises like the hope of the world from the midst of the people.   Around her kneel, beside St. Francis and St. Anthony, six other saints, among them St. Sebastian and S. Bernardino, St. John Baptist and S. Brazio, with two other bishops.   Above, in heaven, Christ blesses her, and two angels seem to sing Magnificat. And in truth this Gonfalon is worth all the trouble of the way, since it is without doubt the most beautiful standard in the world.

From Montone to Città di Castello is near twenty miles by road, but by train from Umbertide or Trestina an easy way enough.

Set on the ruins of the Roman Tifernum, which Pliny knew so well, all its Roman memories seem to have been destroyed by Totila, who destroyed it in 542, and it seems to have remained a desolate village, a mere huddle of ruins, till a few years later its bishop, S. Floridus, rebuilt it.   Was it for this that, through all the hurly-burly of the great quarrel, it remained true Guelf, and that Gubbio was so often Ghibelline?   However that may be, by 1440, in the midst of the useless wars that at that time ravaged Lombardy, the Marche and the Kingdom Città di Castello placed herself, at the suggestion of the Pope, under the protection of Florence, while Cosino de' Medici bought the neighbouring town of Borgo San Sepolcro from him for twenty-five thousand ducats. It is about this time that we first hear of the family of Vitelli, who made themselves lords. Thirty-four years later, in 1474, we find the Papacy, by means of Cardinal Giuliano della Rovere, attempting to reduce these too power-ful vassals of the Holy See. He laid siege to Città di Castello, which alarmed the Florentines, who sent forces to Borgo. Federigo of Urbino then appeared on the scene, and whether by persuasion or terror induced the Vitelli to make terms, none too favourable however, with the Pope. Sixtus IV., the assassin, complained bitterly to Lorenzo il Magnifico that Florence had helped the insurgents. The Papacy had, however, not yet done with the Vitelli. In 1502 Vitellozzo Vitelli was invited by Cesare Borgia to a conference at Sinigaglia, where he was strangled. Thus Città di Castello came again directly into the power of the Papacy, which it was not able to shake off till in 1860 Italy was united, and the Papacy as a temporal power finally, it might seem, disposed of.

Città di Castello produced no great painter, her best being that Francesco, who was of the school of Raphael. Under the Vitelli, however, she was the patron both of Raphael and Signorelli.

Raphael painted his first signed picture, the first picture really his own, after his arrival in Perugia, for the Gavari Chapel in the Dominican church here, at the order of Vitellozzo Vitelli. It must have been executed in 1501 or early in 1502, before the Vitelli were driven out by Cesare Borgia. The picture is now in the possession of Mr. Ludwig Mond, who had it from Lord Dudley, and but for the signature, as Vasari says, 'it would certainly be taken for Perugino's work.' The composition is exactly similar to the Crucifixion which Perugino had just finished for the friars of S. Fran-cesco del Monte at Perugia. It was here in Città di Castello, too, that Raphael in 1504 painted his Sposalizio,

I

now in the Brera. There are, however, to-day no pictures by Raphael in the city. Her glory lies in the work of her guest Luca Signorelli. Though one of these pictures, the S. Sebastian, was painted for the church of S. Domenico, and the other, a Madonna and Saints for the church of S. Francesco at Montone, they are both to-day in the Città di Castello, one in the old convent, now the Museo Civico, the other in Palazzo Mancini. The S. Sebastian was painted in 1496, about the same time as the Standard of Urbino, and in spite of its bad condition it is a work of surpassing beauty. One feels, however, a real disappointment in the figure of the saint, as though for once Signorelli had been touched by a certain sentimentalism, to be found, I think, nowhere else in his work. Above the Saint, God the Father leans from heaven, and below five soldiers with superb and splendid gestures string their bows. Two of them are nude but for the striped loin cloth Signorelli loved so well, the others are dressed in Renaissance fashion. Not far away certain burgesses and women look on at the tragedy, as indeed they must often have done in those days, while in the distance one sees a street leading steeply up a height to a Roman amphitheatre, filled with a bustle of soldiers.

The Madonna and Saints, in the possession of the Mancini family, is a late work, in which perhaps a certain weariness may be discerned. It bears the following inscription, hidden by the frame : *Jacobus Vannutius Nobilis Cortonensis olim episcopus Perusinus Hoc Deo Max. Et Divo Honophrio sacellum Dedicavit : cui in Archiepiscopum Nicænum Assumpto Nepos Dionisius successit, et quanta vides impensa ornavit aequa pietas. MCCCCLXXXIV.'*

In the Archivio of Montone, Miss Crutwell tells us,[1] 'a deed, dated September 10, 1515, was discovered, which

---

[1] In her excellent book on Signorelli : *Luca Signorelli* (Bell, 1899), p. 99.

speaks of an altar-piece presented by the master as a free gift to a certain French physician, Luigi de Rutanis, in gratitude 'for services rendered, and for those which he hoped to receive in future.' The altar-piece was discovered by Signor Giacomo Mancini in a cellar in Montone, almost destroyed by damp and neglect, and since its restoration it is perhaps hardly fair to discuss more than the general lines. . . .' The Virgin stands with something of the weight of a statue on the Cherubim, while on one side is S. Sebastian, and on the other S. Cristina, with 'a terribly realistic millstone hung round her neck.' Above, two angels hold her crown above her head, and below S. Jerome and S. Niccolò di Bari stand with open books in their hands, reading. Beneath Madonna's feet opens the soft Umbrian world about Trasimeno. And, indeed, this landscape is the most charming part of the picture, full of air and the softness of country sounds, the call of the shepherd to his sheep, the wind among the trees.

The Museum contains little else of much interest, certain works of the della Robbia school, a Madonna, an Annunciation, two *Putti* with garlands and a lunette from the church of S. Cecilia—the Adoration of the Magi.

The city itself, however, is one of the most charming in the upper valley of the Tiber. Its old walls, dating from the early years of the sixteenth century, still hem it in, and then it still possesses many interesting buildings of the fourteenth, fifteenth, and sixteenth centuries, the palaces of the Vitelli for instance, the Palazzo del Governo, the Palazzo Comunale, and the Duomo. Not one of these, however, is half so beautiful as the view of the valley and the hills that one gets from the Giardino Pubblico to the west of the Duomo. Through the valley the Tiber flows towards Rome and the sea, and above and beyond rise the mountains, those majestic and indestructible peaks which were before the foundation of any city, and have looked with the same in-difference upon Etruscan, Umbrian, and Italian; that saw Totila pass by with his Goths, and Cesare with his Spaniards, and have yielded themselves only to the love of the youth Raphael, or that great old man Luca Signorelli, who loved them.

XIV

THE WAY TO URBINO

I SET out for Urbino as early as five o'clock one golden
morning in the middle of July. Gubbio was a little
languid after the festa. The steep, narrow streets seemed
quieter and graver than' ever before, and the whole country
more like a deep garden, silent and almost conventual under
the soft, ineffable sky. It is a way long but beautiful that you
follow, at first through a great ravine, where a noisy stream
splashes over the strange red rocks. The world here appears
never to have awakened, and the barren hills seem to have
escaped the creating gesture of God. Soon I came to Scheggia,
and took the highway of the Roman armies, Via Flaminia.
It was from here I first saw the summits of the Furlo, white
and immaculate, like great angels standing in the sunlight,
their feet on the iron of the world. Presently I came into
a vale full of trees—oaks and chestnuts, and by noon I was
in Cagli, where I slept. Rising about four o'clock in the
afternoon I set out to see Cagli, which appears to be devoted
to tannery. It was for Raphael's sake that I stayed at Cagli,
for Giovanni Sanzio, his father, has more than one fine
painting there. I came upon one of them in the church of
S. Domenico, in the second chapel on the left. The whole
alcove, for it is little more, is painted in fresco by Giovanni,—
Madonna with her Son and many angels, together with St.
John Baptist and St. Dominic, St. Peter and St. Francis.
While above, in a kind of lunette, he has painted a great

landscape with the Resurrection in the foreground. From the roof God the Father, surrounded by many musical angels, blesses us.

This great man—for he seems to have been something more than a great painter, so near to the splendid court of Urbino —came under the influence of the three great men among his contemporaries, Piero della Francesca, Melozzo da Forli, Luca Signorelli. He is said to have invited Piero della Francesca to Urbino in 1469, and to have entertained him as a guest in his own house. At that time Urbino was at the height of its splendour, full of learned men from all Italy, the delight of artists as much for the treasures that the dukes had collected there as for the civility of their court. And Giovanni Sanzio, at that time probably the leading painter at court, was in a position to offer hospitality to Piero della Francesca; he appears to have done so very willingly. It was, however, Piero's pupil, Melozzo da Forli, who would appear to have influenced Giovanni most strongly. The great painter of the Resurrection at Borgo San Sepolcro, of the frescoes now destroyed at Loretto, of the story of the Cross at Arezzo, found in Melozzo da Forli, it would seem, a kind of St. Paul; and it was through him, as I think, that Piero's ideas were circulated through the schools rather than by Piero himself; and it was of Melozzo rather than of Piero, though he speaks of him also, that Giovanni tells us in his *Cronaca*, written in verse, now in the Vatican. Simple and grave, his gentleness, his nobility, are what we should wish for in the father of the most serene and perfect of all painters. That he was known to Mantegna, we are assured partly by his work and partly by his *Cronaca*. He visited Milan. It seems not unlikely that since the influence of Mantegna would appear to be by no means small in the Umbrian school, especially in such painters as Piero della Francesca and Fiorenzo di Lorenzo, it was through

Giovanni Sanzio that the great northerner first penetrated into mystical Italy.

Close to his frescoes in a chapel of the Tiranni family in S. Domenico, we find a Pietà with S. Jerome and S. Buonaventura. We shall meet this great man again in Urbino; but it is not there, but here, in the church of S. Domenico, that we find him at his greatest. The serene sunlight that was Raphael seems already to have touched him here where he stands, in the dawn of that perfect day; and, indeed, as it is said, the young Raphael himself, a boy of nine years old, lives as the angel to the right of the Blessed Virgin.

It was still very early in the morning of the next day when I set out from Cagli. Before me the Furlo lifted its white brows for the sun to kiss in the dawn I could not see. It was not long before I was in the midst of that fantastic fairyland, with its strange, horrid cliffs, its threatening crags, its changing lights, and tremendous gateways. On any day but that it must have inspired me with a kind of terror, but the sun was so golden, the sky so serene, that I felt nothing but the mysterious beauty of a scene so fantastical. I was, as it were, on the roof of mystical Italy, which lay beneath me like the great sunny nave of a Romanesque church—the high altar was at Siena, the south transept ended in the silence of Orvieto, the north in the holy city of Assisi, and the great west door where all the nations waited to enter was Rome. As I went upward, higher and higher, with the roar of a mighty torrent in my ears, I seemed to hear the deep breathing of the great organ that was soon to fill that church with some splendid chant. And suddenly it came to me in a kind of profound breadth and depth and simplicity, as of some ancient tone of the plainsong. In a great land of oats and cornfields, with grave uplifted hills, green and perfect and beautiful with the wild rose, many waters swept by me with their song, and in unending suavity those great uplands carried the chant to heaven with the Gloria of the Sun. It was like the evening canticle of the world, splendid with the beauty of the flowers. Ah! shall I ever again hear that grave and perfect chant? shall I ever on some fortunate day find again that profound, monotonous music over the hum of the world? All that we have suffered and dared to hope, all our helpless love and despair, are expressed in the sorrowful and noble music that surprises us in those lonely, forlorn mountains.

XV

URBINO

IT was evening when I came suddenly, almost at a turning
of the way, upon that once splendid city of Urbino. It
was as though I beheld the havoc of heaven. Time, like a
proud and terrible angel with his legions, had laid her low.
In a kind of towering ruin she seemed to lie before me awaiting with strained, despairing eyes the benediction of evening.
Far away to the west I knew Siena pointed her white hands
to the sky, while southward and west Orvieto knelt upon her
barren hills, beautiful because of the blood of Christ. And
lowly in the valley of the Tiber, towards the Eternal City
where the Church awaits even to-day so patiently her
victory or deliverance, Assisi crouched beneath Subasio, a
little brown city vowed to God. Is it strange, think you,
that amid all this patient faith, this curious ·unconsciousness
of material things, a kind of ecstatic dream of the Kingdom
of Heaven, Urbino should stand upon her hill, still in the
attitude of attention and service, like a great Caryatid from
whose immortal shoulders some temple has fallen away?
Between Urbino and those mystical cities of Umbria, one by
one out of the night the great angels of the Apennines
appear, on whose shoulders Heaven rests, on whose foreheads
gleam imperishable stars. You will not find Urbino full of
joy, as Florence or Siena are; it might seem that within her
walls it is necessary to remember death every hour of the
day. Have not her kings, even in the splendid years, deserted

her for a cell, being in love with death before their angel
came? Yet on her hills uptossed, like great white breakers
almost, against the cliffs of the Apennines, she is even to-day
a kind of miracle. It is true she possesses pictures of some
importance, churches of a certain forlorn beauty, a ruined
palace, a broken heart; but what are these to us who pass
by? She is a dead city, that I have loved.

Far out of the tourist's path, till 1898 Urbino could only
be reached after a long journey by diligence. Since then,
however, a small line of railway has made it more easily
accessible from Fabriano. But even now what was one of the
most splendid cities of the Renaissance, that gave birth to
Raphael and harboured Piero della Francesca and Luca
Signorelli, whose court was the most refined in Italy, serv-
ing as a pattern for the *Cortegiano* of the Count Baldassare
Castiglione, is without a decent inn. Lying there on the
hills, still beautiful and proud, Urbino seems to bear a kind
of pathetic witness to the power of mortality, against which
neither brass nor stone may endure.

That Count Baldassare, sent by Duke Guidobaldo to the
court of King Henry VII. of England, who made him a knight,
is perhaps our best witness to the splendour of the city and
the exquisite refinement of the court of Urbino. Castiglione
came to England as proxy for Duke Guidobaldo at his instal-
lation as a Knight of the Garter in 1503. It is said that on
his return 'his conversation of all that he had seen in a
country so imperfectly known as England was greatly relished
by the Duke, and his anecdotes of its court, its wealth, and
its wonders long continued to enliven the palace circle of
Montefeltro.' What Count Baldassare saw must indeed have
surprised him, 'the choicest spirit' of Duke Guidobaldo's
'elegant court.' In 1611, more than a hundred years later,

an English traveller, on his return, writes as follows of the manners of Italy in comparison with those of England :—

'I observed,' says this traveller,[1] 'a custom, in all those Italian cities and towns through which I passed, that is not used in any other country that I saw in my travels; neither do I think that any other nation of Christendom doth use it, but only Italy. The Italian, and also most strangers that are commorant in Italy, do always at their meals use a little fork when they cut their meat. For while with their knife, which they hold in one hand, they cut out the meat of the dish, they fasten their fork, which they hold in their other hand, upon the same dish, so that whatsoever he be that sitting in the company of any other at meat should unadvisedly touch the dish of meat with his fingers from which all at the table do cut, he will give occasion of offence unto the company as having transgressed the laws of good manners in so much that for his error he shall be at the least brow-beaten if not reprehended in words. . . . The reason of this their curiosity is, because the Italian cannot by any means endure to have his dish touched with fingers, seeing all men's fingers are not alike clean.'

And indeed it is so we must ever think of Italy, the first-born of the modern world. That civilisation, as we might say, that ritual of life—life itself being, as some of those great men of the Renaissance were not slow to observe, a kind of religious service—was very punctually and strictly observed at Urbino in the sixteenth century. There on the hills under the imperishable Apennine, the Renaissance, in all its liberty and beauty and splendour, was played out—yes, almost like a play. The most refined and learned of all the courts of Italy, it was there all the wit and genius of the Latin race, about to lead the world towards its emancipation, gathered from time to time. Surrounded by the finest scholars and

[1] Coryat's *Crudities*, ed. 1776, vol. i. p. 106.

the noblest gentlemen of Italy, Duke Guidobaldo lived a life that reads almost like a fairy tale, till suddenly that pestilence which was Cesare Borgia fell upon him and his country, and he fled to Mantua.

And in truth Urbino to-day, in the tragic sunset of a summer day, looks as though Cesare Borgia had but just passed by.

. . . . .

It was with Count Guido Montefeltro in the middle of the thirteenth century that the family, so illustrious in the history of Umbria and Italy, first comes to our notice. A Ghibelline, he went to Pisa with the rest from Tuscany and Romagna to greet the young Conradino who had come into Italy to dispute the crown of Naples with Charles of Anjou. Later, he appears again as captain-general of the Ghibellines, forcing all Romagna to be subject to him. Forlì was the capital of his conquest, and it was there he endured a siege by Giovanni di Appia, general to Pope Martin IV., extricating himself by one of those stratagems which, as Villani says, 'established his reputation as a sagacious man, more cunning than any Italian of his time, masterly alike in war and diplomacy.' However, Forlì was eventually surrendered, and Guido made his peace with the Pope. Not for long; as general of the Pisans against the Guelphs of Florence and Lucca, he was again censured by the Pope; and in 1295 we find him again in the dust and again forgiven. Meantime the Franciscan enthusiasm, almost a religion in itself, swept over Italy. Thousands forsook all and embraced a life of poverty and devotion. Among them was Count Guido. From the dreams of St. Francis he had learned a kind of introspection, so that he came at last to doubt the sufficiency of the Pope's pardon. Throwing away his county and his coronet, breaking his sword, which had never been rendered to his enemy, he went to Assisi, and, putting on the coarse habit of the Franciscans, sought forgiveness of God and peace for his own soul in the tiny cells of what had suddenly become a holy city. Pope Celestin, utterly unfitted for the crown of gold and iron and thorns which the Popes wore so resolutely, so uneasily during those restless years, soon abdicated, making way for Boniface VIII. The new Pope, however, was soon at war with the Colonna, that mighty family which all through the Middle Age was alternately expelled from and returning to Rome. A general was a necessity. Remembering the experience and the victories of Count Guido, he sent for him, 'silencing his religious scruples by a preliminary absolution for the sin of reverting to worldly schemes.' Count Guido, that strange monk of Montefeltro, but lately the most 'cunning and sagacious' general in Italy, counselled 'deceitful promises as the surest means of conquest.' So we find him in the Ghibelline Dante's *Inferno* a miserable soul without hope, to whom the whole of the twenty-seventh canto of the *Inferno* is devoted. Count Guido died in 1298, on September 29th, and is generally supposed to have been buried at Assisi. Thus the great family of Montefeltro dawned on Italy—a race of soldiers and leaders of men who, from their eyrie in the Apennines, swooped down on Italy at the head of innumerable legions, Florentine, Pisan, or Papal, as the case might be.

The next century seems to have been devoted by the House of Montefeltro to fighting their neighbours the Brancaleoni, the Malateste, and the Ceccardi. Eventually Urbino would appear to have expelled the family; but in 1376 it was recalled in the person of Antonio, the great-grandson of Guido il Vecchio. It was he who, 'emancipating himself from the spell that had bound his race to a falling cause, gave to his posterity an example of loyalty to his overlord the Pope.' He appears to have been a somewhat liberal ruler, bent on reform, which may well be, since he was a returned

exile.   At any rate, both Cagli and Gubbio welcomed his rule,
and after a struggle of nearly ten years he won Cantiano
from the Gabrielli.   He died in 1404.   He had three children
—Guidantonio, who succeeded him, Anna, and Battista.

It was Guidantonio who in 1420 received the Golden
Rose from the Pope, becoming later captain-general of the
Florentines in their war against Lucca.   Apparently through
no fault of his own he was defeated.   Eight years later, in
1438, he lost his second wife, whom he dearly loved, and from
this blow he never recovered.   He retired to Loretto, perhaps
with the same malady at his heart as that which had sent
Guido, his ancestor, to Assisi.   Loretto was considered one
of the holiest places in Italy, as possessing the Santa Casa.
It was there later that Domenico Veneziano and Piero della
Francesca were to paint their frescoes, so soon to be destroyed.
It was during his retirement at Loretto, while Federigo, his
natural son, ruled as vicegerent in Urbino, that Guidantonio
founded the Duomo and the Church of San Donato (1439).
In 1442 he died, and was buried in the church he had so
lately founded and dedicated to San Donato.   His 'cowled
effigy' may still be seen there, the spurs he wore as a great
knight hanging from the sword-hilt, the splendid blade
sheathed for ever.   His son Oddantonio, born in 1427,
succeeded him at fifteen years of age.   The terrible story of
this prince reads like some dreadful fiction.   His reign began
well, for Pope Eugenius IV. gave him the title of Duke; he
was the first of his race to bear it.   But he would seem to
have been of a weak and vacillating nature, suffering any
and every sort of influence to master him.   Coming under
the spell of that strange and fascinating personality, Sigismondo Malatesta, Lord of Rimini,[1] he was little better than
wax in his hands.   Sigismondo was one of the strangest
figures in all the years of the Renaissance.   A man of im-

[1] For a study of this typical Renaissance Despot and Humanist, see
my *Sigismondo Malatesta, Lord of Rimini* (Dent, 1906).

mense culture, exquisite taste, and profound understanding
of beauty, he was at the same time a great patron of art, a
great lover, and, if we are to believe Pio II., one of the most
astonishing criminals in history. The patron of Piero della
Francesca, who painted his portrait, and Leon Battista
Alberti, who designed and built his great pagan temple out
of the old Church of San Francesco, he was capable of a real
passion for philosophy, for Greek art, for learning, and was
guilty of the most terrible vices. He is accused of murder-
ing two of his wives, and his children were all illegitimate;
he was crafty, he was cruel, but he was not a barbarian. He
entertained at his court Porcellio, Basinio, Trebanio, the
poets; Valturio, the finest engineer in Italy. Pisanello, the
great medallist, struck medallions for him, even as Piero and
Alberti painted and built for him. He passionately loved
his mistress, the divine Isotta, for whose sake he seems to
have built his marvellous temple at Rimini. His noble
qualities, which might well be imitated by any modern
prince, have been overwhelmed by the renown of his vices
and his crimes. Cunning and boastful he was in his youth,
as later too, and a soldier of fortune. His ambition, very
noble at times, as when with enthusiasm and tears he brought
back from the sacred soil of Greece the bones of the great
Platonist Gemisthus Pletho, was eaten away by selfishness,
his splendid intellect hampered by conceit, his love spoiled by
lust. Thus from the enthusiasm and joy of his youth he came
to no serene old age, but to a brutal cynicism which his profoundly æsthetic temperament and mind were unable to combat.
The Pope burnt him in effigy, and on his tomb in the pagan
temple of San Francesco, where upon every arch and string-
course, in every piece of sculptured work, appear the elephant
and the rose, his emblems and his insolent and yet splendid
legend, there may also be found this brutal, pathetic jest:—

'Porto le corna ch' ogn' uno le vede
E tal le porte che non se lo crede.'

It was this man who, according to the folk of Urbino, brought about the fall of the weak and foolish Duke of Urbino, Oddantonio, whose city he desired. He sent two young men of vicious habits, Manfredi Pio da Carpi and Tomaso Agnello da Rimini, to Urbino, who succeeded easily in debasing his mind and morals, making of the prince who promised so well a mere devil. At last, at the instigation of Serafius, a physician, whose beautiful wife had been seduced by Manfredi, the revolution that Sigismondo so desired was awakened, and Oddantonio together with Manfredi and Tomaso was murdered. Dennistoun quotes from an old chronicle in the Oliveriana library an account of what followed: 'On 22nd July 1444 at lauds [about 3 a.m.], Oddantonio was slain in his own hall, and his familiar servants Manfredi de Pii and Tomaso de Rimini along with him; and forthwith the people of Urbino in one voice called for Signor Federigo, who at once took possession of the state.'

Federigo was the natural son of Guidantonio 'by a maiden of Urbino.' The Pope, on 22nd December 1424, formally made him legitimate when he was yet but two years old. While he was still young Federigo, who was destined to attain to so much splendour, was sent as a kind of hostage to Venice. It was while in that city that he came under the influence of Vittorino de Ramboldoni da Feltre, the learned professor of Mantua. This great man was a Greek scholar of no mean attainment, and his ideal of education soon took possession of the greatest princes in Italy. He taught Greek, Latin, Grammar, Philosophy, Mathematics, Logic, Music, and Dancing at the Casa Zoisa, the 'House of Joy,' where he had settled in 1425 at the invitation of Gianfrancesco II. of Mantua. Nor did he neglect athletics; in the meadows of the Mincio shooting and fencing matches were arranged, together with the game of *palla*. Such scholars as could not afford to pay him he taught for the 'love of God.' His pupils included the noblest names in Italy; all the children of the Gonzaga house were educated at Casa Zoisa, and no doubt met the Duke Federigo in the lecture-room and the meadows. Later Duke Federigo placed the great scholar's portrait in his palace at Urbino, with this inscription : ' In honour of his saintly master Vittorino da Feltre, who by word and example instructed him in all human excellence, Federigo has set this here.' It was to this man that he owed the fact that his court was famous throughout Italy, as was also that of his son, for culture and refinement and learning. During a hundred and ninety years from Federigo's accession Urbino, unlike any other city in Italy, was free from oppression and disorder, and was governed by the princes of two dynasties, beloved and respected, who followed the tradition Federigo had from Vittorino da Feltre.

Much of Federigo's reign was occupied in fighting. A great general, he seems to have humbled most of his enemies, including Sigismondo Malatesta. Before he had reached his eighth year he had been married to Gentile Brancaleone, and this marriage proving barren, he had in 1454 obtained the Pope's brief of legitimation for his sons Bonconte and Antonio. In 1460, however, he married Battista Sforza, daughter of the Lord of Pesaro. Piero della Francesca in his pictures on the back of the portraits of Federigo and Battista in the Uffizi, has painted a kind of allegory in memory of the marriage. During the next few years he was still engaged in war, during which time the state was managed to a large extent by his wife, who appears to have been popular. It was after he had been married about four years that he seems to have won the leisure to attend to government at home, and to devote himself to those things which Vittorino had taught him to love.

It seems to have been in 1454 that Federigo began to build the beautiful palace which to-day crowns the hill on

K

which Urbino stands. Perhaps the finest palace in all Italy, it was the work of Luciano Laurano, helped, it may be, by Baccio Pontelli. Castiglione, in his *Cortegiano*, writes of the palace as follows: 'Among other laudable actions, Federigo erected on the rugged heights of Urbino a residence, by many regarded as the most beautiful in all Italy; and so amply did he provide it with every convenience that it appeared rather a palatial city than a palace. He furnished it not only with the usual plenishings of rich brocades in silk and gold, silver plate, and such like, but ornamented it with a vast quantity of ancient marble and bronze sculptures, of rare pictures, and musical instruments in every variety, excluding all but the choicest objects.'

But it was as a book-collector that Federigo excelled. 'To the right and left of the carriage entrance into the great courtyard are two handsome saloons, each about forty-five feet by twenty-two, and twenty-three in height. That on the left contained the famous library of manuscripts collected by Count Federigo; the corresponding one received the printed books, which, gradually purchased by successive dukes, became under the last sovereign a copious collection.'

It was on the 20th August 1474, towards the end of his life, that, with an escort of two thousand horse, he entered Rome, the Pope meeting him in the great doorway of St. Peter's to give him the dignity of duke. This honour, which was his due, conferred with splendid rituals and ceremonies, was not the only dignity which fell to him. On the 18th August 1474 Edward IV. of England gave him the Garter, even at that time one of the most splendid honours in Europe.

This truly great man died on the 10th September 1482, leaving a son aged ten years to succeed him. Prudent and wise, he was as good a soldier as he was a prince, and as generous a patron of learning as might be found in Italy.

'In person,' says Muzio (whom Dennistoun quotes at great length, together with many others), 'In person Federigo was of the common height, well made and proportioned, active and stout, enduring of cold and heat, apparently affected neither by hunger nor thirst, by sleeplessness nor fatigue. His expression was cheerful and frank; he was not carried away by passion, nor showed anger unless designedly. . . If his kindness was notable in camp, it was much more so among his people. While at Urbino he daily repaired to the market-place, whither the citizens resorted for gossip and games as well as for business, mixing freely with them and joining in discourse, or looking on at their sports, like one of themselves, sitting among them or leaning on some one by the hand or arm. If in passing through the town he noticed any one building a house, he would stop to inquire how the work went on, encouraging him to beautify it, and offering him aid if required, which he gave as well as promised. . . . Once meeting a citizen who had daughters to marry, he said: "How are your family? Have you got any of your girls disposed of?" And being answered that he was ill able to endow them, he helped him with money or an appointment, or set him in some way of bettering himself.' Hundreds of anecdotes and stories are told of him by the chroniclers and historians, all going to show how much he was beloved, and with reason; nor is there any that I can find which is to his discredit.

His young son Guidobaldo I. succeeded him. You may see his portrait to-day in the Colonna Palace in Rome, painted by Sanzio, as you may see those of his father and mother, painted by Piero della Francesca, in the Uffizi. At the age of seventeen he married Elisabetta Gonzaga, the youngest daughter of Francesco, Marquis of Mantua, but by her he had no children. His household, if we may judge from the precise rules we possess which governed it, was as orderly as his father's. In his peacful reign he was able to devote himself almost entirely to study and to the chase. His only trouble seems to have been that he was childless. He had adopted his nephew, Francesco Maria della Rovere, as his heir, and kept him near him at Urbino. Suddenly into the quiet serenity of those days in the woods and the gardens, or the great beautiful palace itself, a kind of tiger leapt. Cesare Borgia, that brutal genius, fell upon Urbino suddenly. Without a thought of defence Guidobaldo, together with his nephew, fled to Mantua. Cesare Borgia ransacked the palace and carried his priceless booty to the Vatican, where the devil himself, masquerading as Pope Alexander vi., waited to receive it. Let it be said in extenuation of Guidobaldo that he was physically a weakling. Once or twice he managed to make headway against the Pope, and the Pope's son, but never for long. He retired to Venice really a beggar. Suddenly, almost as suddenly as Cesare Borgia had leapt on Urbino, Alexander vi. died. In a moment Cesare's magical empire departed from him, and he himself was a fugitive. Guidobaldo returned to Urbino, and, though much of the booty was never restored to him by the Church, passed the rest of his life among his treasures in the retirement of his court. It was then that that Golden Age began for Italy which in its expression and production has never since been equalled. Every sort of scholar came to Urbino : great poets, painters, sculptors, architects, engineers, doctors, priests, quacks of every kind, fools and nobles, dancing-masters and beautiful women, musicians and preachers flocked to the court of one of the most humane princes Italy had ever seen. It was then that Castiglione wrote his *Cortegiano* and his life of Guidobaldo ; it was then that Sanzio entertained Piero della Francesca, that Melozzo da Forli came to court, and Luca Signorelli painted his work in San Spirito. In 1505 Pietro

Bembo, that fine scholar and stylist, came to Urbino. Born in Venice in 1470, he was in 1505 already famous. A *protégé* of the d'Este princes, he had seen Lucrezia Borgia enter that quiet household. This wanton and beautiful princess, whose acquaintance with every sort of vice was surely unique, seems to have become almost a child again in the serene life of the court of Ferrara. All her hateful childhood and youth seem to have fallen away from her and left her almost a girl again. A great friendship sprang up between her and Pietro Bembo. Their correspondence, which lasted from 1503 to 1516, is in great part published. And it is there, as I think, in those rhetorical letters in praise of the virtue rather than the beauty of so famous a princess, that we find the best refutation of the inevitable slander as to the purity of their affection. Coming to Urbino in 1505, Bembo stayed there during six years; it was there he met Giuliano de Medici, to whom he owed so much. Going to Rome in 1512 in the company of Giuliano, Leo X., who was made Pope in the following year, appointed him his secretary. How often in his later life he regretted the unfettered existence of those days at Urbino appears from his correspondence again and again.

The duke, who presided over this court of learning and art, was never in good health. A weakling from his birth, it was necessary for him to take his pleasure rather in the somewhat colourless delights of the library and the salon than in the field. 'His passage,' says Dennistoun, 'from mortality was peaceful; and death, which he considered desirable, spread like a gentle slumber over his stiffening limbs and composed features. At midnight of the 11th of April 1508, his spirit was released from its shattered tenement.' Thus died the last of the House of Montefeltro.

He was succeeded by the first duke of the House della Rovere. Francesco Maria. This passionate man was a soldier rather than a scholar. His adventurous reign is full of murder and war. 'He was a prince of very violent temper,' says Symonds; 'of its extravagance history has recorded three remarkable examples. He murdered the Cardinal of Pavia with his own hand in the streets of Ravenna; stabbed a lover of his sister to death at Urbino; and in a council of war knocked Francesco Guicciardini down with a blow of his fist. When the history of Italy came to be written, Guicciardini was probably mindful of that insult, for he painted Francesco Maria's character and conduct in dark colours. At the same time this Duke of Urbino passed for one of the first generals of the age. The greatest stain upon his memory is his behaviour in the year 1527, when, by dilatory conduct of the campaign in Lombardy, he suffered the passage of Fründesberg's army unopposed, and afterwards hesitated to relieve Rome from the horrors of the sack. He was the last Italian Condottiere of the antique type. . . . During his lifetime the conditions of Italy were so changed by Charles v.'s imperial settlement in 1530, that the occupation of Condottiere ceased to have any meaning.' Driven from Urbino by the Pope Leo x. who conferred his dukedom upon Lorenzo de Medici, he would by no means submit, but was not strong or rich enough to beat the Pope. In 1522, however, Francesco Maria returned to Urbino. Leo x. was dead, Lorenzo de Medici was dead, and Catherine his heir, soon to be Queen of France, did not press her claims.

Francesco Maria's son Guidobaldo, by Leonora Gonzaga whom he had married in 1509, succeeded him. Of Guidobaldo II., surnamed Guidobaldaccio, there is little to say. He quarrelled with his subjects and retired to Pesaro, where he built the great palace, now the Prefettura, opposite the Church of S. Domenico. In the autumn of 1574 he appears to have gone to Ferrara to visit Henry III. of France. On his way back to Pesaro 'during the great heats,' he fell ill and died on the 28th September. On the 30th January 1548 Guidobaldo had married Vittoria Farnese, by whom he had a son and two daughters. It was this son, Francesco Maria II., who succeeded him, the last Duke of Urbino. He was born on the 20th February 1549. His autobiography, extending from his birth to the marriage of his son, is an extraordinary work, full of curious information. It is this sad and mystical Duke whom Mr. Shorthouse has drawn so vividly for us in *John Inglesant.* He seems to have felt something of the same irresistible desire for solitude that forced Guido il Vecchio, his predecessor, into a Franciscan cell at Assisi. Married first to Lucrezia d'Este of Ferrara, whom he did not love, he permitted her to return to Ferrara, and later married Livia della Rovere. It seems to have been in his loneliness, deserted by his wife, that he became occupied with those haunting thoughts about religion which were so eagerly fostered by the Papacy that in 1631 they resulted in his bequeathing his Duchy to the Church. In youth we read that he used a flame vanishing into air as his device, with the motto, *Quies in Sublime*—'There is rest on high'; later he took a terrestrial globe with the legend, *Ponderibus librata suis*—'Self-poised.' He grew more and more into a kind of uninstructed and ungoverned monk. His son by his second marriage, Prince Federigo - Ubaldo, was ruined in his youth. Spoiled by his father, 'taught to regard his subjects as dependants on a despot will,' he died in 1623 a victim to his own lusts and debaucheries. From this blow Francesco Maria never recovered. We see him, a kind of querulous shadow, pass across that fantastic stage at Urbino, ready to listen to the ranting of madmen and fanatic Lutherans and mad monks. Meantime he was in reality the plaything of the Pope. As the cat deals with the mouse, so the Papacy dealt with this poor half-witted creature. In 1624 the last Duke of Urbino died, and his Lordship became the absolute property of the Holy See.

. . . .

In spite of all the patronage and splendour of the Counts and Dukes of Urbino, there is little enough left to-day in their city to remind us of the host of artists they entertained at their court and employed in decorating the magnificent palace where they lived, and the churches they endowed or protected. The palace is, indeed, spoiled and changed, though it be still the finest monument in Urbino. Built by Luciano Laurano, the Illyrian (1468-1482), the master of Bramante, for the great Federigo, 'the Great Christian' as Mahomet II. called him, it was the greatest and the most splendid of all these palaces of the Signori which were built in the early Renaissance, and even to-day it is unique in Italy. It is not certainly in its size, or even in its proportions, that its beauty lies, but in its fitness and in its harmony of splendour and strength. It does not impose itself upon us as so many of the fortress palaces of Italy, built both before and after, do, but is content to please us with a certain quiet and homely beauty that, as it seems to me, is just the quality one looks for in a palace that was not only a place of refuge or offence, but a home, a home where life came little by little to have an exquisite but simple ritual, and where one might happily entertain one's friends. As you wander to-day through those corridors, out of which the beautiful rooms open, so bare now, or turned to the meaner uses of our time, through the doorways and past the mantel-pieces with their friezes of dancing angels or vines carved by Domenico Rosselli, you come at last to the little study of Duke Federigo, where the walls, all of *intarsia*, once shut out for him the noisy world of battle and intrigue, so that in complete silence he might meditate, as he was used to do, on the divine life of the soul, while he looked, as we may, out across the city to the indestructible Apennines, or, climbing up to the platform of that great north tower, gazed really across his dukedom.

In Duke Federigo's day, and for long after, till indeed Urbino came again into the hands of the Pope, the palace was celebrated throughout Italy for its great library and its gallery of pictures. The library is gone, having been taken to Rome in 1657, but some of the pictures remain, though the greater part of these too are scattered, many of them hanging in the Uffizi and Pitti Galleries. Of the works which remain, the most celebrated is Titian's 'Resurrection,' a late work which, like the spoiled 'Last Supper' by the same master, also in this gallery, once was used as a banner on the Feast of Corpus Domini : both pictures, however, were framed in the sixteenth century.

Not far away, on the wall at the end of the room, hangs a picture or study in perspective by Piero della Francesca, while a work by Giovanni Santi, a Madonna and Child with SS. John Baptist, Sebastian, Jerome, and Francis, with its donors, the Buffi family, seems to be the only work in the gallery by an Urbinese. The 'Last Supper,' which includes portraits of Duke Federigo and Caterino Zeno, the Persian ambassador, is by Justus van Ghent.

Close to the palace is the new Duomo, built in 1801. Its sole claim on our notice is that in the sacristy there is a fine picture by Piero della Francesca, 'The Scourging of our Lord.'

Opposite the palace is the Church of S. Domenico. There is nothing to see within, but over the door is a terra-cotta by Luca della Robbia, a Madonna and Saints, carved in 1449.

Returning to the great Piazza, one climbs the farther hill, passing on the left Number 278, the house in which Raphael was born. Raphael's father, Giovanni Santi, held a distinguished position at the court of Urbino; he was both poet and painter. He had come to Urbino in 1448, having seen, two years before, his native village of Colbordolo in the Foglia valley laid waste by Sigismondo Malatesta. He must have been quite a boy at the time, and no doubt assisted his father in Urbino in the sale of corn and oil, by which he got his living. They seem to have flourished, for in 1464 they bought this house in what was then the Contrada del Monte, and is now the Contrada Raffaello. It was not till he was about forty years old that Giovanni married Magia Ciarla, the daughter of a tradesman in the city; she brought him a dowry of one hundred and fifty florins, and on his father's death in 1485 he inherited the chief part of the property of that successful old man; so that we may suppose he was relieved of those domestic anxieties of which he complains so bitterly in his rhyming 'Chronicle of the Life of Duke Federigo.' He had three children by Magia, but two of them died in infancy; his son Raphael, called so may be because the Archangel Raphael was the protector of youth, was born on Good Friday, March 28, 1483. He seems to have been very delicate as a child even, and his mother, fearing to lose him also, nursed him herself. The faded fresco, once in the court-yard, but now removed to one of the rooms of the house where he was bórn, may well represent mother and son.

Raphael was but eight years old when he lost his mother, and six months later found himself in the care of a step-mother, a certain Bernardina di Parte, the daughter of a goldsmith, who brought his father a dowry of two hundred florins. Less than two years later Giovanni Santi died. A quarrel about his property between his brother, a priest named Bartolommeo, and Bernardina, who had given birth to a daughter, followed. Meanwhile Raphael was cared for by Magia's relations. But we know nothing of his boyhood. Vasari tells us that in 1495 Giovanni took him to Perugino in Perugia, but in 1495 his father was already dead and

Raphael but eleven years old ; besides, between 1493, when
Perugino married a young wife in Florence, and 1499 he was
but seldom in Perugia. If we are to look for Raphael's
first master we shall find him, according to Morelli and Mr.
Berenson, in Timoteo Viti of Urbino, a few of whose pictures
are still left in the Pinacoteca in the ducal palace. Certainly
Timoteo Viti left Francia's workshop in Bologna, whither he
had gone five years earlier, in 1495, and settled in Urbino,
where, in 1501, he married. He seems never to have left
Urbino afterwards, so that we may well admit that of all
those masters who influenced Raphael, and they were not
few, Timoteo Viti was the first, and, it may well be, the
strongest.

The Contrada Raffaello leads up to the Fortezza, whence one
may have a fine view of the city and the mountains ; but from
the Piazza at the bottom of the hill the Via Bramante leads
to the church of S. Spirito, where are two fine grave pictures
by Luca Signorelli. These two pictures of the Crucifixion
and the Pentecost formed originally a standard painted in
1494 for this church.[1]

One returns once more to the Piazza, and taking Via Mazzini,
follows downhill through Via della Porta Vecchia and Via
Barocci to the Oratorio di S. Giovanni. Here the walls are
covered with frescoes of the stories of the Blessed Virgin and
St. John the Baptist by the two brothers Lorenzo and Jacopo
da San Severino. Born in the little town of San Severino, not
so far away in the Marche, the ruined picture of the Marriage
of St. Catherine in the Cistercian church there proves Lorenzo
to have been twenty-six years of age in 1400. It was sixteen
years later that he and his brother painted this oratory,
which is a beautiful and radiant monument of their labour.

So in the summer days one may wander very pleasantly and
quietly about this old and beautiful city that seems so majesti-

[1] See Pungileoni, *Elogio St. di Giov. Santi*, p. 77.

cally lonely among the mountains. Yet it is not in her works of art, or even in her actual buildings perhaps, that her secret charm lies. There are times that come ever more rarely as we grow older, when in a moment almost we seem to understand the true character of a person or a place; when suddenly the merely superficial mediocrity of the world disappears, and between two heart-beats we are face to face with reality. Perhaps it is thus the realities of the great world steal upon our virgin souls in childhood, cutting us off from heaven, telling us entrancing stories to which we cannot but listen, enthralled as we are by this beautiful and mortal world, this delightful and mortal flesh. It must be thus our powers and passions are developed, unconsciously for the most part. It would seem that the world whispers to us in our childhood secrets that we never remember, but that leave their indelible mark—moods that we are subject to, that have conquered us, desires and needs that we have not willingly developed, knowledge that we would, how gladly, forget. It was some such moment as this that was prolonged for me at Urbino, when at evening I would watch the shadows pass over the mighty foreheads of the mountains, those brows that the sun has kissed when night falls since the beginning of the world; and turning towards the dear city at my feet I understood how few are the years even of brass eternal.

XVI

FABRIANO, GUALDO TADINO, AND NOCERA UMBRA

IT was in the heat of the day I first came to Fabriano, by the little line that runs thither among the mountains from Urbino. More than a thousand feet above the sea, Fabriano lies in a valley between two heights. Famous as the birthplace of Gentile da Fabriano, there seems to be nothing from his hand to-day, in a town devoted, as it has been for centuries, to the manufacture of paper. Allegretto Nuzi, however, the great master of Gentile, has left a few panels in the Municipio and the churches of this his native place. Born early in the fourteenth century, Allegretto's name appears on the register of painters at Florence in 1346 ; he died in Fabriano between September 1373 and September 1374.[1] His earliest dated work (1315) is, however, not in Fabriano at all but in the Museo Cristiano of the Vatican. It is a triptych, that comes from the Ospizio of the Camaldolesi di Roma, while his most famous work, a triptych, Madonna and Child with angels between two saints, painted in 1369, is in the Duomo of Macerata. Other works by him are a diptych, in Berlin, of Madonna and Child, and the Crucifixion, and a poliptych in Apiro, both of which are signed. Here in Fabriano there are, as I have said, many of his beautiful, forgotten panels, which in their richness of colour and hierarchical beauty are

[1] A. Venturi, *St. dell' Arte Ital.*, tom. v. p. 839. (Milano, 1907.)

among the loveliest things in Umbria. It is in the Duomo
that we find most of his work, a poliptych, for instance, of
Madonna and Child between four saints, while above in the
cusps are four half-figures of Blessed and a Crucifix. In
another poliptych, beautiful but ruined, we see the same
arrangement, only the saints are different; but his most
characteristic works here in the Cathedral are those panels—
fragments of an Ancona, each containing two figures, St. John
the Divine and St. Anthony, St. John the Baptist and
S. Venzano. That hierarchical beauty, with all its solemnity
and richness, whose secret might seem to lie in a certain
exquisite stillness, is fully expressed at last in the marvellous
fragment, a triptych of Three Saints, preserved in the
Municipio. There we see S. Antonio of Padua bearing a
lily, S. Agostino with an open book, and S. Stefano with a
palm and a closed book. But the 'subjects' of this work are
less than nothing; it is in the expression that its beauty lies,
the richness of colour, the purity of the blues and reds and
whites, and the glory of the gold. These three figures have
in truth stepped out of the service books, and are still caught
in the mystery of the Middle Age; something mysterious
and inexplicable surround them, something that Gentile has
not known how to express, caught as he has been by the
beauty of the world, that Ottaviano Nelli seems to have seen
for a moment in the Madonna del Belvedere, but that escaped
him ever after, and that in Umbria, at any rate, has found no
real expression save in the work of this neglected master.
Taking something, as he did, not only from Orcagna but
from the Sienese, much that is so distinctive in Gentile's
work may be traced to him. If he began, as in the Madonna
and Child in the Vatican, in the poliptych of the Duomo of
Fabriano, as the disciple of Ambrogio Lorenzetti, in his
most characteristic work, the Quattro Santi of the Duomo, and
the Tre Santi of the Municipal Gallery, he is his own master,

expressing with something of the hardness of ritual, its glitter and love of order and precision, the words of the Divine Office through which, as in his pictures, a strange, inexpressible light seems to shine.

There is another picture by Allegretto, a S. Antonio, with people kneeling round him, in the Municipio, and another in the Fornari collection signed and dated 1372.

It is but ten miles from Fabriano to Fossato, and but fourteen to Gualdo Tadino. There is nothing to be seen at Fossato, but Gualdo Tadino is as well worth a visit as any place in Umbria. Set high up above the plain of Chiaggio, it still preserves a few ruins of the ancient Tadinum, through which the Via Flaminia forces its way between Rimini and Rome, and then it was here that Totila met his death at the hands of the eunuch Narses. 'In his march from Ravenna,' says Gibbon, 'the Roman general chastised the garrison of Rimini, traversed in a direct line the hills of Urbino, and re-entered the Flaminian Way, nine miles beyond the perforated rock, an obstacle of art and nature which might have stopped or retarded his progress. The Goths were assembled (A.D. 552, July) in the neighbourhood of Rome, they advanced without delay to seek a superior enemy, and the two armies approached each other at the distance of one hundred furlongs between Tagina[1] and the sepulchres of the Gauls.[2] The haughty message of Narses was an offer not of peace but of pardon. The answer of the Gothic king declared his resolution to die or conquer. "What

---

[1] Taginae, or rather Tadinae, is mentioned by Pliny, but the bishopric of this obscure town, a mile from Gualdo in the plain, was united in 1007 with that of Nocera. The signs of antiquity are preserved in the local names—Fossato=camp ; Capraia=Capræa ; Bastia = Busta Gallorum.

[2] Refers to the battle in year of Rome 458.

day," said the messenger, "will you fix for the combat?"
"The eighth day," replied Totila, but early the next morning
he attempted to surprise a foe suspicious of deceit and prepared for battle. Ten thousand Heruli and Lombards of
approved valour and doubtful faith were placed in the centre.
Each of the wings was composed of 8000 Romans; the right
was guarded by the cavalry of the Huns; the left was covered
by 1500 chosen horse, destined, according to the emergencies
of action, to sustain the retreat of their friends, or to encom-
pass the flank of the enemy. From his proper station at the
head of the right wing, the eunuch rode along the line,
expressing by his voice and countenance the assurance of
victory; exciting the soldiers of the emperor to punish the
guilt and madness of a band of robbers; and exposing to their
view gold chains, collars, and bracelets, the reward of military
virtue. From the event of a single combat they drew an
omen of success, and they beheld with pleasure the courage of
fifty archers, who maintained a small eminence against three
successive attacks of the Gothic cavalry. At the distance of
only two bow-shots the armies spent the morning in dreadful
suspense, and the Romans tasted some necessary food without
unloosening the cuirass from their breast or the bridle from
their horses. Narses awaited the charge, and it was delayed
by Totila till he had received his last succours of 2000 Goths.
While he consumed the hours in fruitless treaty, the king
exhibited in a narrow space the strength and agility of a
warrior. His armour was enchased with gold, his purple
banner floated with the wind, he cast his lance into the air,
caught it with the right hand, shifted it to the left, threw
himself backwards, recovered his seat, and managed a fiery
steed in all the paces and evolutions of the equestrian school.
As soon as the succours had arrived, he retired to his tent,
resumed the dress and arms of a private soldier, and gave the
signal of battle. The first line of cavalry advanced with

more courage than discretion, and left behind them the infantry of the second line. They were soon engaged between the horns of a crescent, into which the adverse wings had been insensibly curved, and were saluted from either side by the volleys of 4000 archers. Their ardour, and even their distress, drove them forward to a close and unequal conflict, in which they could only use their lances against an enemy equally skilled in all the instruments of war. A generous emulation inspired the Romans and their Barbarian allies, and Narses, who calmly viewed and directed their efforts, doubted to whom he should adjudge the prize of superior bravery. The Gothic cavalry were astonished and disordered, pressed and broken, and the line of infantry, instead of presenting their spears or opening their intervals, were trampled under the feet of the flying horse. Six thousand of the Goths were slaughtered without mercy in the field of Tagina. Their prince, with five attendants, was overtaken by Asbad of the race of the Gepidae. "Spare the King of Italy," cried a loyal voice, and Asbad struck his lance through the body of Totila. The blow was instantly revenged by the faithful Goths; they transported their dying monarch seven miles beyond the scene of his disgrace, and his last moments were not embittered by the presence of an enemy. Compassion afforded him the shelter of an obscure tomb; but the Romans were not satisfied of their victory till they beheld the corpse of the Gothic king. His hat, enriched with gems, and his bloody robe, were presented to Justinian by the messengers of triumph.'[1]

Gualdo Tadino is the birthplace of Matteo da Gualdo, one of the many Umbrian painters influenced by Benozzo Gozzoli. His works, scattered in the churches of this little city, in Montefalco and Assisi, show some likeness to the work of

[1] Gibbon, *Decline and Fall of the Roman Empire*, cap. xliii.

L

Boccatis, and Benozzo indeed seems to have influenced him through his pupil, Mezzastris of Foligno who with him painted the Cappella dei Pellegrini at Assisi. In the country about Gualdo Tadino, in the Chiesa di S. Pellegrino and the Chiesa di S. Maria di Nasciano, you may also find Matteo's works; in the first a poliptych with the Madonna and Child adored by a choir of angels between S. Giovanni Battista, the Archangel Michael, S. Giacomo, and S. Pellegrino, while in the cusps are God the Father, S. Bartolommeo, a pope, and two other figures; under, there is this inscription— TPRE. DONI. AGNELI. FRACISCI DE GYALDO M. CCCC. LXV. In the church of S. Maria di Nasciano one finds a picture once signed by him, a triptych with the Madonna and Child in the midst surrounded by angels and two saints, S. Sebastiano and S. Rocco. In the cusps are the Annunciation and the Presentation in the Temple.

Gualdo Tadino itself, however, is by no means wanting in the pictures of her son. The Municipio has certainly five of them—a triptych with Madonna and Child between St. John Baptist and St. Catherine, and, in the incomplete predella, the Baptism of our Lord, the Last Supper, a miracle of St. Catherine, and two saints, is signed M. CCCC. LXXI. Mactheus de Gualdo Pinxit. Die xxvii Aprilis. The Anconetta, with Madonna and Child between St. Francis and S. Bernardino, St. Margaret and St. Catherine, is also signed; above is a little tabernacle with angels between two *tondi*, in which are the half-figures of S. Ludovico and S. Bonaventura. Here, too, is a small oblong picture of the Annunciation, and a lunette of the Coronation of the Blessed Virgin, and under, two saints, of whom one is Beato Angelo da Gualdo. This last work seems to show Sienese influence, even the hand of Sano di Pietro.

One of the most curious and charming of Matteo's works is that Pala d'Altare in the church of S. Maria Assunta, where we see the genealogical tree of the Blessed Virgin growing from its root in Adam till it blossoms in her, while its fruit was the second Adam.

The great treasure of Gualdo Tadino, however, does not lie in the work of Matteo her son, but in the magnificent poliptych of Niccolò da Foligno in the Duomo. In the midst is the Madonna and Child surrounded by a choir of angels in adoration, while at the sides are St. Peter, St. Paul, St. Francis, and S. Bernardino. Above, in half-figure, are St. Anthony of Padua, St. Sebastian, St. Ludovic, and the Archangel Michael; while in the pinnacles in the midst is the Ecce Homo, and at the sides S. Cristoforo, S. Chiara, S. Lorenzo, and S. Venanzo; in the *pilastrini* the Apostles. Below, in the predella, certain Franciscan Santi e Beati (*non senza qualche nota umoristica*), angels and *putti*. This magnificent work is perhaps the masterpiece of a man who was after all the greatest truly Umbrian painter before the advent of Perugino, not only in the quantity and variety of his work, but in its quality also. It is a work of his school we see in that Crucifixion, with two saints on either side, which stands here in the Duomo. But for another example of his own work we must leave Gualdo Tadino and follow the road for ten miles down the valley to Nocera Umbra.

Nocera stands as loftily as Gualdo Tadino, above the Flaminian Way, some three miles from the railway station that bears its name. Celebrated as it is all over Italy for its mineral waters, it is a quiet place enough, very delightful in the summer heat, while its old churches—the Duomo, for instance, and the Madonnina — keep still some few pictures.

Niccolò's poliptych is in the sacristy of the Duomo. In the midst, under a pavilion, Madonna kneels in worship of her little Son, while behind, angels, from the nurseries of heaven, sing Gloria in excelsis. At the sides stand S. Lorenzo,

S. Rinaldo, S. Feliciano, and S. Francesco. Alone in the midst Madonna is crowned Queen of Angels; at the sides are half-figures of St. Sebastian, St. John the Baptist, St. Paul, and St. Catherine. Above these again are half-figures of the four doctors of the church.

There is little beside to be seen in Nocera, and yet one is loath to leave this quiet country of hills, where the mountains begin to humble themselves to the sweetness of the valley. Little to be seen! Yet here, as elsewhere, one sees what is in one's heart. They are not the best of us, perhaps, who will hurry away down the narrow valley to Foligno in the valley of Spoleto.

THE UMBRIAN SCHOOL OF PAINTING

XVII

UMBRIAN ART

IN Umbria, that true Italia Mystica, among the hills which in the profound silence of the sunshine of early summer, under a calm and soft sky, are really like vast precious stones, Painting for the most part was content to be just a Religious vowed to God. She sometimes comes to us as in the work of Bonfigli, which is perhaps the greatest treasure of the Pinacoteca at Perugia, with something of the sweetness of the nun, the oversweetness of which men have always been so suspicious; finding therein something not quite sane or amiable; troubled in spite of a deep outward serenity by a subtle ugliness that has really only just missed a profound beauty. Or again, as in the magnificent work of Piero della Francesca, she appears with all the vitality and energy of life and yet with a kind of horror on her countenance, as in the face of the Risen Christ at Borgo San Sepolcro. And at last in Perugino himself we seem to find a real duplicity in the cloying and exquisite sorrow that does not really affect the soul, in his Crucifixions; the insincerity and too delightful innocence of his warriors and captains in the Cambio; the affectation of his Nativity at Perugia; the awful facility of much of his work. That school of painters which in Umbria, and especially in the valley of Perugia, painted, in the fifteenth and early sixteenth centuries, so tenderly, so emotionally, as it were, the story of Christianity may be studied perhaps better in Perugia itself than anywhere else in the world. There, gathered from church and convent, we find the works of Taddeo Bartoli, of Boccatis, and above all of Bonfigli and Fiorenzo di Lorenzo, housed in the Pinacoteca in the Municipio, and splendidly arranged in order for us, so that we may appreciate the gradual progress of the school towards such perfection as may be found in Perugino, Pintoricchio, and their followers. It is an expression chiefly of a profound and delightful sentiment that we find, far indeed from the intellectual travail of Florentine Art, or the magnificent acceptance of life that the Venetians show us. It is full of a very gracious spaciousness, at least in the greater men, that is noble, and surely at one with the splendour and expanse of vale and hill in the country itself. They were not great men, these Umbrian painters ; perhaps only Piero della Francesca and Luca Signorelli, who were not really Umbrian at all, can rightly be called that ; but they were great artists capable of giving a host of people intense pleasure, charming them with the gentleness of their work, the emotion almost of tears, to be found in the story of Christ and Madonna ; the softness of the landscape and the luminous and perfect sky that have through them perhaps become in themselves religious ; the sheer beauty of all that, quite thoughtless and unphilo- sophical though it may be. It is, too, in these men that we find the expression of an emotion very different from the thoughtfulness and science of Florence with her desire for liberty and good government. Here in Perugia painting is one thing, liberty quite another. It is strange to remind oneself that, while Perugino was at work on his softest and gentlest works, the Baglioni and Oddi were slaughtering one another and the Perugians in the streets ; that the fiercest and most ferocious tyrants and bravos of the Renaissance were filling the streets of the city, and even the cathedral, with blood and the cries of the wounded and the heaps of the dead. But it is well to remember, too, in calling to mind those tumultuous days in Perugia, that at Urbino was established the most cultured court of Italy or of the world— a court whose influence was no doubt felt not only everywhere in Umbria but throughout Italy, reconciling civilisation with a race so warlike, and gradually forming the spirit of the modern world.

Divided even in the earliest times into two schools which had their centres in Gubbio and Perugia, Umbrian painting is really provincial in the true sense of the word, the hand-maid of the Church, touching life only very rarely, intent for the most part on the service of the sanctuary ; having, indeed, no life at all, no possible life, apart from religion. Unlike Florence and Siena, Umbria had no Giotto nor Duccio to point out the road she should follow in her Art. For whereas Giotto made it for ever impossible for Florence to ignore painting as such, its problems and difficulties, while Duccio assured Siena of her great pictorial future, Umbria in these early years produced no great leader ; how should she, out of touch with life as she was, busied rather with action, frittering away her life in infinitely tiny and cruel quarrels, or dreaming of the lives of the saints that she possessed in so great an abundance, weeping with St. Francis over her sins, or listening to the voice of Christ with the Blessed Angela of Foligno, ready to burn the world under the passionate eloquence of S. Bernardino, or praying night and day with Beata Colomba of Rieti ? In those first years of the fourteenth century, when Giotto, Duccio, and the sculptors were busy recreating the Art of the world, Umbria was for the most part silent, her soul imprisoned in the mystery of her soft hills, very scornful of man, seeing that her ways so often ran with his blood, the which seemed to her less precious than the meanest of her dreams. And yet Umbria was not isolated from the world as Siena was. Only she was so much nearer Rome, that Eternal City which, busied always with action, government, dominion, has produced no really great artist; has, indeed, never cared overmuch for Art for its own sake, but has used it rather as a means of expressing her own glory in glorious days; impatient of it always under the Popes, and ready at the first whisper of scandal to cast it from her for ever.

All the art of Italy is really an alien in Rome. She in her tragic and actual life, perhaps the most tremendous force in the world, ruined every beautiful thing she touched, harnessing it to her chariot, or dragging it a splendid captive through her highways. So, having found Raphael, that scholarly and serene soul, she drugged him with her enchantments, and compelled him to paint some of the most beautiful frescoes in the world on the awkward cramped walls of the Vatican, thinking of them chiefly as a decoration, but spoiling them as just that by her desire for reality, for the expression of life where it was most out of place. It is only the splendid genius of Raphael that has saved us from feeling the awkwardness, the difficulty, of the spaces he had to fill.

It was the same with Michelangelo. That destroying genius, terrible in his isolation, who seems to be always brooding over some immense sorrow, is only not overcome by her because he has already been overwhelmed by his own personality, a more exacting master. Even his strong will, however, she bends at last, desiring that he shall forsake his true vocation, sculpture, and decorate with his unsatisfied genius the private chapel of her master the Pope. In that place where for centuries the vicegerent of God, not always observant of that Peace with mankind proclaimed in the dawn so long ago, has been chosen, Michelangelo created a terrible and immense crowd of sorrowful figures, each one of which seems to accuse the Papacy and God Himself of some tragic crime committed upon mankind—Adam, who so languidly, so reluctantly touches the outstretched hand of the Creator; pitiful humanity and our beautiful world drowned in that bitter unforgivable flood; the mighty Sibyls bowed under the thoughts they dare only express in mysteries; the tortured Prophets, the sacrificed messengers of God, the Athletes, and the Slaves. And above all, dwarfing everything, ignoring everything, stands the huge fresco of the Last Judgment, in which Man in all his beauty condemns God, and, as it might seem, rises from the ease and peace of the grave only to pronounce sentence on life for ever.

This profound and wonderful vision of life by no means decorates the chapel of the Popes; it dwarfs it. The air is so full of figures that we can see nothing. It is a torture to gaze upon that roof, physical as well as spiritual. We are overwhelmed by a crowd of passionate and insistent figures, so that it is impossible to look at anything, seeing that they all so eagerly claim our attention. To compare this chapel with the Upper Church at Assisi is to understand the extraordinary difference between the fourteenth century and the sixteenth, between Rome and any other city, between what Giotto conceived decoration to be and what Rome had forced it to become. In that quiet, empty church in the city of St. Francis, how perfectly Giotto has understood the limitations of reality; nothing is thrust upon us, nor is there any overwhelming passion. Our real emotion will come, not from the quiet frescoes on the walls, but from the miracle of the Mass itself, said there so rarely and with so simple an earnestness. And at least we may there follow undisturbed the fair words of the liturgy, and become a little reconciled in the exquisite monotony of the plainsong, while in the Sistine Chapel we should be devoured by uneasy dreams.

But Rome has ever been the insatiable mistress of the greatest men, luring them to every sort of destruction, and encouraging them in their mightiest follies; for her what valour has not been spent, what heroic love has not been given always in vain, what terrible dreams have not ravaged and spoiled the world that she might go more proud! The greatest geniuses she has slain like slaves, the most priceless love she has spent like dross. Washed in the blood of the martyrs, and of innumerable creatures with whom after all we share the world, she, the most beautiful, the most splendid adulteress, has taken Heaven captive, and in all her troubles proclaimed that visionary city as her true Capitol. She, the head and fount of our world, the true capital to whom the mightiest cities are but provincial towns, is sufficient for herself; nor has she ever touched an alien beauty without spoiling it. First it was the Art of that Greece whom she had humbled that she strove to learn, always as one might learn a trick, always in vain. Then she forged out of the mysticism of Jesus of Nazareth the mightiest weapon of practical politics, and where He seemed to deny life she gave it to us more abundantly. And at last, it was the Art of Renaissance which she destroyed; for after Michelangelo and Raphael comes the Baroque.

And yet while I speak thus of her as of one who has but little of my affection, I love her—ah, how dearly!— the one immortal city, the splendid burgonet of the world. Over the earth she has cast out her people, and because of her I live, and am free, and may look towards heaven without fear. When her enemies destroyed her temples and her gods, trampling into the earth even the fairest statues, the loveliest goddesses, she, in gentleness and love of a world she mothered, contrived others not less lovely in their stead. She led me to the embrace of Christ and showed me the beauty of the world. What were my England, whom she found naked and a child, without her, and all the splendid years, the dreams, the victories? The kings of the world have knelt to do her reverence, and the peoples have flocked to kiss her stones. As a beautiful and splendid empress she has scorned the byways of life, her progress has ever been along the fair imperial way. She has turned from Life and Pleasure and Beauty neither for the cursing of peasants nor for the brutal threats of the Teutonic barbarian. When our hand was in hers how happy were we—how fair our country, how merry our people; and now that we have parted from her for a moment, with what distraction we regard one another! One by one the fair and beautiful things have fallen away, the merry days no longer come, and Christ, once so gentle and so fair, is not any more divine, but from very far off demands a sober and a sombre world, bereft alike of beauty and of pleasure, since the way is so difficult, our enthusiasm so narrow.

But, O Rome, I will remember splendid days, and forget the wrong my fathers did! If they have denied life, thou hast kept it safe for me through all the tumult of the years. I will no longer remember their dim, sad thoughts, the anger at thy light, the boasting, and the fatal wars. For in quietness and in peace thou hast guarded the ancient things, the reverence, the fidelity, the beauty, that are from of old. And seeing that I only live because thou hast given me life and all precious things, the Songs that lift up my heart, the Law by which I live, the Poetry that is very beautiful, Madonna Mary to pray for me and Christ to hold up my soul in His hands,—so thou hast taught and I believe —shall I not love thee with all my heart, with all my mind, with all my soul, and with all my strength? for thou only art still as lovely as in old time, thou only art our capital, thou only, O Rome, in all the world, mayest still remember the deeds of Scipio, the face of Cæsar, the words of Virgil, nor is there any other city whose brows are bound with immortality.

The school of Art which flourished in Rome for so brief a period in the thirteenth century, had almost entirely disappeared by the year 1310. That fatal year saw the Papacy transferred to Avignon, not to be restored to Rome till, sixty years later, St. Catherine led Pope Gregory XI. by the hand into the Eternal City. In those sixty years a school of painting that really restored Art and Beauty to the world utterly perished.

So early as the year 1210 the Cosmati were decorating the Roman churches with mosaics. And so it is in a little church at Cività Castellana, where we may still find their indestructible work—Christ in Benediction and the Symbols of the Evangelists—that we see what are really the beginnings of the new Art in Italy; the work of Laurence and his son Jacob, 'Magistri Doctissimi Romani,' as the inscription tells us. Here and there in Rome you may come upon their work still, in S. Alessio and at Aracoeli. That Jacob whose name is so piously preserved in the inscription at Cività Castellana would seem to have had a son named Cosmas, and the 'new Vasari'[1] tells us that in the graceful chapel of the Sancta Sanctorum we may find his name inscribed 'on the left-hand pilaster of the entrance'—Magister Cosmatus fecit hoc Opus. It is then to this family that we must give the honour of the revival of Art in Italy. Long before Giotto or the fabulous Cimabue, who for Vasari at any rate are the first names of the Italian revival, the Cosmati had been at work in the capital of Christianity, seeking their inspiration in classical work, forming thereby a genuine school of Art, a Roman school, which in the work of Pietro Cavallini and his pupils was to make so deep an impression on the Art of Italy in the achievement of Giotto and the rest. In S. Maria in Trastevere in Rome, we may still find mosaics of the school—the Birth and Death of the

---

[1] Crowe and Cavalcaselle, *op. cit.*, vol. i. p. 86.

Blessed Virgin, the Annunciation, the Nativity of Our Lord, the Adoration of the Magi, and the Presentation in the Temple. Ghiberti gives these works to Pietro Cavallini, a pupil of the Cosmati, an artist of the first rank, whose work without doubt gave Giotto the hint he needed. In S. Cecilia in Trastevere, his best work, perhaps, has lately been discovered—frescoes of the Last Judgment, in which we may see very easily the influence of the antique. And it is not only in Rome that we find the work of this great master and his school, but in the Upper Church at Assisi also. That great Franciscan church built in 1228, and consecrated by Innocent IV. in 1253 as a monument to the memory of St. Francis, who lies buried beneath its foundations in the faintly coloured rock of Monte Subasio, is really an immense museum of Art. There the Roman school of Pietro Cavallini painted the walls and the roof with the Creation of the World, the Creation of Adam, the Creation of Eve, Abraham and the Three Angels, the Temptation, the Betrayal of Jesus, and the Nativity.[1]

But with the school of Pietro Cavallini, so splendid in its vigorous and inspired achievement, we see at once the finest and the last work of the school of Rome. Working as it was perhaps up to the moment in which Pope Clement V. departed to Avignon, left without any patrons or employers, the school ceased to exist. And so we find that when, in the beginning of the fourteenth century, the Franciscans wished to continue the decoration of S. Francesco, it was to Florence and Siena they turned rather than to Rome.

All Giotto's work in S. Francesco is strongly influenced by the works of the Roman school, and if we allow that his frescoes of the life of St. Francis in the Upper Church were painted in 1302-1306,[2] it may well be that he was in

[1] Crowe and Cavalcaselle, *op. cit.*, vol. i. p. 96, note 3.
[2] See on this important question, *op. cit.*, vol. ii. p. 14, note 1.

reality a pupil of that school in a stricter sense than we had thought.

How is it then, seeing that Rome had in the thirteenth century a school so splendid that Umbrian Art was almost unaffected by it, that it was to a Florentine and not to an Umbrian that the Franciscans turned for the decoration of their church? The Umbrian school was, as is well known, of late development. Those little cities dotted among the mountains were each so small and so isolated, that it might seem they were incapable of producing a school of Art sufficiently enthusiastic to benefit by the work of the Romans, until they were brought under the direct influence of that spirit which later captured all Italy. Ottaviano Nelli died in 1445, Gentile da Fabriano was not born till 1360, and so we find that the Umbrian school is really a school of the fifteenth century. Such Art as there may have been before the last twenty years of the fourteenth century was too provincial, too naïve, and merely religious—religious as the mere drudge of the Church—to benefit at all from an Art so splendid as that of the Roman school. In the years of exile at Avignon, Roman Art died never to rise again. So it is at last rather from Florence and Siena than from the great city at the head of her long valleys that Umbria learned the art of painting, when in 1360 Gentile da Fabriano was born, and fifty years later Piero della Francesca first saw the light in the little town of Borgo San Sepolcro.

It was in Religion, the latest passion of the capital of the world, that in those early years Umbria achieved so much; her saints are not the least famous upon earth. And even in Painting, that great ornament of Religion, she later accomplished not a little. Raphael was born in Urbino, and learned the art of Perugino at Perugia, and although it was not until after he had been to Florence that he became of any real importance as an artist, something of the serenity of his native country lingers about his work always—something not proud, but humble, not unsatisfied, but contented. Nor is Michelangelo without his debt to Umbria, though it be in less direct fashion. How much he learned from Luca Signorelli is perhaps in the case of so overwhelming a personality a matter of little importance. It could not have been so much that we should ever feel the debt. Yet no one can look at Signorelli's frescoes in the Cappella Nuova in the Cathedral at Orvieto and not feel something of the new genius that was about to burst on the world. It is not, however, as an Umbrian that we consider Raphael to-day, but rather as a Roman, as a classic painter of the high Renaissance, in whom already we begin to see signs of decadence; a Roman, and therefore influenced by men from all provinces and cities and countries. Nor of course can we claim any real part in Michelangelo's work for Umbria. His ideas, the expression of which may have been in part suggested by Signorelli, are his own. No one of his own day understood them; those who were his disciples succeeded in carrying the ideals of the great sculptor—for even as a painter he is a sculptor—to the ridiculous and the brutal.

Seeing then that Rome, to whom she looked so naturally down her long valleys, was unable to satisfy her in her desire for Art, Umbria looked first into her own heart, and finding there little but dreams turned towards Siena, a city as mystical as herself, a city too of great saints, and learned much from her.

Umbrian painting begins with a certain Oderisi or Oderigi of Gubbio, whom Dante has placed in his *Purgatorio*[1] as a man so earnest in the study of his art as to have had little time for anything beside. Vasari, in his life of Giotto, says that Oderigi lived in Rome; that he was an excellent

---

[1] *Purgatorio*, canto xi.

M

miniature painter, living' on terms of close friendship with
Giotto. He tells us further, that he himself had 'some few
remains from the hand of the artist, who was certainly a
clever man.' Dennistoun tells us that he died in 1299; but
indeed we know nothing concerning him; no work certainly
from his hand has come down to us, though it is said that
some miniatures in the missals in the archives of S. Pietro
in Rome are his. His pupil Guido Palmerucci has left
us some wall paintings in the chapel of the Palazzo del
Commune, together with a S. Antonio—all that is left of
a large painting which covered one of the walls of S. Maria
dei Laici in Gubbio.[1] Palmerucci died in 1345, and Martino
Nelli, the first of that family, appears to have been contemporary with him. Poor painter as he was, very little is left of his
work in Gubbio to-day—a ruined fresco over a fountain in the
Via Dante, and one or two other fragments, are all that remain
to us of the work of a man whose very name would have
perished but for the work of his son Ottaviano. With this
man Umbrian Art really begins; the greatest of the Gubbian
painters, his work is sometimes marvellously lovely. Like
splendid miniatures, his paintings are gay with colour, they
seem to be composed of curiously cut antique jewels. Too
large to fit into the corners of the service-books, these
pictures of Ottaviano Nelli's doubtless served somewhat the
same purpose as the tiny pictures that greet you as you turn
over those ivory leaves. They too were painted in the
service of Religion, and even as the miniatures in the
missals remind the priest, not without a certain serene
joy, of the facts of Christianity, so these larger miniatures
over the altar or upon the wall bring to the mind of the

[1] Perhaps, too, a Tondo with Madonna and Child and a picture of
the Annunciation, part of an Ancona, in the Municipio of Gubbio,
but see Mason Perkins in *Rassegna d'Arte*, June 1907, and Venturi,
vol. v. p. 637.

worshipper, how much more vividly than words can do, the story of Christ and Madonna—beings really to be worshipped seeing that they are seated on so magnificent a throne, dressed in such gorgeous apparel, gazing so unconcernedly upon humanity. It is perhaps in these huge miniatures that we find the living influence of forgotten Oderigi.

Ottaviano had many pupils, but not one of them came to any fame. It is in Fabriano that Umbrian Art finds her true expression, in the art of Gentile da Fabriano, the pupil of a certain Allegretto Nuzi, who was painting in Florence in 1346, in which year he appears in the register of the painters of that city. Two pictures by him at any rate have come down to us—a Virgin and Child, now in the Lateran, and an altar-piece in the Sacristy of the Duomo at Macerata, the one dated 1365, the other 1369.[1] It is here doubtless that we find the influence of the school of Oderigi, so soon to be forgotten in the work of Gentile da Fabriano. Scattered up and down Italy—in Florence, in Rome, in Milan, in Perugia, in Pisa, and in Orvieto — you find Gentile's work to-day, always with something of the delight in beauty and in exquisite things that is so characteristic of the school of Siena, with much too, perhaps, of the glowing, glittering colour of Ottaviano Nelli and the Gubbian school. A new kind of happiness comes to us from his pictures. He of all men has looked on Umbria for the first time and found her so fair that he dare hardly tell us of his delight. In such a dawn it was, he seems to say in his great picture in Florence —in such a dawn it was, as I myself have seen over the clear, soft hills, that Mary and Joseph, with our Lord, fled into

[1] A triptych with St. Augustine, St. Antony of Padua, and S. Stefano, in Municipio Fabriano. Part of a great poliptych with St. John Ev. and S. Antonio Ab. in cathedral of Fabriano. Two other works in Cathedral of Fabriano, and a S. Antonio between the groups of worshippers in the Congregazione di Carità di Fabriano. See also *Venturi*, vol. v.

Egypt. I know the very flowers by the way, they were so many and so fair, since by that road went the Prince of Life. For the first time in Umbrian painting a painter has ventured to tell us that the world is fair. Long and long ago Umbria had dreamed of heaven and listened to the very voice of Christ, that voice as of many waters, confusing the simple sounds of the world, till suddenly she seems to awaken in Gentile da Fabriano to a kind of apprehension of her own loveliness. It was but for a moment that life was able to disturb her in her contemplation. When Gentile died, he left no successors. Into the enchanting, distracting music of the world sweeps again that voice of many waters, drowning everything in its own perfection and sweetness. Gentile died in 1427; in him the Umbrian school pure and simple found its greatest painter; with him it came to an end. There were, however, numerous isolated schools of painting among the mountains, which were almost entirely local in their development. Of these the earliest would seem to have been that of San Severino, where Giacomo and his brother Lorenzo painted about the year 1400. It is in their work, and more especially in that at Urbino, where, in the Oratory of St. John Baptist, they have painted the story of that saint, that Morelli has thought we first meet with portraits of men and women 'full of life and expression.' A namesake of one of those painters, whose work is in the National Gallery, signed 'Laurentius II.,' was painting so late as 1481.

But it is in another of these little cities that we find the founder of the school, if school it may be called, which later attained to such fame under Perugino. Foligno, that little town in the valley not far from Assisi, produced a painter in the middle of the fifteenth century in Niccolò da Foligno, called by Vasari Niccolò Alunno. Born about 1430, he was almost certainly the pupil of Benozzo Gozzoli, who, between

Rome and Florence, painted much in Umbria. Mystical poet as he is, he thrusts upon us his sincere grief or joy in the life of Christ or the Blessed Virgin in so irresistible a fashion that we are captured almost at the first glance. 'The result is,' as Mr. Berenson has well said, 'that with precisely the same purpose as the later Bolognese, he holds our attention, even gives us a certain pungent, dolorous pleasure; while we turn away from Guido Reni with disgust unspeakable.'[1] And it is not only of a painter so enamoured of the flesh as Guido Reni that Niccolò disgusts us, but even of Perugino, whose affectations and insincerity are intolerable beside the simple beauty, the sincere religion of the founder of the Perugian school. Nor is Niccolò without claim upon our notice as a painter pure and simple. Pictorial though he be, as indeed is all the school, his line and colour are full of emotion, his figures move with the true impulse of life.

The influence of Fra Angelico and Benozzo Gozzoli, almost universal in Central Italy, is found in the works of Bonfigli of Perugia, a more naïve but less divine interpreter of the promises of Christ. Coming to Umbria in 1447, and to Perugia herself in 1457, Benozzo Gozzoli probably taught Bonfigli something of his art—that art which is so pretty, so charming a treasure of the Pinacoteca Vannucci to-day. Here at last, in this so timid intelligence, we find the roots of that charm, that sentimental beauty, which has so captured the world—the roots of what afterwards flowered so luxuriantly in Perugino and Pintoricchio—a particular effect of light, a suggestion of gold in the air, something of that serenity which Perugino knew so well how to express. His angels, of which there are so many in the Pinacoteca, are among the most charming things in the world; crowned so fantastically with roses, they are as delightful and almost as affected as anything in Perugino's work. It is not for him to devote himself

---

[1] Berenson, *Central Italian Painters*, p. 87.

to the art of painting, seeing that he is intent on quite
another service—to wit, the illustration of the lives of
Madonna and the saints.   What in the way of science he has
learnt from Fra Angelico or Benozzo Gozzoli—that teacher
of the third class from Florence—he has learnt as it were by
heart without any real consciousness of its value.   And since
there is so little thoughtfulness in his work, he remains a
delightful but less spontaneous, less original illustrator of
heaven than Fra Angelico, without the genius and the science
of that master, but charming, lovable, as exquisitely
obvious as Perugino and all the school which is in itself
the one feminine school in Italy, content to be charming and
delightful; and refusing thought, having perhaps no need
of it.

Meantime another master, greater than any living Umbrian,
had appeared in Piero della Francesca.   Born at Borgo San
Sepolcro in 1416, his work was certainly one .of the most
astonishing achievements of the age.   He appears to have
painted in Perugia as well as in Urbino, Arezzo, and Loretto;
and in Rome his work was destroyed to make room for that
of Raphael.   Fiorenzo di Lorenzo, who was working in
Perugia in 1487, a pupil, it may well be, of Benozzo Gozzoli,
or even of Bonfigli, seems to have met this curiously thoughtful painter early in life.   How different is his work ever
after !   With the single exception of a picture by Piero della
Francesca, Fiorenzo's work is perhaps the chief delight of the
gallery at Perugia.   He was the realist of a fortunate age.
In those delightful little panels—if indeed they be his—in
the Gabinetto di Fiorenzo di Lorenzo we see all the passionate
and languid figures of those ferocious years at their happiest
moments, posing before their fellows, or listening to the
loving words of S. Bernardino of Siena.   The beautiful
palaces of marble, set in I know not what perfection of landscape, jewelled with tiny lakes under a lofty and perfect sky,

are, as it were, the creations of one who understood the dreams of this people, so capable of mysticism, so eager for power, for heaven, for the lives of their foes. A kind of music seems to thread its way through his delicate landscapes, and in the Marriage of St. Catherine and the Nativity fresco to break into a concord of sweet sounds long drawn out, unwearied and full of joy.

Fiorenzo's work lends a spirit of antique cheerfulness to the Pinacoteca at Perugia beyond anything of the sort to be found in the somewhat cloying sweetness of Perugino. He seems to have seen the very spirit of the fifteenth century objectively, almost as Piero della Francesca sees his subjects—as though she were a stranger in Florence or Perugia, through whose fierce and rugged streets she trips, a vision of new beauty. In this series of eight pictures of scenes in the life of S. Bernardino of Siena a new elegance transforming the old religion, almost certainly aiding it profoundly in its encounter with the new spirit, seems to have come into the Piazza and the streets of the old warrior city—something infinitely more subtle and perhaps more sincere than the sentiment of Perugino. Fiorenzo's two pupils—for so I take them to have been—Perugino and Pintoricchio, made the school famous—painted in the Sistine Chapel, in Siena, in Florence, and in their day were as famous as any painters in Italy. Perugino, indeed, probably manufactured, for there is no other expression for his methods, more religious pictures than any other painter in Italy. He managed a kind of workshop of pious paintings, employing many pupils and workmen, and allowed their feeble and sentimental work, often quite unworthy of him, to appear as his own. But in spite of every disadvantage inherent in so brutal a commercialism, his achievement is secure. As what has been called by Mr. Berenson 'a space-composer,'[1] he has few equals in all the history of his Art.

[1] Berenson, *Central Italian Art*, page 95.

If his pupil Raphael surpassed him, it was rather by reason of his teaching, perhaps, than by any original comprehension of space that Raphael possessed.

The achievement of Pintoricchio is different. His touch is much heavier than Perugino's, as we may see to-day by comparing their work in the Sistine Chapel. In him we see really the goal of the purely pictorial school achieved—a perfect 'illustration,' a lovely and ornamental explanation of the subject. Not that the subject is everything, but that movement, life, painting, are nothing, and the most important thing in his work certain delightful ornamental thoughts— poetical, charming—which the painter has given us on certain subjects, such as the Nativity, or St. Catherine disputing with the Doctors, or the Life of Pius II.

But after all, here in Umbria, it is a splendour of space, a light that never was in any other sky, a breadth and nobility of landscape, a softness over hill and valley, that we must look for rather than the terrible travail and earnestness of the Florentine school. We are in Italia Mystica—the country of St. Francis; heaven here is really more precious than earth. And it is perhaps the expression of this mood of the soul that has brought Perugino his fame, though it may well be he himself had something of a contempt for it.

So unimportant in comparison with the schools of Florence and Venice, less even than the school of Siena in the History of Painting, the Umbrian school yet brings us the most famous and beloved name in modern art—Raphael Sanzio. But it is not as an Umbrian we think of Raphael, but rather as a Roman painter. He learned from so many and so various teachers—from Lionardo, Francia, and Bartolommeo, no less than from Giovanni Sanzio, Perugino, and Pintoricchio. And yet even in his latest work—the Transfiguration, in the Vatican—after he has encountered all the greatest intelligences of his day, how he brings back to us the soft distances, the spacious golden air of Umbria! In his youth his work had been so like to Perugino's that in Florence he had been encouraged to persevere in it in the hope of one day achieving or even surpassing the charm, the soft and lovely excellence of his master. How perfectly he has learned every lesson, how humbly he has listened to every teacher! It is easy to see that his youth was spent in Umbria. His personality, never very strongly marked, seems to have absorbed all or almost all that was best in his contemporaries, and to have added something of the serenity, the quiet delight in beautiful things for their own sake, the loyalty to the old great masters, that were so conspicuously his own. It is as a scholar among masters that we see him, content even to the end of his life to learn and to absorb everything that was fair with which he came in contact; not the art of painting only, but scholarship, philosophy, history, poetry, the classics also, transforming them into his own terms, and finding in them the serenity and beauty of his own nature, as we have scarcely been able to do in the centuries since his death. Without the great nervous strength of so profound, so subtle a personality as Leonardo, or the immense physical virtue of Michelangelo, he died at thirty-seven years of age. And he is like a relic from the classical age; some perfect, serene god, blithe and beautiful, discovered, as it were, by some happy fortune, in a time so in love with pagan culture as the sixteenth century. And even as his work has something of the indestructible perfection of the antique, its precise virtue, its ideality, so in his own body he was beautiful and delicate. His nature was so transparent that everything that was really life-giving shone through it as the sun. The disorder, the tragic rebellion of Michelangelo were impossible for him. He could never have been sufficiently lawless in his imagination or passions to violate the instinct of reverence. And so we find in him a kind of impotence that, after all, overwhelms even a nature so strong and so impetuous as Michelangelo at last.

Of all that imperious and splendid age, glittering with many cruelties, shadowy with subtleties that in the end made Art impossible, Raphael is the saviour. The presence of his nature is like a fair soft light over everything, or like a perfect flower in the midst of a battlefield. Rather than any saint or soldier, or philosopher, or man of genius, he serves as the type of the Renaissance at its highest ; and his impotence— if we may so call it—is nothing more than the failure of all art to express, to do more than shadow forth, that perfect state which Plato has seen lying in the heavens, which St. Paul has assured us is eternal there.

XVIII

PIERO DELLA FRANCESCA

IN Vasari's *Lives of the Painters* there is much that modern
criticism, working for the most part negatively, has
destroyed or at least questioned, and having robbed us as
in so many instances of much that we had come to regard
with a kind of affection, it has yet dealt with Piero della
Francesca in a more friendly fashion, re-establishing for him,
as it were, a reputation that our fathers had forgotten.
Vasari regards Piero chiefly as a kind of inspired mathe-
matician, a painter devoted to the study of perspective, rather
than as a subject for æsthetic criticism. But for us, long
after the disputing as to the subjective or objective quality
in his work shall be hushed, he will remain a painter of rare
power and beauty, so that we shall find ourselves in sympathy
with him when Perugino, with all his facile and effeminate
beauty, has become a burden, and the perfection of Raphael·
has failed to satisfy our desires.

Born at Borgo San Sepolcro, according to Vasari, about
the year 1406, he was the son of Benedetto dei Franceschi
and of Romana di Perino. His father who, Vasari says, died
before his son's birth, would seem in reality to have lived
till 1465, so that the boy's education was by no means left
entirely to the care of his mother. Of his early youth we
possess unfortunately no details at all, but at fifteen years of
age he became a painter, probably in the studio of Domenico
Veneziano, though it was not till the year 1439, Veneziano

being then in Florence painting in the Ospedale and in
S. Maria Novella, that we hear of them as working together.
From 1439 to 1445 he would seem to have remained with
Veneziano, but actually we know scarcely anything of his
life during those years.   But in 1445 the Brotherhood of the
Misericordia at Borgo San Sepolcro commissioned him to
paint an altar-piece for their chapel.   This is the Madonna
della Misericordia, which during the year 1903 was removed
from the Chapel of the Ospedale and placed in the Municipio.
It may well have been after he had finished this picture for
his birthplace that, in the company of Domenico Veneziano,
he proceeded to Loretto to paint certain frescoes in the old
Church of Our Lady of Loretto.   It would appear that, the
plague becoming very severe during their stay, they were
forced to depart because of it.   There is nothing by Piero
to-day in all that strange place ; it seems probable that he
worked in the old church which was destroyed in 1465, when
the present Chiesa della Santa Casa was begun for Pope
Paul II. by the Florentine Giuliano da Majano.   Whether
Piero proceeded to Rome in the company of Domenico
immediately after leaving Loretto is uncertain.   But Nicolas V.
who had sent for him, when he came to Rome, set him to
paint that room in the Vatican where Raphael, having been
compelled to destroy Piero's work, has painted the 'Disputa'
and 'The Deliverance of St. Peter from Prison.'   It has been
suggested, and is indeed almost a tradition, that the strange
effect of light in the latter fresco was suggested to Raphael
by one of the frescoes he destroyed, no doubt unwillingly.
It is remarkable that in the fresco at Arezzo where Constantine
lies sleeping in his tent during a vision, Piero has achieved in
a moment, as it were, the whole secret of light—light conceived
not simply as mere sunshine but as a kind of spirit fallen
on everything, gracious and splendid even in the shadows,
which are certainly no mere masses of indifferent obscurity

but pools of cooler light only less luminous than that sword of heavenly flame which has flashed from heaven and swept a path through the moonlight for the message of an angel.

It may be that Piero was in Rome from 1447 to 1451, or from 1451 to 1455, but actually in the year 1451 he was at the court of Sigismondo Malatesta, one of the most extraordinary and interesting of the many curious personalities of the Renaissance. This strange and wayward dreamer was at the same time a man of action of the most brutal sort. His crimes, mysterious and incredible almost, are too horrible to dwell upon. He murdered two wives, and at last died the husband of the beautiful and learned Isotta degli Atti, who had long been his mistress. In his own honour and because he loved her, he rebuilt the Cathedral of S. Francesco at Rimini, consecrating a chapel, 'Divae Isottae Sacrum.' The beautiful church remains one of the most interesting monuments in Italy. For in Sigismondo's brain there was a dream which he seems to have shared with Pico della Mirandola—a dream that suggested the possibility of the gods of Greece and Rome being after all only in exile, awaiting, perhaps, man's return to sanity and the desire of life. But, egotist as he was, he himself was his own god, and so it is really for himself and for the woman he loved that he employed Alberti to build his temple and his tomb, where upon every arch and string-course, in every piece of sculptured work, appear the elephant and the rose, his emblems, and his insolent and yet pathetic legend: 'Sigismundus Pandulphus Malatesta Pan. F. Fecit Anno Gratiae MCCCCL.'

So it was in this temple of Malatesta in the Cappella delle Reliquie that Piero painted the beautiful fresco of Sigismondo kneeling before his patron saint, which we find in its own place to-day. Sigismondo himself is seen in perfect profile, a method of portraiture that seems to have been especially dear to Piero, for he used it many times, and certainly instructed others in the advantage of this manner. It is so we see the Duke and Duchess of Urbino, now in the Uffizi, and a certain portrait attributed to him in the Poldo Pezzoli Collection at Milan, of a lady supposed to be the wife of Joannes de Bardi, which however is only very doubtfully his own. But here in Rimini in this strange church we see the figure of him who built it, in full length, kneeling before his saint, St. Sigismund of Burgundy. Behind Sigismondo are two magnificent hounds, and you look into the picture at a landscape full of the splendid spaciousness of Perugino, with something over all how different from anything Perugino ever painted, even in his youth. Some profound and noble energy, some altogether gracious strength and measured sweetness, disengage themselves from this fading picture made so long ago. It is fulfilled with the air of the mountains, those strong and fresh winds that since God brought them out of His treasures have touched no earth but this. And amid all this freshness, this mysterious nudity of Nature, as though one were looking on a landscape before the creation of man, between two beautiful pillars hung with garlands Sigismondo kneels, inscrutable, with half-closed eyes, his beautiful hair low on his forehead and almost covering his ears, his hands clasped as though to quiet his unruly spirit, his lips shut close as though to hide some curious smile.

Having finished his work at Rimini, it is possible that Piero proceeded to Rome. However this may be, Vasari suggests that he returned from Rome to Borgo San Sepolcro on account of the death of his mother. It must have been about this time, certainly after he had painted the fresco at Rimini, that he painted the magnificent series of frescoes in S. Francesco at Arezzo, by far the most considerable piece of work that he achieved during his whole life. The legend of the Holy Cross, its history from the beginning of the world until it was discovered by the Emperor Heraclius, and later by St. Helena, is one of the most curious dreams of the Christian mind. No longer upheld in its entirety by the Catholic Church, it is nevertheless true in its intention, since for the Middle Age at least the Cross was indeed a lovely branch of the Tree of Life which is in the midst of the Paradise of God. And even as the earth in the beginning held that which bore the secret of immortality, so it was at last in the sweet soil, very deep in the ground, from which we too were made, that the mother of the emperor found the cross of palm, of cedar, of cypress, and of olive, and 'waited what God would do.' The beautiful legend told by Jacques de Voragine in the thirteenth century, and translated into English by William Caxton, is but one, albeit perhaps the loveliest, of those histories he thought worthy to be called 'legends worth their weight in gold.' And it is this golden legend that Piero has painted so vigorously in the choir of S. Francesco at Arezzo. How far are we in contemplating these frescoes from the passionate asceticism, the unearthly beauty of Fra Angelico! It is as though a new desire had suddenly been born into the world, a desire for life, where Fra Angelico after all would have been content with death, or would have seen life in exquisite distorted fashion down the transforming vista of mortality, with all the changes of the grave between him and that perfection of life. But with Piero it is different. What magnificent vitality he has given to these beautiful women, how valiant are his men, how puissant his angels! And above all, he has filled earth and heaven with radiant light. It is in the clear and nimble air, in the fair white light of our real and beautiful daylight, that he alone of his contemporaries has dared at last to paint man and woman in all the sweet energy of life, full of that long breath of God which at dawn in a garden first gave us life. The air, exquisite as a precious stone faintly coloured with the thought of God, caresses the fair flesh of his figures as in our world, only he has given it some perfection which we can only hope to see. For his light is the light of the profound air of heaven, and he seems to rejoice and be glad in it, as the musical lark which adventures nearer than we dare to the sun, which is as the smile of God. He has already discovered that there is no black in all our world. Along the low horizon of the east he has laid the shadow of the fingers of God, which is the fairest sunrise; and it is the flash of an angel's wings that obscures the moonbeams with light, while through the tired eyelids, delicate and translucent, of the great emperor, dazzles the Cross, itself a glowing jewel, which brings his heaviness to an end with a vision of morning. These clouds for ever a-sail so delicately in his sky, what are they but light expressed and made visible, more fragile than the sunbeams, of which indeed they are the delicate, white daughters, made not of earth, but of dew and light and the jewelled fragments of the sea. They have the shape of the wings of angels, and they are as fair as the fairest. They are the ships of heaven burthened with light. They are the children of the sun; from him they set out whiter than snow in the dawn, to him they will return at evening, drenched through and through with the colour of heaven. For Piero alone of all his fellows seems to have observed a new form of energy in light itself; to him it is the one thing that is very precious. He perhaps understood that the act of creation began and ended with *Fiat Lux*. From that moment life began, and lasts while the sun, or the light, or the moon, or the stars be not darkened, or the ceaseless dawns that encircle our world be not finished, or the luminous night shall still climb out of the reluctant sea, until the shadows flee away because there is no more light under the sky, since it has fled back into the eyes of God.

One lonely and magnificent figure he left behind him at Arezzo in the cathedral—a figure of St. Mary Magdalen, very noble and reticent. She adorns no altar, but in a quiet corner of the great church—a little lonely, because, perhaps, unlike the great multitude of the saints, she has loved much, and seen, and understood, and has suffered great experiences, and only learned to acquiesce at last in the scrupulous orderliness of God because of love—she stands very sorrowful, since she alone of all those clouds on clouds of saints really understands. Well, it is always so; we find Piero emotionally under the influence of the Middle Age, and yet himself perhaps a kind of emancipator or deliverer from its mysticism, at times hardly less astonishing than Luca Signorelli, his pupil. For he, too, was occupied rather with his art than with the expression of ideas about religion. He was the first painter, perhaps, to study perspective scientifically. Problems of light, the action of light on beautiful faces or hair, the action of light upon light, would certainly seem to have fascinated him almost all his life long. And yet he has not discarded the ideas that were then gradually becoming less insistent in the world, but in all their modesty and beauty he has used them without question as a means of attaining a beauty bought with much toil and feverish endeavour. His Magdalen is not the ecstatic and splendid courtesan that we see in Titian's canvas, but a beautiful and lonely woman, who will ever remember that lingering dawn in the garden, when, in the midst of her passionate weeping, the gardener came so quietly and spoke her name, and in a moment she knew Him whom she had loved.

So Piero, having finished his work at Arezzo, returned, perhaps, to his birthplace; and it is there, indeed, that we

N

find the most extraordinary of his works. The 'Resurrection
of Christ' in the Municipio at Borgo San Sepolcro is, perhaps,
the most beautiful representation of the triumph of Christ in
the world.   It is not easy to see it.   You journey over the
mountains from Arezzo for hours amid all the clear beauty
of Tuscan hills, that have something not Tuscan about them—
a softness, a glamour, that is found, perhaps, only in Umbria ;
and at last in the valley of the Tiber you come upon a tiny
city at the foot of Monte Maggiore of the Central Apennines.
There, amid all the quietness of a country place, in the cool
rooms of the Municipio are set such works of Piero as remain
in his birthplace—an altar-piece in oil and tempera, till lately
in the Ospedale della Misericordia, and two frescoes, San
Ludovico and the Resurrection.   The fresco of the Resurrection comes upon us with a kind of surprise ; we had not
suspected Piero of so much thoughtfulness.   It is as though
he had listened to some voice, or seen a vision, or on some
fortunate day been led away the captive of Love, for him as
for Dante, a Lord of terrible aspect, who has shown him the
places of Death and Sorrow.   In the cold light of the earliest
morning, mere sunless dawn as yet, Christ has risen, and
is standing in His tomb.   His experience is in His face, the
dawn of a knowledge, perhaps, of the sorrows of humanity.
It is as though for the first time He had really understood
the power of evil, to which, after all, we are so unwillingly
the slaves, the hopeless misery of that state of imperfect
love.   The noise of hell has furrowed His face, and He has
only just escaped into our quiet world.   Beneath that terrible
and beautiful figure, inspired for the first time with thought,
down whose endless vistas his soul has fled these three days
and nights, lie four soldiers, sleeping in the noiseless twilight.
Behind the green trees on the right the first exquisite frail
light of dawn is coming to comfort the world, and with the
return of the Prince of Life the first day of spring has come ;

already the flowers have blossomed and the trees budded behind Him as He came out of the sunrise, and when He shall turn at last into the garden, where Mary will find Him, those bare boughs, that naked hillside, that brown and sterile earth will quicken too, even as the hills that He has already crossed. All the passion of His encounter with Death and the dead is graven on His face, and though men sleep He can know no rest; He is up before them, and the whole long day is waiting for Him.   He is stronger than Time, which has swept everything away, for He who made Death has struck him dead again.   Ah, in looking on this fresco, one seems to understand that for all those years before He came there is only silence. For Piero has expressed not only the old magical truths of Paganism and Christianity, the joy of the world at the coming of spring, the triumph of the Prince of Life in a world pallid with the fear of Death, but the subtler and more terrible thoughts, too, of the age of thought that was just then dawning for the world.   He seems to see a God no longer delicate and exquisitely pitiful, gracious and victorious in an encounter where the end was not doubtful for a moment, but one innocent and almost ignorant of evil and the tragedy of mankind; really at home only in heaven, or in the desert of Judæa on the banks of the Dead Sea, a place of stones and precipices too desolate for thought. We see this figure standing almost dreadful in solemnity in the waters of the Jordan while John pours the water from the shell over His head, and the white Dove hovers above Him in profound stillness, in the Baptism now in the National Gallery.   The desolate country, of a cool brown and grey, stretches away over hill and valley beyond the city, which later brought the tears to His eyes when He thought of its unavailing joy.   Three angels stand aside surprised and afraid, so terrible has the Christ become after even so long in the company of men.   And again the same figure, a little younger, a little less lamentable, less tragic or isolated, stands attentive, as John Baptist in .the Perugia altar-piece, while above this a sweet and valiant angel, under the pillars of some cool colonnade, speaks his message to Madonna.   And again, the same figure, as I think, lies dead and helpless on His mother's knees in a beautiful Pietà now in Perugia.   For Piero, certainly, Christ has no form nor comeliness; His beauty is departed from Him.   As a child He is already rather strange than beautiful; and as the youth whom John baptizes, He would seem already to have felt the weight of the world heavier than a hundred crowns.   As He lies dead upon His mother's knees, something of that heavenly beauty, mysterious and symbolical, may be found, for Death has kissed Him at last and given his inscrutable peace; but in the majestic figure of the risen Christ we find, indeed, a real and perfect beauty, the dream of the world since the beginning. In that figure, standing there in the tomb, I seem to find the calm and intense majesty of the statues. He looks vaguely out at the world, and yet not at the world, comprehending it for the first time, perhaps; and it is not any profound joy you find in His countenance.

In a lovely picture of the Nativity in the National Gallery, full of cool greys and I know not what perfection of simple morning, a tiny choir of angels sings the *Gloria in Excelsis*, while He who is come so humbly into our world lies with arms stretched out to His mother, who worships Him.   Well, on His return from Hades at the dawn of a day so different, something of that same vague helplessness seems suggested, perhaps, by the very intensity of His look or His loneliness. He seems almost to be aware of a virtue within Himself, which is wasting itself uselessly. His perfection, His strength is the forlorn hope of the world. The sorrows of the world have not wearied Him, but have entrenched His face with the scars of thought. A whole multitude, vast and tremendous, has drunk of the well of His tenderness, and He has only just escaped from their terrible desires.

Thus, one finds in Piero's work much of the thoughtfulness of Luca Signorelli, his pupil, together with a freshness and a beautiful kind of strength that is rare in Luca. Vasari says that he became blind; but one is relieved in thinking thus of his dejected old age—he died in 1492, aged eighty-six—to know that any such statement is quite unauthenticated. 'Sanus mente, intellectu et corpore,' he says of himself in 1487; it is hardly the language of a blind man. His work has a kind of suggestiveness very rare in Art—a kind of distinction that is certainly, as I find it, the expression of a personality of great strength. For without personality Art is the feeblest of pretensions. Everywhere in his work we find the same exquisite vitality, reticent and scrupulous, but profound as his Umbrian sky. In thinking of him we seem to understand the strength that had been hidden beneath the sweetness of Fra Angelico and the true mediæval painters.

XIX

MELOZZO DA FORLÌ

MELOZZO DA FORLÌ, another pupil of Piero della Francesca, is certainly one of the most remarkable painters of the Umbrian school. Born at Forlì in June 1438, if we are to believe his epitaph, formerly in the Church of the Trinità at Forlì, he lived fifty-six years and five months, dying there, as we learn from a manuscript quoted in the *Commentary on the Life of Benozzo Gozzoli*, in the Le Monnier edition of Vasari, on November 8, 1494. His work is so rare, his legend so scanty, as to leave us with little more than the name of a painter who must have been famous in his day, painting, as he did, for Pope Sixtus IV., inscribing his name in the book of the Academy of St. Luke, of which he was one of the original members, Melotius Pi. Pa.—Melotius, Painter to the Pope. For Federigo too, the famous Duke of Urbino, he painted many pictures, decorating the library of the palace at Urbino with representations of the seven Arts.

That Piero della Francesca was his only master remains doubtful at the least. That great painter was not at Urbino before 1469, in which year Melozzo was over thirty years old; but that Piero influenced him in his work is obvious to any one who will study the few pictures that remain to us of all Melozzo's work. We possess none, indeed, which does not show the influence of Piero.

Cardinal Francesco della Rovere was elected Pope with the title of Sixtus IV. in 1471, and in 1472 we find Melozzo in

Rome. Sixtus IV., famous as the builder of the Sistine
Chapel, was also notorious for his nepotism. And so it was
for Cardinal Riario della Roverò that Melozzo painted the
tribune of the Church of SS. Apostoli. His work was
destroyed in 1711, but a much repainted fragment—a figure
of Christ—is in the Palazzo Quirinale to-day, and certain
figures of angels in the Sacristy of S. Pietro. This
marvellous fresco represented the Ascension, and the tradition of certain feats of foreshortening which Melozzo had
contrived has come down to us to-day. Something of its
splendour, its emotion, its moving beauty, may be seen in the
figures preserved in St. Peter's—two angels playing on
musical instruments, in which some exquisite emotion seems
to be expressed, some delicate kind of joy in the return of the
Prince of Life to His heaven. Certainly we find there a new
spirit, very different from the isolated and tragic solemnity
of the work of Piero della Francesca. A graciousness wholly
Umbrian—something of the ineffable and serious joy of the
hills and valleys of that land which always seems as though
it had been especially blessed—disengages itself from these
paintings. And yet we feel the presence of Piero, if only in
the bold solution of that problem of foreshortening, in the
evident interest in the scientific part of painting in a man of
whom Giovanni Santi, his pupil, sings :—

> 'Melozzo, dear to me,
> Who to perspective farther limits gave.'

About this time Melozzo painted in the library of the
Vatican, then newly restored by Sixtus IV. and placed under
the guardianship of the learned Platina, a fresco, now transferred to canvas and much damaged thereby, in the Vatican
Gallery. We see Sixtus IV. enthroned, with Platina kneeling
before him, while Cardinal Giuliano della Rovere, afterwards
Pope Julius II., Girolamo Riario, Cardinal Pietro Riario, and

Giovanni della Rovere, the Pope's nephews, surround him. Long attributed to Piero della Francesca, this picture, almost more than any other by Melozzo, shows his master's influence. In a great and beautiful hall Sixtus sits, while Bartolommeo Sacchi, surnamed Platina, kneeling at his feet, points to an inscription in which we read of the blessings the Pope has conferred on Rome. The two Cardinals, Pietro the sensualist, a Mendicant, Giuliano the unimpassioned intellectual, together with Girolamo, the Lord of Forlì (who, it may be, brought Melozzo to Rome) and Giovanni, stand beside the Pope. Something of that delight which Piero had in painting beautiful perspective may be found here too, together with an impersonal, unemotional effect very rare in Melozzo's work.

In the little town of Forlì, in the plain between Bologna and Rimini, where he was born, there still remains one of his rare works—the Pesta Pepe. It was originally painted for a sign over a shop. We see a figure in violent action beating with both arms a heavy pestle in a mortar. The foreshortening is astonishing. 'Nowhere, perhaps,' says Mr. Berenson, 'nowhere, perhaps, as in his renowned "Apothecary's Apprentice Pounding Herbs," does painting show such embodiment of the joy in mere living, the play of muscles and the use of limbs.'

Melozzo is said also to have painted seven pictures for the palace at Urbino in the reign of Federigo. The two pictures, now in the National Gallery, representing Rhetoric and Music may perhaps be his; they are ascribed to him, but it is doubtful whether they are really from his hand; while at Windsor there is a portrait of Federigo, also given to him; and Morelli speaks of another, which I do not remember to have seen, in the Barberini Palace in Rome. But at Loretto, in the Chiesa della Santa Casa, Melozzo has painted with a certain solemnity, a rare gravity very characteristic of Piero, a series of prophets. It is possible that he studied the work of his master here in Loretto before it was destroyed in 1468. What those frescoes were which Domenico Veneziano and Piero della Francesca painted at Loretto before they were driven away by the plague, we shall never know. Vasari says they painted the roof of the Sacristy, and that Signorelli completed their work. This, however, is impossible, since Luca Signorelli painted in the present church, which was only begun in 1468, while it must have been about 1447 that Piero was working in the old church.

Melozzo da Forlì, in comparison with Luca Signorelli, that great intelligence, is a painter of deep emotion. There are no great ideas in his pictures, nor does his work suggest to us that there was a great intelligence behind it. His temperament, deep and strong, carries him away, so that we rather feel his intense emotion, his victorious joy, than understand his thoughts. Something of Piero's science is there, a delight in the difficulties of painting; but above all, we find a triumphant sense of life and movement, a kind of ecstasy, a delight in living and moving things for their own sake.

XX

LUCA SIGNORELLI AT ORVIETO

IN Vasari's life of Luca Signorelli, his kinsman, there is perhaps something more than is usual even with him of that delight in human nature which is so characteristic of this sixteenth-century writer of imaginary portraits. A real love and reverence seem to have inspired Vasari with a kind of gravity as he wrote of this painter from Cortona, who first made it possible for him to study Art. It is perhaps chiefly as an old man, very noble and quiet, that we remember Signorelli after reading those pages; and occupied as he was all his life in business important to Art and to Italy, we shall ever think of him as an old man blessing a little child, passing his last years among those who loved and honoured him, a superb and aristocratic figure, with something of the serene sincerity that in that courteous age might be expected to surround such an one.

It is strange that one who in his day was so beloved should have been so disregarded in our own. 'In his paintings,' says Vasari, 'he showed the true mode of depicting the nude form, and proved that it can be made, although not without consummate art and much difficulty, to appear as does the actual life.' And as an artist it is so we must regard him really as the rediscoverer of the perfection, the sufficiency of the human form, the true master of Michelangelo, who did not scruple 'courteously to avail himself' of his achievements—perfecting them, fulfilling them with his

own spirit and invincible personality, and so justifying as it
were the lesser genius of Signorelli by his own devastating
victory.   And so for the most part while we applaud Michelangelo, we forget his forerunner, who has but little philosophy
to give us; whose work, loyally following that of his master
Piero della Francesca, is almost impersonal; who was consumed by no immense sorrow, nor bitterly unsatisfied by
love, nor overwhelmed by the tragic power of his imagination,
but a man of quiet days, interested chiefly in his Art which
he seems to have practised wholly from a love of it; splendid
in his life, taking much pleasure in clothing himself in handsome vestments, dressing, as the gossip of the time is anxious
to tell us, always in silk, holding with a certain pride many
offices in his native city, and especially courteous, as Vasari
repeats, to all who approached him, both to those who desired
his works and to his disciples.

Born at Cortona in 1440, Vasari says that his earliest
work was done for the Church of S. Lorenzo in Arezzo in the
year 1472.   But of all his work, frescoes and banners and
paintings in oil, done in Arezzo, but two remain—a Madonna
with Saints and Prophets, painted in his old age for the
Compagnia of San Girolamo, now in the gallery; and three
parts of a predella containing the Birth, the Presentation in
the Temple, and the Marriage of the Blessed Virgin, now in
the Sacristy of the Duomo.   The earliest work of which we
have any knowledge is now in Milan in the Brera.   It is a
Flagellation painted in oil on a panel, in which we may discover easily enough the influence of Piero della Francesca,
and it may well be, something of Donatello too, in an evident
desire for the truth as regards the human form.   How great
was the influence of Donatello on Luca Signorelli it is perhaps
impossible to tell; other masters, as Antonio Pollaiuolo, for
instance, may have intervened between the great sculptor
and that passionate student of anatomy who was to influence

Michelangelo so profoundly; but even in so early a picture as the Flagellation—early, I mean, in his long life, though it was not painted until his fortieth year—we find him occupied after all chiefly with the human form, interested really only in that, in its vitality, its vigour, its nobility; so that we turn from the almost ignoble Christ to the splendour of the two men who strike Him with the knotted cords, or to that figure which binds Him to the pillar with such energy, or to the young man who stands with half-drawn sword exquisitely scornful of Him who bears this shame with so much lowliness of spirit and humility. And indeed, for Signorelli, conscious of his strength, and used rather to inflict such punishment than to bear it, there seems to have been but little comeliness or beauty in a spectacle so humiliating. The profound spiritual insight of other and earlier masters was denied him. Of all men of his time he was the least a mystic. The subtleties of the soul that appealed so strongly to Leonardo da Vinci have nothing to do with him. Something of an exquisite and affected elegance we may find, perhaps, in the figure of one of the men who, daintily almost, swings his body with the blow; but even here in his earliest known picture, it is rather the grandeur of the human body, its sufficiency and perfection, that attract him than any mystical emotion or beauty.

In 1479 we find him appointed to the Council of XVIII. in Cortona, and a little later to the Priori and the General Council, which offices he held almost to his death. That he was in Rome in or about 1484, that he painted the frescoes attributed to him in the Sistine Chapel, the criticism of our day is doubtful. But about this time he painted an altarpiece in the Duomo at Perugia, which of all the pictures now in that city is perhaps the most delightful. Madonna sits on a high throne, behind which hangs a garland of flowers; two angels sing in heaven, and around her stand St. John

Baptist, S. Onofrio, S. Ercolano, and S. Stefano, while seated
on the steps of the throne a naked angel tunes a lute. The
almost fantastical realism of this picture is redeemed by
a sense of beauty at once serene and strong. That angel
tuning his lute, so unembarrassed by the great saints and
the very Son of God so near him, seems to embody the
spirit of all Signorelli's work. The dreams he had ex-
perienced in Florence, the work of Donatello and Pollaiuolo,
come to us, how sedately, from amid all the unexpressive
work in the picture. He has conquered his dreams, and
has expressed them, and he seems here to have assimilated
almost everything that he took from his masters, and to
have had his way with it; so that the figure of that angel
is but the first of those legions of nudes that are to come
from his hand, not all redeemed from their mere strength
by the power of his genius, but all living often more nobly,
but never perhaps with more natural life than in that delicate figure for whom the Madonna waits, till to the music of
his lute he shall be prepared to begin some exquisite canticle.
The same or nearly the same figure of Mary may be found
in the 'Circumcision' of the National Gallery, but in that
laboured old picture there is nothing of the lightness, the
ecstatic perception of beauty, of the delight in physical perfection, that we find in the Perugia altar-piece. Just that sort of
perfection Signorelli perhaps never touched again; something
of it, however, with how much more contrivance of joy and
certainty of touch, together with a serenity of purpose that is
wanting ever after, we find in the great picture of Pan, now
in Berlin. That serious, dreamy god sits there enthroned,
enchanted by the sound of flutes, his vine staff in his hand, the
crescent moon over his head. Through the dreaminess of the
summer afternoon, the soft music of the flutes, the beauty
of those who surround him—that unattainable beauty to
which he himself, his rude goat feet daintily crossed, can

never attain—come to him with a kind of sadness; and while one sleeps and another seems to be awaiting an interval in which to utter some profoundly beautiful word, Pan himself has drifted away into another world, and in his pitiful imperfection has attained to that kingdom of the soul of which those around him, with all their perfection, are ignorant. Some vision of his own death seems to have come to him, and he sees humanity approaching its final success by means of his discouragement and decrease, by the passing away, the forgetfulness, as it were, of such a day as this, such unconsciousness, such serene contentment. His fantastic body, and even that too exquisite youth who pipes to him so daintily, so precisely, must be exiled from their kingdom; and one day this music, so pleasant now, will be changed to weeping, and on a night of a great star and the strange unaccustomed voices of angels, little figures distraught with grief will be heard wailing to each other, frantic and despairing, 'Great Pan is dead, great Pan is dead.' Is it the birthday of Christ that he foresees in this golden summer afternoon, the sound of the angels' wings, their message of goodwill, or only the wind among the reeds, and the pleasant, tearful voice of Psyche seeking for Eros?

And indeed in the work of even so realistic a painter there is more than a little of that strange dream, which reconciled Paganism and Christianity, than at first sight might appear. Pico della Mirandola, whose fascination even Sir Thomas More in sixteenth-century England understood, had died in the very year in which the Pan is supposed to have been painted. So thoughtful, so superb a man as Signorelli, the friend of Lorenzo de Medici (to whom he was able to make gifts), must have known of Pico, and even perhaps have met him. It is strange at least that in a picture, now in the Uffizi, he has painted the Madonna and Child surrounded by flowers, and in the background, instead of the shepherds, we see four splendid and naked youths, almost the very gods themselves, who we may remember had taken service as shepherds and goatherds at the coming of the new religion. This deep and serious soul who was later so exercised by thoughts, not of death, but of the life after death, the tragical ending, not without splendour, of this beautiful world, may well have been affected by a dream so courteous and so delightful as that of Pico della Mirandola.

In 1491 Signorelli was painting in Volterra, and it is in his work still there in the Duomo and the Municipio that we find, for the first time perhaps, the influence of Perugino; something more spacious and softer in his work, that is to become so pronounced in the Magdalen at the foot of the Cross, now in the Accademia at Florence. But it is in the Annunciation, in the cathedral at Volterra, that we see the influence both of Piero della Francesca and of Perugino, the earlier master, with his curiosity as to the science of perspective, the action of light and energy, predominating. While at Perugia Luca must often have seen that lovely altar-piece which is to-day one of the chief treasures of the Pinacoteca; and here in Volterra he has painted a variation of that masterpiece, a variation that is by no means so successful as the picture of his master. For in the strong, reticent work of Piero what profound energy—almost passionate—he has given to Gabriel; the angel seems only just to have stopped in his flight, to be filled even now with a sense of speed, of a great space swept by his wings, a great distance overcome by their uplifted beauty. He has fallen on his knees with a new energy, and is fulfilled with a vitality swift and godlike, visible even in his reticent gesture, the arms folded across the bosom, as though to suppress some profound joy or excitement. Madonna, under that beautiful colonnade, in which we may see all the curious scientific knowledge of distance and light that Piero had acquired so laboriously and yet so magically, bows in grave self-surrender to the command of God.

How differently has Signorelli conceived of this Annunciation of the Prince of Life. A youth of delicate, sexless beauty surprises Madonna as she comes, perhaps, from some church. He is running towards her, and points with one hand towards the sky, while in the other he bears a lily from the gardens of heaven. Nor in Madonna is there anything of the reticence of Piero, but a certain Peruginesque affectation and insincerity. Yet, even as in Piero's picture, she stands under a colonnade, but less lovely by far. In another picture, now in Florence, painted in his old age, we find the same subject treated more successfully. It is a predella, and the angel hastens from the mountains across a tiny valley towards the Virgin, who is sitting under a porch musing. In this predella picture how much freer is the artist, how much more himself than in the picture at Volterra!

About the year 1497 we find Signorelli at Monte Olivetto, a little monastery not far from Siena. His work there, however, was left unfinished, and, if we may judge from the overpainted frescoes, ruined and crude as they are to-day, can never have really interested him. It is true that now and then we catch a glimpse, as it were, of the great work at Orvieto, but surely Sodoma has filled the walls with a finer knowledge of decoration. Later, we hear of Luca at Siena, and then at Borgo San Sepolcro, where he painted the Crucifixion now in the Municipio—a somewhat disappointing work, laboured and unimpassioned, and yet, by reason of some sweetness not to be defined, magical and full of light.

It is seldom in all his work, up to this time, that he has led us to suppose him capable of the great work that was yet to be done at Orvieto. 'Unequalled in the art of the fifteenth century,' says Morelli of the series of frescoes on the walls

of the Cappella Nuova in the Duomo of that city, unequalled
by reason of a certain 'passion, vehemence, and strength.'
It would appear that it was after severe study in Florence,
whither he had gone from Siena to see the works of 'the
living masters as well as those of the departed,' that he
undertook to paint in fresco the chapel begun fifty-three
years before by Fra Angelico.   In that strange Romanesque
church, with its superb and astonishing façade in the Gothic
manner, Luca Signorelli has painted the story of Antichrist
and the Last Judgment, together with Heaven and Hell, and
other like subjects.   'He there represented,' says Vasari,
'scenes descriptive of the Last Judgment, with most singular
and fanciful invention.   Angels, demons, earthquakes, ruins,
fires, miracles of Antichrist, and many other objects of
similar kind are depicted in this work, with crude forms,
varied foreshortenings, and many beautiful figures, the
master having imagined to himself all that shall go to make
up the terrors of that last tremendous day.   By this performance the artist enlightened the minds of all who came
after him, for whom he has indeed greatly diminished the
difficulties attendant on that mode of representation; nor
am I surprised that the works of Luca were ever highly
extolled by Michelangelo, or that for his divine work of the
Last Judgment, painted in the [Sistine] Chapel, he should
have courteously availed himself, to a certain extent, of the
inventions of that artist, as for example in the angels and
demons, in the divisions of the heavens, and some other parts
wherein Michelangelo imitated the mode of treatment
adopted by Luca, as may be seen by every one.'   And indeed
it is only the colour and, perhaps, a rather brutal insight into
the secrets, the structure, of the human form, which should
have been redeemed, as Michelangelo contrived to redeem
it, by a more delicate perception of texture and surface,
throwing a glamour almost spiritual in its beauty over that

o

beautiful and yet pitiful humanity, whose loveliness is after all but dust gathered into life for a moment by the smile of God, that makes him less than the painter of the Sistine Chapel.

The paintings in the Cappella Nuova begin with the Preaching and the Reign of Antichrist. In the foreground, surrounded by every sort of person, he stands upon a marble pedestal, speaking to the crowd the words which the devil whispers into his ear. This superb and beautiful figure is itself a masterpiece; so beautiful that at a distance we might mistake him for the Christ Himself; on a closer view we see the keen and hateful face of the despoiler. At his feet lie numbers of golden vessels and heaps of money, with which he would cheat the world of what little soul remains to it. In the background a beautiful temple stands, with many coming out and going in, all armed; while further off we see, as in a vision, the coming of Antichrist, hurled from heaven, bringing war in his advent, even as Christ shall bring peace. Nothing can exceed the conception of this picture in its strength and splendour. In a sombre world, from which all joy seems to have departed, this tremendous drama takes place, not without a certain piteous agony. That woman who so reluctantly sells herself is but typical of a thousand others who would, how gladly, have escaped the hard choice thrust upon them. It is not so easy to escape. Where shall she go, for nothing is without money and without price? What shall she do? she seems to ask herself, as she passionately protests against a bargain so sordid as that which he with the lean, eager face and the open money-bag offers her. The grave, sweet heaven, full of the sunset, serene with the last light of the day, undisturbed by even the most profound tragedies of humanity, seems almost hateful in its calmness and purity. And suddenly, into that stainless sky, a mighty angel soars, and sweeping earthward hurls the Antichrist into a waiting world.   In the corner of the fresco, sombre and with clasped hands, stand Signorelli himself and Fra Angelico—the one stern and almost unmoved, the other sad and full of pity for his bright world which has been so spoiled.

Opposite this fresco Signorelli has painted the Resurrection of the Dead.   Two angels, mighty and splendid, sound the trumpets, from which stream the banners of the Resurrection, and the dead stand forth from the grave.   All, or almost all, gaze upwards towards heaven—some with surprise, some with horror, some with a kind of indifference.   In one group at least we see a remembrance of life in the loving greeting exchanged between friends.   Luca has dived into the secrets of the grave: not content with the unveiled human form in its action and beauty, he has here introduced the skeleton, horrible and almost obscene, too grotesque for pity; the grinning skull, amid all the beauty of humanity, gazing with vacant, empty sockets towards the sky.   Next to this fresco Luca has painted the 'Damnation of the Wicked.'   It is perhaps in its movement and passion the finest of the series. The devils, almost human and yet so brutish, fight and at last conquer the despairing souls of the wretched.   The human form in every gesture and attitude is realised with an energy and an insight almost miraculous.   This fresco would seem to be continued on the window wall, where we see Charon's boat approaching, while the dead, in terror, await it on the shore.   Opposite to this fresco, on the other side of the window, continued on the side wall to the Reign of Antichrist, we see the Paradise.   On the window wall the angels soar, almost like a musical melody, as it were, in plain-chant; while on the side wall we find a wonderful study of the human form, no longer agonised, but serene in every attitude of adoration; and above, the very angels of God.   Over the doors of the chapel we see the signs of the end of the world, with effects of light and shade, as though some celestial army, splendid with spears, were marching across heaven, darkening the world, their swords flashing with the brightness of the face of Christ.

Beneath the technical excellences of these frescoes, their qualities of decoration and movement, there lies a magnificence of intellect and imagination as surprising as it is splendid. Luca Signorelli was a kind of poet as well as a painter of great achievement and genius. To a genius as great in mere pictorial power and strength as Perugino's, he adds a power of vision, grave and austere, evidently derived to no small extent from Dante, that we shall look for in vain in any true Umbrian. He sees the world, life, the human body in a new way—a way as different from that of Piero, his master, as it is also different from that of Pollaiuolo. That great master of movement might perhaps be amazed at the power Luca, evidently his pupil, shows even there, so passionate, so full of vitality are the gestures, the attitudes of his numberless crowds.

One other great work he left behind him in this chapel—a Pietà so lovely that, of all his work, only the Entombment in the Duomo at Cortona can be compared to it. A great angel, in all the celestial strength of his immortal youth, supports the drooping figure of Christ with a tenderness rare in Luca's work.

This great artist, who delighted in living splendidly, and loved to dress himself in beautiful garments, was a greater man than we have been willing to admit; full of grave thoughts and passionate dreams, about which he is so reticent that, but for the occasional glimpse of his nature which he permits us in his work, we might think of him as merely immersed in certain half-scientific studies of anatomy and perspective and movement. But we come to understand at last that he is really a modern, as concerned with humanity and thoughts of our world as Michelangelo, one of our very selves, who has already shaken off the dreams and languor of the Middle Age, the mere excitement and curiosity of the early Renaissance, and has attained to our point of view, our vision of life and of man.

Is it, after all, in that picture of the school of Pan, the exile and the death of the gods, the shadowy Advent of Christ that he wishes to suggest, or some sentiment of kinship, of brotherhood with Nature, that, in looking on the fields, or the woods, or the sea, strikes at our very hearts; something of what the Greeks had imaged in Pan, that pathetic sweet god, a spirit in the whispering reeds, or the wilder places among the rocks, or in the woods, or on the mountains, for whom we feel an indescribable emotion, a kind of want, a longing so keen, that we know we cannot be reconciled at sunset, until we see the stars—or in winter, until we have seen the snow? That strange stirring of the spirit at the thought of the earth from which we sprung was not unknown even in those days. Already it had driven Petrarch to the summit of Mont Ventoux, and it was not for nothing that St. Francis made his canticles, or Alberti said that when he saw the meadows and the hills covered with flowers in springtime, his heart was sorrowful; and when in autumn he saw the fields golden for harvest and the orchards of apples, he felt such grief that many saw him weep because of his sadness. The sight of jewels, too, of flowers, or of fair landscapes cured him of sickness. And so we find Signorelli, who consorted with princes, who was loved by Lorenzo de Medici, when he was old, and the men of Cortona carried his picture on their shoulders from Cortona to Arezzo, during a visit to his kinsman in that city, meeting in the house Giorgio Vasari, then a little boy of eight years old; and hearing that he would learn nothing at school save how to draw, Luca turned to Antonio, the father and said to him : ' Antonio, let.Giorgio learn by all means to draw, that he may not degenerate ; for even though he should hereafter devote himself to learning, yèt the knowledge of design, if not profitable, cannot fail to be honourable and advantageous.' And turning to the child he said, 'Study well, little kinsman.' Then hearing that he was suffering from some childish ailment, he bound a jasper round the child's neck with his own hand with an infinite tenderness. We read, too, that when he lost his son, he would not part with him until he had made a drawing of the young body, pathetic and beautiful, so that he might remind himself every day of a thing so frail, which he had found so precious.

It is of this man, so reticent, so wise, so tender, that we think as we gaze at the frescoes of the Cappella Nuova. He, too, seems to have understood the ecstasy and sorrow of love, the beauty and pity of life, the darkness of the grave, the disillusion that life brings, the exquisite things that we have perhaps just missed ; but you will find no rebellion or hatred of life or mankind in his work. He understood and concerned himself with what he found most beautiful—the human form, poetry, music ; courteously faithful to a world that was equally unfortunate in so much, and yet so to be desired. And when he came to die, it was, be sure, as one who had realised already that even that debt too must be paid to the utmost farthing ; that the body he had so loved, which he had clothed so nobly, and had studied with such infinite care, must be compounded once more with the earth from which it came, in no ignoble end, but with a certain order and momentary tears.

XXI

BENEDETTO BONFIGLI

NOT the least delightful among those earlier Umbrian
painters, so scrupulously concerned with religion and
the beauty of religious meditation, Benedetto Bonfigli would
seem to have been born in Perugia about the year 1420, some
seven years before the death of Gentile da Fabriano. A painter
of but little importance we may think; concerned not so
much with Art as with the representation of religious truths,
and almost by chance a kind of historical painter, in the
Cappella dei Priori, where he has painted so languidly, and
yet with a certain sweetness—at least in the early frescoes—
the story of the city as it had come down to him; the
wonderfully heroic actions of S. Ercolano, his life, his
death, and all the wonders of that distant past. But as the
master of Perugino, as the only visible founder of that
school of Perugia which became so famous, which has been
so beloved, Bonfigli appears to us as a painter of more
importance than his weak but charming work at first
suggests.

Though he seems in his day to have travelled as far as
Rome and Siena, it is really only in Perugia that we find his
work. Mr. Berenson mentions an early picture in a private
collection in London, and he is represented in Berlin and in
the Opera del Duomo at Empoli; but beyond these three
pictures, all his work is still in his native city—in the
Pinacoteca for the most part, with here and there a standard

or a panel in the churches, which have rendered their treasures to the municipal authorities, one may believe, not without a certain sadness.

The pupil perhaps of Boccatis, who was working from about 1435, it is really a glimmer, faint and evanescent, of Florentine genius that we see in his work—the influence of Fra Angelico and Benozzo Gozzoli, and it may be of Fra Lippo Lippi. Among these bright and soft Umbrian hills two of those painters have left not a little of their work; and in Perugia herself there are still some of their paintings, very carefully made on a prepared canvas covered with stucco and laid on wood—not the least interesting of their pictures, seeing that they are unrestored. And at Spoleto, at the head of that long valley, Fra Lippo Lippi produced the most splendid of all his works—the frescoes in the apse of the Duomo, where we may see even to-day the Annunciation and the Adoration of the Shepherds, and Madonna crowned by her Son, very tender, and strong with vitality, so characteristic of Fra Lippo, who must surely have influenced the mystical painters of the surrounding cities profoundly. But even so early as 1454, when Bonfigli was at work on the frescoes of the Cappella dei Priori, we hear of Fra Filippo as one whom the Perugians would have liked to engage to paint their chapel; and in 1461 he comes himself to judge of the work done there, and praises it. Consider, too, the Madonna of the Frate, now in the Uffizi; how blonde she is, how delicate and full of grace her fine modelled features— the small, soft chin and wide brow are pure and fair as a bright lily before any hand has touched it. And then look at Bonfigli's Adoration, and it might seem that her younger sister held the Child while the three kings came with their gifts to greet Him. Her hair falls in little golden curls over her temples, that are delicate and almost transparent in their fineness; and over her hair some dainty lace-work, that has fallen in so many folds, hardly covers her head or her slender throat. Her wide brow, and the delicate arched brows that we find in so many fifteenth-century paintings, are characteristic of her, certainly the first of her race in Umbria.

Another painter beside Fra Filippo was named in the contract of 1454—to wit, Domenico Veneziano, the master of Piero della Francesca. That somewhat vague personality moves behind the work of more than one Umbrian, and we find him perhaps here too in a certain uncouth vigour and robustness so manifest in Bonfigli's Bambini. But after all, Bonfigli's masters must, as it seems to me, for ever remain unknown. The documents are silent, and what gossip of the time we possess would appear to be misleading. In the Adoration in the Pinacoteca at Perugia we find at least a new personality in Umbrian Art. The drawing is very weak, the whole picture really just a chance or almost accidental combination of colour on the wall, refined upon by an unconscious artist who was anxious about nothing save the story he was telling with a certain peevishness, a certain impatience. Mark how unamiable she is, that strange country virgin! There is almost the shadow of a frown between the pure brows. And those three emaciated child angels, how sorrowful they are, how mechanically they assume the attitude of prayer! And in that far country across the curious hills that divide us,—is it from Bethlehem? —a great army seems to be moving, rushing out of the gates of the city with stamping of horses and bright armour and spears, and all the splendour of the eve of battle. Never again, as I think, is Bonfigli quite so uninitiated, so naïf in his workmanship; but even here in this picture which I suppose, perhaps without sufficient reason, to have been among his earliest work, he has not forgotten to crown his angels with those strange wreaths of roses, so artificial, so obviously grown in heaven, that we see in all his pictures.

The frescoes in the Cappella dei Priori, begun in 1454 and unfinished at his death in 1496, would seem, since he worked at them so languidly, so intermittently, to have been distasteful to him. That fresco which begins the series in which we see St. Louis of Toulouse standing before the Pope, is, to my mind at least, easily the best. Was it perhaps after seeing this fresco that Fra Lippo Lippi in 1461 recommended that Bonfigli should paint the whole chapel? One might almost think so. And yet in the fresco where St. Louis lies dead surrounded by monks in a church which is really S. Pietro in Perugia, how lovely is that figure of the kneeling youth, who, unconscious of anything but the dead saint, seems to be weeping so passionately!

In 1460 Bonfigli is said to have been in Siena, and later still in Rome, painting in the company of the young Pintoricchio. That visit to Siena, even though it were his first—and, remembering his work, I cannot think it—seems to have been of some importance to him. A new spirit comes into his life, a desire for beauty not divorced from religion but as a handmaid of it, as a kind of realisation of that song of the beauty of holiness. Something of this we see, perhaps, in the picture of the Annunciation in the Pinacoteca. Madonna, a little tearful, kneels on a stool of beautiful workmanship; her eyes, just lifted from the book of prayers which she holds in her hand, gazing at nothing. The angel, dressed in fantastic fashion almost ridiculous, speaks his message, while between him and Madonna, writing the words which the angel speaks, St. Luke sits on his ox, between whose legs is a copy of the Gospel. From the Eternal in the Heavens, the Holy Spirit as a dove descends with a great swiftness, making a passage of light in the soft air. Four child angels, one of a real and natural beauty, with outstretched hands watch the work of God. Madonna is kneeling just outside the magnificent portico of some palace in a kind of courtyard, over the rich walls of which we see the tops of the cypresses and the mountains. Above is a loggia with carved and slender pillars. It is perhaps in the frieze of the wall whereon Bonfigli has painted a sumptuous sort of carving, that we find our first surprise. And then something of a larger world seems to have come into the picture with the impersonal detached figure of St. Luke, who so calmly, almost with a smile, writes the unforgettable words. How strange is this dream of the Annunciation! And indeed, long after we have forgotten the mere strangeness of an idea so natural perhaps to mystical Umbria, we remember that soft delicate Madonna with the peevish lips and the delicate temples. It is said, I know not with how much truth, that in the Adoration Bonfigli has introduced the portraits of his sister as the Madonna, his nephew as the Child, and his brother as the youngest of the three kings. It may be so; but it is another woman, younger and more charming, who is so distracted by the message of the angel amid all the beauty of that Renaissance palace in the Annunciation, and who prays with so much simplicity and sweetness in perhaps the most beautiful picture of all his work—a Madonna and Child much damaged, yet retaining something of the memory of Fra Angelico in its simplicity, its spirituality. Who was she that was so unhappy, a little wilfully, we may think perhaps, her future being so splendid? We shall never know. Fra Filippo had painted in his pictures over and over again the woman he loved. It may be indeed that Bonfigli did so too. How peevish she is, how discontented, how delightfully unhappy! Was she, perhaps, his wife who quarrelled with him, so that their differences have been noted in the public records? Or was she just a vision that even to-day, if we are fortunate, we may chance to see in that very city?—something so delicate and wonderful and altogether lovely, that for ever after that fierce, rude city seems to have been changed for us; living ever in the memory as some place almost out of the world, so that in thinking of her all the tumult of our life is hushed, and the soul itself silent in order that all our dreams and visions may come to her and be touched by her delicate hands and made perfect. For her voice is as the sound of distant waters, and our thirsty days are ended in a moment when she speaks; her eyes have looked at heaven and remembered the stars, and the sun has lingered in the coils of her hair, and her hands are softer than the bright lilies which will reconcile us with death at the last. I cannot forget the sound of her footsteps or the folds of her dress, and the gesture of her hands is a perpetual benediction. Ah, how I have envied those she is even now making so happy! for where she is one might say God smiled. At home in winter, when the world is hushed by the fall of the snow, and the earth made pure again from heaven, I have seemed to see her coming, delicate and altogether precious, across the spotless fields, her golden hair trailing in the night like a shower of stars, her little feet whiter than the blossoms of the snow. And when my spirit was perhaps stooping under my life, was it not her eyes that looked on me and refreshed me, and tenderly lifted up my soul, and ever since has she not held it softly in her hands? and I know as I know the sureness of the stars that she will not let it fall.

Those banners which Bonfigli painted to be carried in procession, one of which, the Gonfalone di S. Bernardino, is now in the Pinacoteca, are almost peculiar to the Umbrian school. Another of these strange painted canticles is in S. Fiorenzo, and yet another in S. Maria Nuova. The one in the Pinacoteca is, however, not the least curious. Above sits the great figure of Christ surrounded by angels, while below are gathered the priests and people of Perugia, in front of the Oratorio di S. Bernardino and the Church of S. Francesco, intent on some ritual or service. Between our Lord and the people, S. Bernardino himself stands, listening to the words of Christ. It is evidently a portrait of the saint—the lean, emaciated face still in a kind of mystical contemplation. The terrible emotion of the orator, from whose lips fell words not of love only but of burning scorn and terrifying denunciation, is hushed. His whole figure is burning in a kind of ecstasy, he seems like a flame almost motionless in heaven. It is said that the people gathered together outside the Oratorio di S. Bernardino are busied with the ceremony of the blessing of the candles by Pope Pius II., which happened in 1459. However this may be, surely one of those women who stand so unconcerned in the corner of the picture is the Madonna of the Annunciation? Pale and graceful she stands, still a little unhappy, while before her a nun kneels in passionate prayer; yet she is so indifferent that she has almost let her candle fall.

The banner of S. Maria Nuova is less beautiful, and it may be from another hand. Christ between the sun and moon surrounded by saints and martyrs threatens the people of Perugia with an arrow, while Death mows them down with a scythe. The saints appear to be interceding. At S. Fiorenzo there is another Gonfalone, also commemorating some pestilence; a long inscription in verse, upheld by an angel, prophesies to them in the manner of Jeremiah. In Corciano there is another, and indeed the list of those ascribed to Bonfigli is long. It is in these banners that Bonfigli really ceases to be an artist and becomes a mere agent of the Church. Certainly, with the possible exception of the one in the Pinacoteca, they can make no claim to beauty. It is not in them that we shall find the master of Perugino, but in those pictures, a little bitter and yet sweet withal, which have been gathered together from many places into the Pinacoteca. Without the passion and the profound sense of beauty which Niccolò da Foligno possessed, and which make him so interesting a pupil of Benozzo Gozzoli, Bonfigli yet contrived to give his pictures that suggestion—though it is scarcely anything more than a suggestion—of sentiment and charm which in Perugino came at last to be so loved, which seems to us at times so sickly, so insincere. Sometimes his angels are really beautiful, more often they are peevish and unhappy, with a kind of childish grief that looks almost like a simper on their old young faces. As an historical painter, or rather as a painter of tradition, he was unsuccessful, evidently feeling himself incapable of telling a story or composing in the larger way of Gozzoli. And yet there is something golden in his work, something of the soft beauty of his birthplace, that Perugino was to turn to such good account. In thinking of him one might almost say that his chief fault was that he learnt so little from Piero della Francesca, or Signorelli, or the Florentines. The father of Perugian painting, he gives but the faintest clue to the work of Perugino or Pintoricchio; and though he was born in the fifteenth century it is rather as a kind of primitive we come to regard him, indifferent alike to Art and to life, occupied as he was as a kind of craftsman in the business of the Church.

XXII

FIORENZO DI LORENZO

IT is perhaps to the work attributed to a more obscure painter that in Perugia we shall turn from the Madonnas of Bonfigli or the work of Perugino, finding there something that is lacking in those painters—a vitality and energy that it had, perhaps, from Piero della Francesca, and a thoughtfulness learned from the Florentines.

Scarcely anything is known of the life of Fiorenzo di Lorenzo; the contemporary, or nearly the contemporary (for it is probable that he was somewhat younger) of Bonfigli, it is possible that he was his pupil. But there is a deep and simple loveliness in some of Fiorenzo's work that is far beyond the cold and heavenly beauty of Bonfigli even at his best, as in those children he has crowned with roses and gathered round the Virgin and her Son to sing some song that, unheard by us, has brought that curiously sweet unearthly look into her face. Fiorenzo has forgotten the angels in the delight of life and the tragedy of our world. In reality he has made the attempt, only to fail at last in his successors and pupils, to break through the mysticism of the Umbrian school that was even then becoming so affected, and to introduce a new motive—life itself, according to him, being indeed worthy of immortality. For him the sky is almost as luminous and as spacious, at least in his youth, as ever it is in Perugino's paintings. Space—it was the idea that had absorbed the attention of Piero della

223

Francesca, the dream that had led him down innumerable vistas of Roman colonnades, the real secret of the beauty of his birthplace, as it is of the charm of all Umbria, and, indeed, of Italy. And at last, in a man who is absolutely Umbrian, we find an appreciation of all that. It was like a vision of the æsthetic history of his country—that Raphael and Bramante were later to reveal so triumphantly to mankind. It was the fundamental idea of the Latin genius. How exquisitely that idea of space, as a very noble thing in itself, is revealed in Santa Maria Maggiore, for instance! It is as though the very aspect of the world here in Italy had been betrayed to captivity; the very soul of sanity apprehended and made visible before the magnificent mad dreams and visions of the Middle Age had tampered with humanity. There is nothing Gothic in the Latin genius; an Italian fails to understand the intense individuality, the personal abasement, the betrayal of humanism and of man, to be found in a Gothic cathedral; to him the grotesques of the French churches would be just madness. He under his soft sky is profoundly distressed by the thought of the gloom and rain and mist of the North. His music is the plain-song; his mystery is sunshine. And there he finds, perhaps, a mysticism more profound than in the North, with all its obvious groping after God in semi-darkness, we shall ever understand. Fiorenzo peopled space with sunshine. It was his profoundest emotion. For ever a-sail in the sky, we find those luminous clouds that are like a flight of doves hesitating during a single breath, and so still for ever. Perhaps, after all, they are in their delicacy and delight only the very light itself made visible, half crystallised or half turned, magically, into the sunniest vapour, visible where all is invisibly visible in the infinite heaven of Italy.

In the Pinacoteca in Perugia there is a number of

Fiorenzo's works, and yet he is a rare painter. In the National Gallery there is a part of an altar-piece, and in the Pitti Palace a small Adoration of the Magi, attributed to Pintoricchio, his pupil, or follower at any rate; in Vienna, in the Academy, there is a tiny Madonna and Saints in Glory with worshippers below; and in Berlin a Madonna, also given to him by Mr. Berenson, and out of Umbria almost nothing else.

The beautiful fresco—an Annunciation—on the outside of the Portiuncula at Assisi has now disappeared, sold it has been said to an American.[1] In the Church of San Francesco at Deruta, a tiny village on the hills not far from Perugia, there is a fresco of SS. Romano and Rocco—a plague picture—with a view of Deruta below, dated 1475.[2] And at Montone, in the Church of S. Francesco, another fresco, which Professor Lupatelli gives to Fiorenzo in some small part, and that is all. Our study of him, then, is practically confined to what has been collected within the Pinacoteca at Perugia.

In the Sala di Fiorenzo di Lorenzo, in the Pinacoteca of that noble old hill city, there is a fresco of Madonna with her Son and St. Catherine of Alexandria and a bishop, probably St. Nicholas, on either side. It is, even in its ruin, one of the loveliest things that Fiorenzo ever painted. The Child—always in some way with Fiorenzo the least pleasing figure in the picture—is placing the ring on the finger of S. Catherine. Round His neck is a necklace of beads, from which hangs a charm, a piece of branching coral, as common to-day in Italy as in old time. Madonna is seated on a long bench, and the wall behind her at one time was evidently

---

[1] This fresco is now at Fenway Court, Boston, U.S.A.

[2] For an account of this picture, as for much else of interest regarding Fiorenzo di Lorenzo, see *The Problem of Fiorenzo di Lorenzo*, by Jean Carlyle Graham. Loescher, Rome, 1903.

P

elaborately decorated. Christ stands on her knee. In her left hand St. Catherine holds a palm branch—her sign of martyrdom—and a sword. She is undoubtedly the most beautiful figure in the picture. The little fingers of the hands of these figures are all curiously bent, a very characteristic affectation of Fiorenzo's — indeed, I know no genuine work by him in which it is absent. The collar-bones, too, are prominent in the middle, and a little excessive and knotted. This beautiful fresco, so much simpler and sweeter than much of his work, is free from any horror of mysticism or madness of monastic zeal. It is as calm and as lovely as an Umbrian evening. The level light of the valleys is caught for ever and preserved even in the spectre that it has become—a few exquisite and faded colours on the wall, where we perceive lovely ghosts smiling at us very gently, as though to remind us that, after all, all things pass away and nothing remaineth. How far are we in this picture from the grotesque affectation and insincerity of that other Madonna with the Child and two angels, together with four saints[1] (No. 43) in the same room ! Here, though the picture is undoubtedly Fiorenzo's, there is almost nothing of beauty. Of the four saints St. Peter is almost humorously vain and empty ; he holds his keys, and is painted in a very characteristic fashion. St. John, on the left hand of the Madonna, is scarcely less sincere ; from his head fall innumerable corkscrew curls. Blessed Paolino, to the left of St. John, is undoubtedly the finest figure in the picture—he looks out at the spectator. On the right of St. Peter, at the other extreme of the picture from the St. Francis, is St. Benedict with his branch of budding palm, bearing in his hand an open book. Madonna sits with her hands pointed in prayer, worshipping the Child, who, with His arms folded in an ecstasy of affectation, appears to be summing up the effect

[1] Dated 1472.

he is producing on the spectator. There is nothing to redeem the picture from ugliness, save the figure of Paolino and, perhaps, the angels; yet, in spite of this, it is intensely interesting, even to the æsthetic critic, by reason of its characteristic handling. Here are all the signs of Fiorenzo, all his pet affectations—the curiously pointed ears, almost faun-like, the bent little fingers, the high and prominent collar-bones, everything, indeed, that marks this picture as his own quite apart from any exterior evidence. There remain two undoubted paintings by Fiorenzo: one a kind of niche,[1] with St. Peter and St. Paul on either side, and above, the Madonna and Child, with cherubs and angels, which he has signed— a beautiful piece of decorative work; the other a triptych, a Madonna of Mercy with the Child and two angels. Two tiny figures kneel before them in monastic dresses. On one side are S. Mustiola and St. Andrew, on the other St. Peter and St. Francis. Below is a predella with various saints— perhaps S. Bernardino, St. John Baptist, a Pietà, a St. John, and others. It is quite a lovely piece of work, a little ruined, but still full of beauty and very characteristic.

It is not, however, in these, the undoubted works of a master who has suddenly become so famous, that we shall find ourselves chiefly interested in the picture gallery at Perugia; for saving the first of them they are not remarkable for great beauty, and are certainly less lovely than other works attributed to him, which we shall now proceed to examine.

'The Nativity,' or 'The Adoration of the Shepherds,' is said by Mr. Berenson to be an early work. Exquisite in its charm and in its drawing, it is perhaps a little harsh, a little crude in colour. The yellow of St. Joseph's robe is too hard and raw for our sophisticated eyes, though certainly something may be allowed for the fact that here in a gallery

---

[1] Dated 1487.

the picture is subject to a blaze of light that the painter did not contemplate. It is, however, in the figure of the Virgin that the charm of the picture really lies. A young girl, for she is scarcely more, she kneels before her Child whose tiny arms are stretched towards her. Her hands are pointed in prayer, but she gazes at her only little Son, not as at the Desire of all Nations, but as at the Desire of her heart. The beautiful soft robe which covers her expresses the lines of her slight figure so well, that indeed we are aware of it— Turris Eburnea—in all its fragile gentleness, its dainty youth-fulness, its perfection. Her hair is coiled behind her neck and scarcely reveals the ears, that really are Fiorenzo's own. So with every dainty elegance, eloquent of his love, the painter, who doubtless loved her, has told us it may be of his earliest glimpse of heaven. Behind her many angels, unre-garding, sing perhaps 'Magnificat.' The shepherds, three in number, kneel behind St. Joseph, a little surprised that, after all, it is no rhetorical splendour of which the angels sang. A great dog gazes meditatively from the corner; and Christ, the very Jesus Parvulus, is fallen among the flowers, that, as with Persephone, would seem to have sprung up in a kind of sudden resurrection of spring at His coming. In that magnificent fresco of the Resurrection at Borgo San Sepolcro Piero della Francesca has something of the same idea, in that, with the dawn, Spring (who it would appear had for the moment hidden her face), suddenly returns, and the trees are in leaf and the corn high, and the wild flowers like an army of many coloured angels have run down the byways of the world. So Christ lies a little child among the flowers—great heads of silver dandelion seed, and anemones, and starwort —on the skirt of Madonna's robe.

But I at least should hesitate to give this picture to Fiorenzo; and for more than one reason. Madonna herself, certainly the figure upon which most pains have been expended, is utterly unlike anything else of Fiorenzo's. Perhaps she is a Florentine with her daintiness, and her exquisite lines, and her fragile beauty. Fiorenzo's Madonnas are too heavy; the Umbrian girl is not, and certainly was not, sufficiently civilised, sufficiently refined for a painter even to have found in her such a natural daintiness and sweet reticence of beauty. Perhaps she is a Florentine not unknown to Ghirlandaio, or perhaps Pintoricchio painted her. In his work at Spello her sisters, less lovely, but her very sisters, gather in quietness, seldom looked at by the stranger, and even yet as unvulgarised as on the day Pintoricchio painted them. Moreover, in the gallery in Perugia where she herself lives, Pintoricchio has a Madonna at the moment of Annunciation, who is her very self painted in a less happy moment, when she was tired or a little overcome, or perhaps a few years older. It was some one who knew Florence far better than Fiorenzo did who painted this 'Nativity'; and, moreover, the painter of the 'Nativity' was also the author, in part at any rate, of the 'Adoration of the Magi' (No. 4), also attributed to Fiorenzo; and for this reason: in both the pictures, German influence is to be found. In the Madonna of the 'Adoration of the Magi' we see, not an Italian girl, for she is without the beauty of any southern land, but the longer face, the more ascetic loveliness of the North. Without doubt this may be explained by the Van der Goes Triptych, now in the Uffizi, which he painted for Tommaso Portinari, the agent of the Medici in Bruges. The middle portion of this triptych, curiously enough, represents the 'Adoration of the Shepherds,' and there lying on the ground is the very Jesus Parvulus we see in the Perugia 'Nativity.' But we are told that the 'Nativity' belongs to Fiorenzo's early period,[1] the 'Magi' to his latest, and we must believe therefore that in his earliest and in his latest time he

---

[1] Berenson's *Central Italian Art*, pp. 90 and 142.

remembered Van der Goes, but that in all his most characteristic work he had forgotten him. It is not open to doubt that this picture of Van der Goes had a great influence on many painters, but it would seem to be impossible that its influence on Fiorenzo was exercised in his youth and in his old age, but never in his middle life. It seems to me that the 'Nativity,' so slightly characteristic of Fiorenzo, may very well be given to Pintoricchio, when in his youth he was influenced by, and in all probability the pupil of, Fiorenzo. Signor Morelli in his *Italian Masters* has an interesting page on the affinity between the early work of Pintoricchio and Fiorenzo, where he points out certain peculiarities in the manner of both artists. And Pintoricchio may very possibly have been to Florence, either in the company of Perugino or alone, although there is no record of such a journey. The 'Magi' has been painted for the most part in tempera, though it looks now like an oil painting; parts of it are doubtless in oil, but for the most part it is in tempera which has been washed over with oil, possibly by the monks with some idea of preserving it. Pintoricchio never mastered oil, confining himself to fresco or tempera. Both these pictures seem to me to have more of Pintoricchio in them than of Fiorenzo, but it may well be they were school pictures which Fiorenzo, the master, designed more or less, but which were painted by his pupils.

Fiorenzo, however, would seem to have been a painter of a variety of styles, for above the door of the Sala di Fiorenzo in Perugia there hangs a most beautiful, though ruined, Pictà, surpassing in loveliness and strength anything else in the room. It is a little in the manner of Piero della Francesca, and the model for the dead Christ may have been the same as that, not only for the John the Baptist in the altar-piece by Piero in this gallery, but also for the Risen Christ at Borgo San Sepolcro. It is possible, however, that

Fiorenzo went to school to Piero della Francesca, and that there is more than a touch of Piero's hand in this fresco. There is another Pietà painted in the manner of the St. Catherine, in the Gabinetto of the Perugia Gallery, very lovely and very like to the 'Madonna and Child with two Saints' (No. 1), which I have already tried to describe. But it is out of all comparison of less account than the Pietà in the Sala di Fiorenzo, which, alas! is so badly hung that it is necessary to mount a pair of steps to see it properly.

It is perhaps, after all, in spite of the beauty of the 'Nativity,' or the calm and exquisite thoughtfulness of the Madonna with St. Catherine and St. Nicholas, to the drawings that Fiorenzo made in tempera of the Miracles of S. Bernardino[1] that we turn almost with relief, as to something into which Life, so languid in his religious pictures, steps daintily, not without delight. For here, if nowhere else, Fiorenzo has escaped for a moment, as we may think perhaps, in the company of his pupils, Pintoricchio and others, from the sacrifice of experience that religion even in its finest expression demands of us. Here in these drawings, exquisite as they are and full of joy, he is at last the realist of a very fortunate age. His young men, slender and lovely, magnificently dressed with a dainty fastidiousness and elegance, swagger across his beautiful landscapes where, in all the glow of miniature work, the pools of water are just precious stones, amethysts or sapphires perhaps, and the skies spaces of light set with clouds that are tiny white feathers afloat in his heaven lost from a cherub's wings in some battle of the angels. It is a kind of ideal youth that we find there, with all the sweetness, the vanity, the confidence, and happiness of just that. It is always necessary for us to remind ourselves that these young men are but the attendants of a great saint who is busied with his miracles. What are miracles to them

---

[1] One of these panels is dated 1473.

or to us ?   We care for them for themselves and are willing
to forget San Bernardino. In one picture of this series of
events in the life of the saint, where a hound gazes out of
the picture, there are two youths who, even in their obvious
surprise and well-bred satisfaction at the miracle they are
watching, never forget the world and their joy of it for a
moment,—they are but typical of the painter's work. In the
same picture is a figure of a kneeling woman, perhaps the
wife or mistress of the injured man, in whom we see a
reminiscence of the Magdalen before the Cross in many an
early picture by Fra Angelico or another.   The curious
rocks towering above their own natural arches show us
for a moment a vision of the later dreams in landscape of
Leonardo, in their curious shapes, their stalactites, their
mysterious beauty.   One is astonished to find so curious an
arbour just outside a palace—or a monastery is it?—that
rises magnificent with marble and brick to the left of the
picture.

Are these paintings really concerned with the miracles of
San Bernardino, or with the most magnificent gentlemen,
Oddi and Baglioni of Perugia?   And so this effort of flattery
or realism, softened and made precious by the years, comes
to us to-day a very vision of ourselves, perhaps, as we were
three hundred years ago.   Here, in the interval that must
elapse between Birth and Death, Fiorenzo has shown us the
joyful world too young to be listless, but a little passionate
with sorrow, a little anxious about love, instinctively beautiful, as we, alas! are perhaps instinctively scientific.   Great
passions would be out of place in a world where all is possible,
seeing that for a few hurried prayers muttered between two
kisses the good saint will, with all the pride of the city as
audience, in his profound simplicity save out of the wreck of
life that which we really desire.   Ah, not great passions! for,
as Fiorenzo knew, it may be they can never be satisfied ; they

prey upon us, and at last to them we shall sacrifice everything and become even as that sorrowful one to whom the
saint hurries, always a little too late, finding himself not the
deliverer but one among the musical throng who follow
that unfortunate one to his grave.   And yet in the crouch-
ing figure, whose golden hair covers her as with a mantle,
what profound expectancy, what trembling, voluptuous
sobbing, what certainty of disaster! Her hair, like old
and beaten gold, streams over her shoulders, her attitude
is about to become more lamentable than Fiorenzo dared
to draw.   She is on the eve of the apprehension of life
which is so sorry.   It is all that the artist allowed himself
to express of what perhaps he had only apprehended for a
moment when he had understood how he had failed to paint
—well, what he desired.

   It was thus by means of a refusal that Fiorenzo, at last
really alone among his fellows, touched life.   The great
things were beyond his genius, he could by no means trans-
pose them into art, he fails to give them any reality.   But
with the lesser things, the actual daily exterior life of the
city, the simple passion of S. Bernardino for doing good,
the vanity of the young men, their anxiety about this vanity,
the expectancy of the young women, how successful he was
—he and his pupils—we see in these few tempera drawings
that are left us.   Perhaps at last he came to think of life not
as a history but as a piece of poetry, the world being after
all for him, as for all of us, just himself.

   His pupils Pintoricchio and Perugino cannot be said to
have carried on his tradition.   In Fiorenzo's mind there ever
seems to have been a dream which he had not the genius to
realise.   Was it contact with Piero della Francesca that had
set this dream free in his soul?   We shall never know.   In
his youth it is said he painted well, and in his age he painted
well; his middle life appears to have been less inspired, less

happy at least, in its expression. The reason for this is lost to us. We know nothing of his life. Only, as for us so for him, the outside world with its elements and forces, its fascinating romance, its passions, and disaster, was as nothing in comparison with that dream of a world in his own soul which he was not able to betray into captivity, and from which no man could deliver him.

XXIII

PIETRO VANNUCCI: IL PERUGINO

IMMERSED, it might seem, in a kind of religious contemplation, Perugino appears to us to-day never to have emerged from the dreaminess of the Middle Age. In spite almost of his masters and the strenuous vitality of that Florentine world that influenced him so much, he was an ascetic, concerned rather with some ideal dream than with the actual world. But his is an asceticism conceived of not as strength, never as just that, but as sentiment, an over-refinement, as it were; so that we find him almost shocked by the mere exuberance of life, seeking for its less strenuous and more quiet moments, and endowing them with a sweetness that at last becomes wearisome, sickly, almost wilful in its deception. The immense intelligence, the clear and perfect 'cerebral power' of his most famous pupil, Raphael, he did not possess; his ideas—if ideas we may call them—would seem to have been just monastic thoughts, that with him are not quite simple or sincere, a little anæmic through loss of touch with the world, a little too pretty and sweet in their make-believe. Judging him by his pictures alone—and, indeed, how else are we to judge him?—he would seem all his life to have been in a continual reverie, touching actual things only once or twice, as in his portrait of Dom Baldassare di Vallombrosa, and even then finding them softened for him with a kind of glamour of holiness or the nearness of the sanctuary, or the strange silence of the monastic life. It is only there and in his landscapes, perhaps, that we find any reality or loyalty to experience and observation. And yet it is not altogether as a sentimentalist that we must think of a man whose achievement was so large, but rather as a kind of poet who very easily and simply, and with a kind of natural success, had learned from his masters all that they could teach him, but was yet imperfect by reason of some want of intelligence, a real intellectual feebleness, so that his triumph is incomplete, is postponed, till Raphael with his profound and perfect scholarship, his immense intelligence, achieves the real victory that Perugino had only seen, as it were, prophetically.

Città della Pieve, where the greatest of the Umbrian painters was born about 1446-47, is a little hill-town, drenched through and through with the sun and the wind. Ruddy and stark on its hilltop, it looks across the uplifted plain towards Perugia, crouched like an eagle beneath the Apennines. A little dead city, above the silence of the long, beautiful valleys, she is really to-day a picture that Perugino himself might have painted—has painted, indeed, in many a fresco and panel scattered over the world. Only some twenty-six miles from Perugia, the capital of the province, this little town no doubt had many of her sons employed in the city, and so it was to Perugia that Perugino came seeking work, so that he might not starve, for he was poor. 'This child,' says Vasari, 'brought up in penury and want, was given by his father to be the shop drudge of a painter in Perugia, who was not particularly distinguished in his calling, but who held the art in great veneration, and highly honoured the men who excelled therein ; nor did he ever cease to set before Pietro the great advantages and honours that were to be obtained from painting by all who acquired the power of labouring in it effectually.' Who this painter was remains doubtful, but it would appear certain that first Bonfigli, and later Fiorenzo di Lorenzo and Piero della Francesca, were Perugino's masters. Whether, indeed, he had another and earlier master than Bonfigli, some altogether unillustrious Perugian, who loved good painting rather than practised it, we shall probably never know. Morelli suggests that Perugino went to Arezzo to assist and to learn of Piero della Francesca, who was working there with intervals of other employment from 1453 to 1469; but there would seem to be no evidence other than the work of the two artists to support this theory. That Perugino was influenced to no small extent by Piero della Francesca is obvious; but it may be, perhaps, that he received no little of Piero's knowledge rather from his pupil Fiorenzo di Lorenzo than from the master himself. In 1472 —Vasari says owing to poverty—Perugino was in Florence, where his name appears in the roll of St. Luke.

It has been suggested by Mr. Berenson, following Vasari in this, that while in Florence Perugino came under the influence of Verrocchio. It may be so; and yet his work at this time at La Calza seems to point rather to Luca Signorelli, another pupil of Piero della Francesca, than to that scrupulous, dry Florentine master, who already had in his studio a youth who was to come to the highest eminence, Leonardo da Vinci. But, indeed, we know nothing of his life in Florence. From his earliest youth it would seem, if we are to believe Vasari, that painter, 'not particularly distinguished,' who had been his first master, had ever told him that 'Florence was the place above all others wherein men attain to perfection in all the arts, but especially in painting.' Vasari also speaks of an Adoration of the Magi, in which Perugino about this time painted the portrait of Andrea Verrocchio; but unfortunately this work, with the rest in the Convent of the Gesuati, was destroyed, together with the church, so early as 1529.

It would seem that Perugino did not stay very long in

Florence, for in 1475 we hear of him in Perugia painting in the Palazzo Pubblico, but no trace remains of his work. In 1478 he was in Cerqueto, where there remains a figure of S. Sebastiano, painted by him in the manner of Luca Signorelli; and, indeed, Vasari speaks of a host of pictures by him which have since disappeared, painted in Florence or its neighbourhood, whereby he seems to have gained reputation beyond the ordinary, so that in 1480 Sixtus IV., della Rovere of Urbino, invited him to Rome to paint in the new chapel he was building in the Vatican, which he desired should be decorated by the first artists in Italy. And it is here in the Sistine Chapel that for the first time we find the true Perugino, the painter of space and light; just there, indeed, the true pupil of Piero della Francesca, and yet successful in this effect of spaciousness in a new way almost, magically filling his picture with air so that the sky is no empty void, but fulfilled with light, deep and limpid and clear with the golden, serious beauty of heaven. It is 'The Delivery of the Keys to St. Peter' that he paints on the wall with a new effect of outdoor life, the pleasant freedom, the splendour of all that, putting into it by reason of its spaciousness, it may well be, a really religious effect, a sense of God. And it is just there we touch, perhaps, Perugino's magic. That clear yet soft landscape, wider than the sea, between the gracious gesture of the mountains east and west, serious by reason, perhaps, of their grave influence, their serene loveliness ever lifting up the eyes of man to the soft sky, seems even to the most inattentive traveller to be blessed. Something gracious seems to have fallen on it, a new light is in the valleys and on the mountain-sides, a light that never was on any Tuscan hills. Something of the lives of the saints seems to have expressed itself in the attitude of Nature, for temperate beauty has sweetness here in a land that is a little ascetic, and yet not cruelly so—a land of dreams truly, yet through which the Tiber rolls towards Rome. And it is just this effect of something blessed that Perugino, almost a realist for once, has caught in his picture in the Sistine Chapel. He paints many another landscape lovelier by far, and full of a clearer air, jewelled with waters, and touched, as it were, by a serener light, so that his effect is often more religious than here; but in this, his only fresco in that chapel of Sixtus IV., we see for the first time the splendour of that space, that art of composing with space which later Perugino brought so near to perfection, and through which Raphael expressed his most profound thoughts. And, above all, this creation of space had for its immediate effect a kind of religious consequence; it was in itself an expression of God. Mystical Umbria had spoken her secret thought that had inspired so many saints whose lives were, perhaps, merely magical to the world. Here, at last, in language which forced the world to its knees, she told her thought and her dream in the work of Perugino. It seems ever to lift up the eyes past the fragile and sorrowful figure in the foreground to the soft sky, so splendid, so lovely, and so deep, where God is, behind that visible air, with all His saints.

It was not till 1491 that Perugino, after many disappointments in Orvieto and in Florence, was in Rome again, this time at the invitation of Cardinal Giuliano della Rovere, afterwards Pope Julius II. There he painted the altar-piece in the Villa Albani, in which the influence of Piero della Francesca seems so obvious. In the midst he has painted the Nativity under one of those beautiful colonnades that Piero had almost invented. Madonna, who kneels before the Child on the ground, is even in feature very like to the Madonna of the Nativity in the Perugia Gallery attributed to Fiorenzo di Lorenzo. And yet how different from that somewhat hard and dry old picture is the exquisite world Perugino has painted. Miles and miles away lies the vistaed earth, and the sky is full of air and light; in the shade of the colonnade two angels kneel between the kneeling figures of Madonna and St. Joseph ; on either side, in separate compartments, kneel the soldier-saints, perhaps St. George and St. Michael, or St. Gabriel, while on one side stands St. John Baptist, and on the other some aged man. Above, in other compartments, are the Crucifixion and the Annunciation, the angel and Madonna, both kneeling under the beautiful cloisters of the Temple, perhaps. And it is just here we find Perugino doing what his masters Piero della Francesca and Fiorenzo di Lorenzo had tried to do—and doing it very much better. He has not the vitality of Piero, but he has learned perspective and all the entrancing magic of vistaed colonnades from him, and yet has subordinated them to the purpose of the whole work. How much more beautiful is his handling of the picture as a piece of composition than that of Fiorenzo ; and yet in spite of their evident presence here how entirely his own is the whole picture ! He has gone one step beyond Piero, and has understood perspective as not merely a material element of pictorial beauty, as not merely a mathematical problem, but as a spiritual element of thought and passion. What is all this space and light, this heaven full of air, but a kind of perspective, a compre- hension of the largeness of the evening sky and earth? And it is as just that, that Perugino has understood it. He goes on painting this new heaven and new earth during his whole life, till we see that it is true, that it is just what we have been looking at down every Umbrian valley, but have not really understood till now. When he leaves this spiritual world that has been revealed to him and turns to figure- painting it is no longer the world that he sees, no longer reality at all, but certain dreams of perfection, too soft and

sweet for truth, a little sentimental, as we might say of one
who desired rather to express an imaginary emotion than
the truth.   It is thus we think of him when we look at that
altar-piece now in the Uffizi, which he painted at Fiesole in
1493.   Madonna sits a little abstractedly with the Child on
her knees; a languid figure, fragile and tearful, stands on
her right as St. John Baptist, while on her left a beautiful
St. Sebastian looks towards heaven, and though the arrow
has pierced his soft flesh, he stands so elegantly and is so
immersed in his prayer that he has not noticed it.   Well,
it is in such subjects that Perugino is least great.   How
insincere are all the figures, how merely charming, how sentimental!   And yet how well he has composed the picture so
that it is by no means crowded, but perfectly constructed,
and with quite simple means.   Throughout the whole of his
life he had been a wanderer, coming to Perugia as a child.
He had lived in Florence, in Rome, in Siena, and in many
a tiny Umbrian city, and in 1494 he seems to have gone
to Venice.   A picture in Cremona of Madonna and Child
enthroned with two Saints may well have been painted on
his way to or from the great sea city; but in the following
year he is back again at Perugia, being nearly fifty years
old, painting there an altar-piece for the Cappella dei Priori,
now in the Vatican.   About this time, too, he visited, it may
be for the first time, the little town of Borgo San Sepolcro,
the birthplace of his master, Piero della Francesca.   Piero
had painted there in the Palazzo dei Conservatori his
wonderful fresco of the Resurrection, but in the picture of
the Ascension by Perugino we find no suggestion of any
influence which such a strange and almost startling work
may have had on him.   More artificial than usual, weaker,
and really a kind of splendid illumination, a huge miniature,
this Ascension has nevertheless something of his magic, if
only in that far-away landscape with the delicate trees so

Q

clear against the sky, and the loveliness that is not beauty but serenity—a charm in everything which he so seldom fails to give even to his most insincere work.

To this year too belongs the beautiful 'Entombment,' now in the Pitti Palace, in which we find a certain enchanting seaside and far-away mountains. Is it really the sea or only a memory of the lake of Perugia, Lake Thrasymene, from whose banks many a fair town climbs up the hills, just as Perugino has painted the little city in this picture. In the foreground we find one of his best pieces of composition—the dead figure of Christ, framed by that little sorrowful company which is come to bury Him. And indeed we may say that it was at this period of his life that he produced his greatest religious works, for in 1496 the fresco of the Crucifixion in the Chapter House of S. Maria Maddalena dei Pazzi was finished. This beautiful fresco, certainly one of the loveliest dreams of that life so full of dreams as to be almost wilfully indifferent to life, is very characteristic of his work at its best. Coming to it through the shadowy street of Florence early in the morning, in the company it may be of some beloved friend, whose serene and quiet spirit has occupied our thoughts on the way through the noisy streets to this little church, so hidden away out of sight, we seem to understand Perugino, his aim in Art, his spirit, his contentment with just that poetical, mystical expression of the serenity of heaven and earth, the holiness of just that, as never before. It was indeed thus that I came with one who is now making others happy, whom I have never seen. Something, I know not what, in the fresh perfection of the morning, or the serene presence of that perfect comrade, seemed to have prepared me for a vision of all that I apprehended in the calm, quiet beauty of the morning and the perfect satisfaction, the contentment, I had in the society of my companion. And indeed it is just that, which

Perugino has expressed in the fresco of S. Maria Maddalena dei Pazzi. The fresco is divided into three compartments, each framed by a beautiful round arch. In the midst, in a country of little hills more delicate than anything we have ever really seen with our bodily eyes, in a kind of heavenly landscape Christ hangs upon the Cross, while St. Mary Magdalen worships Him. To the right and left, in the same exquisite country of delicate streams and trees that the softest wind would make musical, the Blessed Virgin and St. John the Evangelist stand, while two other saints kneeling adore the crucified Saviour. There are but six figures in the whole picture; and it is just this spaciousness, perhaps, earth and sky counting for so much, that makes this work so delightful. Another Crucifixion which he painted about this time, now in the Academy at Florence, seems to confirm one in the thought, in the theory, of the real spirituality of that sense for space and air and all that is meant by 'space-composition,' which are so exquisitely insisted upon in the fresco in the Chapter House of S. Maria Maddalena. For here all that serenity and perfection is wanting, and we find instead a kind of affectation of all that was so perfect in the first picture. Painted for the Convent of St. Jerome, it was necessary to introduce that saint and his lion—that strangely pathetic creature that looks at us so sentimentally, so full of embarrassment, from many an old painting up and down Italy.

In two pictures, both in the Perugia Gallery, one of Madonna and Child, painted in 1497, the other of St. Francis and S. Bernardino interceding with Madonna on behalf of Perugia, we see, as it seems to me, the first glimpse in Perugino's work of that fantastical, elegant spirit, which has done so much to hurt his reputation. It is not that this spirit was nowhere in his work before, but that in these two pictures—in one of them at any rate—it would seem to have obtained supreme command. How insincere are those angels that caper so elegantly with such conscious grace about Madonna, and how impossible are those cherubim that star the 'Intercession of St. Francis'! Perugino, who had taken Piero for his master, has here wandered so far from him, that we could never guess while looking at these works that he had ever come under his influence. The serious purpose, the thoughtful dramatic art, of the great painter of S. Francesco at Arezzo have disappeared from Umbrian Art, and instead we find a kind of reaction towards that older manner, pictorial and entirely decorative, an art in the service of religion, very pretty and thoughtless, and concerned with the emotions. Not passion, but a superficial kind of charm; not the beauty of holiness, that mystical beauty which we find so profound in Angelico, but the dainty piety of beautiful women, who spare a few languid, insipid hours for Madonna in all the exquisite days. Something of the same spirit, and yet with a real and living beauty upon it that is wanting in the two Perugia pictures, we find in the great altar-piece in three compartments, in the National Gallery. But here we find something new also. That dainty, effeminate, and yet sturdy figure of St. Michael is the forerunner of a whole company of youths and captains, the dream warriors of the Cambio, which seem so charming, so unreal, and yet so characteristic of the later Perugino. It was about the year 1500, when Perugino was more than fifty years old, that the Priori of Perugia begged him to decorate the Cambio. He would seem to have agreed with no little gladness and pride. To-day as we enter that somewhat gloomy chamber, so bare and yet so full of the fantastical thoughts of the Renaissance, it is the real Perugino we see, perhaps the most characteristic of all his works, on ceiling and wall. And, indeed, it is true Renaissance work that we find there, less virile than the Florentine, less subtle, and softer too, with still a suggestion of the sanctuary about it, the quietness of a holy place, the languor of the Gregorian chant, the delicacy of the fine vestments and altar clothes, antiquity seen with all the affectation, the daintiness, the make-believe of the Renaissance, with something of its naïve admiration at itself, and its whole-hearted worship of antique captains and old philosophies.

They are no Romans nor Greeks, these fragile warriors with the sweet boyish or even girlish faces, the round limbs and delicate hands. They have never heard of Ares or Mars; to them the brightness of Apollo, the beauty of Aphrodite, have not been revealed; only they have understood the beauty of the delicate wounded hands of Christ, the sorrowful dreams of Mary Madonna, the fatal and fantastic lives of the saints, the ecstasies of the mystics, the eloquence of the preachers. They have not been born into the world with the Aphrodite of Melos, the mother of Love, but with Mary Madonna, Mother of God; and though God be Love, and she His mother, it is of the salt of her tears they have tasted and not of the salt of the sea. They seem to cry for some memory of their greatness to linger with us on the way to death, and almost in pity we are eager to remember them. But, indeed, they have never existed, these delicate, sorrowful Christians that masquerade as Greeks and Romans; they are the dreams of a fortunate age in the midst of misfortune; they are pale sunbeams on a winter's day, ghosts of some golden age in heaven that never came to our earth; already they are fading on the wall, and even while we look they seem to pass away like some exquisite fantastic dream. Endowed with all the ideal grace and humility of Christianity, they seem to tell us of an age of chivalry that never happened: Thermopylæ passed by them in a dream, Aspasia was but a vision seen in some convent on a day of spring, Hannibal is a tale that is told, and Carthage a city in a Book of Hours.

How differently Signorelli would have dealt with his ideas, how little poetry he would have found it necessary to bring to an antiquity in itself so splendid, how little sentimentality he would have thrust upon the greatest soldiers of the world! Was it, perhaps, that the Perugians in their fierce and brutal city needed some such fanciful emasculated dream as this to reconcile them with their own world? Was this, too, an expression of the dreaminess, the mysticism of Umbria? Was Perugino painting merely for his public? Indeed, I think he painted here in the Cambio more for himself than in many a scornful religious picture. This man with the rugged, scornful, indifferent face, that looks at us in this very room, was a dreamer, a poet, a man of emotions rather than a thinker. Taught by Piero della Francesca certain lessons in the science of Art, all his life he remembered them, but does not carry that science any further; is indeed only interested in it when he can find a spirit, poetical, full of dreams, and a world of dreams that may be expressed by it. So he takes the knowledge that Piero had given him, or develops it, not as Signorelli did, intellectually, scientifically, in the true manner of Piero, but in a way entirely his own, applying perspective with all its intricate problems not to the works of man only but to the creation of God. How he has planned out heaven and earth in spaces of light full of air and sunshine! We shall do wrong if we think of his work as an expression of anything but just that emotion. His subjects he might seem to have thrown to his public with a certain scorn, content if he might express his love of heaven and earth. He thinks of Nature so far as he caught sight of her, not as a being like himself, as Wordsworth did, but as the spirit of God. It is perhaps that which we find so delightful in his work, so that even when his sentimentality, his insincerity, his love of sweet, tearful faces, his reiteration of affected sorrow disgust us, we still find his work religious in the true sense, by reason of a certain spirituality that lurks behind those theatrical sorrows of saints and martyrs. For us at least, initiated as we are by our own souls into the genuine and lonely sorrows of the world, it is rather as the painter of Italy, of all that Italy means to us, than as a painter of religious pictures that Perugino appeals to us, and, in a sense, that would make him one of the most religious painters of the world; for it is in the beauty of the world, its joyful summer fields, its uplifted hills and the soft sky we have learned to love so passionately, that we find the best expression of all that we mean by religion. Not Paganism, but an apprehension of the presence of God in His unspoiled work—work which He Himself found so good, which He gave us, too, not to destroy but to enjoy and to cherish, seeing that it must remind us, how inevitably, of Him.

Those delicate warriors that stand at attention so languidly in the Cambio seem to have haunted Perugino for some time. We see perhaps the first of them in the St. Michael of the National Gallery altar-piece, and the same figure appears in a picture of the Assumption, now in the Academy at Florence. Indeed, those four figures, who look so languidly and with such unction towards Madonna as she is carried upward, rather by some irresistible force within herself than by the angels, who merely point towards God in His Heaven, are but four more of the isolated figures of the Cambio. Splendid in their beauty, they are of the same company, and yet how real beside those dreamy Romans and Greeks. Something of the unction of the earliest Latin hymns inspires them—naturally enough, one might think, seeing that they are at one with the subject of the picture. In the same gallery at Florence we may see the two portraits that Perugino painted about this time, of the Abbate Baldassare and of Dom Biagio Milanesi of the Vallombrosa.

At last, in these two portraits he has touched reality very successfully, and it may well be that some will consider these portraits his greatest works. Simple and without the smallest accessories, they show us that for one moment at any rate Perugino touched life and found it beautiful. But it was not in any ordinary human being, full of thoughts of the world, that he came at last to consider the life of man, the realities of the world, but even here too in a man touched by the simplicity, the chaste, lowly ways of the monastery. It was perhaps the only way in which a mind so affected, so shy of reality as Perugino's, could approach reality at all ; and these two portraits remain to show us how simply he dealt with anything he could not utterly transform with his own spirit, could not make his own and endow with the emotions of his own mind.

In the following year, 1501, he was elected one of the Priori of Perugia, and we find him painting not long afterwards four saints and two angels, together with a lovely landscape of hill and river, round a monstrous wooden crucifix, whose terrible wounds and emaciated humanity horrify us even to-day in the Perugia Gallery. The double altar-piece in the same gallery would seem to be rather the work of his pupils than his own ; and indeed the rest of his life is a kind of fading repetition of all his former glory. At Florence, in 1503, he helps to choose the place where Michelangelo's David shall stand, is outvoted, and. his opinion is disregarded ; and because of this perhaps he returns to his own land, Umbria, famous now because of him ; returns, indeed, to his very birthplace, Città della Pieve, and paints there in the following year the Adoration of the Magi, almost for love, since he knew they were too poor to pay the cost. You may see it to-day in all its ruined splendour ; in a more fantastic landscape than he ever painted before, and with a new effect of light streaming as from the gates of

Heaven down the long valley, the three kings and their
company come to worship a little Child. It is a kind of
allegory of his own life, that had been almost as splendid as
a king's progress, and yet always full of devotion to so
spiritual a thing as earth and sky. But all his splendours
were not finished, for in that same year he received a letter
from Isabella d' Este, Duchess of Mantua, minutely describ-
ing a picture she wished him to paint. She had long
desired Perugino to work for her, and when at last he
consented, it was not a Madonna or any Holy Family she
asked, but a battle between Love and Chastity; Pagan in the
manner of the Renaissance, full of a kind of romance.

'My poetic invention,' she writes, 'which I wish to see
you paint, is the Battle of Love and Chastity—that is to say,
Pallas and Diana fighting against Venus and Love. Pallas
must appear almost to have vanquished Love. After breaking
his golden arrows and silver bow, and flinging them at her
feet, she holds the blindfold boy with one hand by the
handkerchief which he wears over his eyes, and lifts her
lance to strike him with the other. The issue of the conflict
between Diana and Venus must appear more doubtful.
Venus's crown, garland, and veil will only have been slightly
damaged; while Diana's raiment will have been singed by
the torch of Venus, but neither of the goddesses will have
received any wound. Behind these four divinities, the chaste
nymphs in the train of Pallas and Diana will be seen engaged
in a fierce conflict—in such ways as you can best imagine—
with the lascivious troops of fauns, satyrs, and thousands of
little loves. These last will be smaller than the god Cupid,
and will carry neither gold bows nor silver arrows, but darts
of some baser material, either wood or iron if you please.
In order to give full expression to the fable and adorn the
scene, the olive tree, sacred to Pallas, will rise out of the
ground at her side, with a shield bearing the head of Medusa,

and the owl, which is her emblem, will be seen in the branches of the tree. . . . I send you all these incidents in a small drawing, which may help you to understand my explanations. If you think there are too many figures you can reduce the number, so long as the chief ones remain—I mean Pallas, Diana, Venus, and Love—but you are forbidden to introduce anything of your own invention.' It was thus the great religious painter of the age was asked to paint a subject which could never have suited a genius so mystical, so little interested in action. But he finished the work, and we may see it to-day in the Louvre. Full of a kind of movement, its mere carelessness, its mixed perspective, show how little he cared for work into which he was forbidden to introduce ' anything of his own invention.'

Later, in Rome, painting in the Stanze at the command of Julius II., meeting there Signorelli and Pintoricchio, both so famous, he worked with a certain enthusiasm, and indeed his work in the Stanza del Incendio is delightful even beside Raphael. On his way back to Perugia, he would seem to have stayed at Assisi, and to have painted a Crucifixion, now spoilt, in S. Maria degli Angeli. But perhaps the loveliest work of his old age is in his birthplace in S. Servi. Ruined though it be, it still holds something precious for us in a new kind of sincerity in that last vision of the Crucifixion. Later still, we find him painting at S. Agnese in Perugia, and at Trevi; and again, with a kind of humility, completing a fresco that his pupil Raphael, then so famous and so lately dead, had left unfinished in S. Severo at Perugia.

He himself was not far from death, which came to him, as it is said, in the plague of 1524. A certain mystery shrouds his burial and all concerning it. Vasari says that he was buried honourably at Città della Pieve; but a later gossip asserts that he died at Fontignano, without receiving the last sacraments of the Church, and so was buried in unconsecrated ground. This assertion has been used to . prove Perugino's irreligion, which it would seem is a question scarcely worth discussing. It appears unlikely that the Church would have employed an atheist to represent for her so many of the most touching scenes in human life, and in the life of Christ, and then have refused him burial at last. And indeed, in thinking of so quiet an artist, it is not necessary to come to any such conclusion. In a sense the most religious painter Italy ever produced, it is rather as a painter of earth and sky, of space, and of all that space came to mean to him, that he interests us. Not content with any description, as it were, of the Nativity or the Crucifixion, subjects so full of the exquisite tragedy of heaven, he desires rather to suggest the very spirit, the serene beauty, of the presence of God, and to allow his thoughts about the world to disengage themselves from his pictures. He was the first painter perhaps who cared for the soft sky, finding there something precious, which we too have seen because of him.

XXIV

PINTORICCHIO

IN Vasari's *Lives of the Painters* but little space is given to the life and work of Pintoricchio, and although we have come to think of him as a painter of some interest and importance, since the discovery of his work in the Sistine Chapel for so long given to Luca Signorelli and Perugino, we shall do wrong to claim for him more consideration than he really deserves; at his best he is but a third-rate painter. So, while as an Italian painter of the Renaissance he may be disregarded almost, as an Umbrian, or a follower of Perugino and the pictorial school of Central Italy, he still has his importance, seeing that he has much of the charm, the prettiness, which, one half believes, have made Perugino so popular; while he is almost without the greater qualities of his master, whose real development is to be found, not in Pintoricchio, but in the Raphael of the Stanze, and in such a picture as the Madonna del Granduca.

Born, as is supposed, in Perugia in 1454, he was at most but eight years younger than Perugino. At his christening he was given the name of Bernardino, not an uncommon name we may believe in those days, when the memory of S. Bernardino of Siena, full of tears and passionate eloquence, still haunted the piazzas of Perugia. Little, poor, and deaf, if we are to remember his first nickname—*il sordicchio*—he was very evidently a youth of great promise—a promise which was to come so early to performance, and so soon to fall into a kind of weakness; a delight in just pretty things, delightful enough in themselves—pretty women, pretty landscapes, and all the life of the animal world, so naïve and charming; the sweetness of the flowers, too, tall lilies, or the wild flowers that are scattered over the fields, together with something of Bonfigli's love for surprising or pretty costumes or dresses. How carefully he notes the folds of a girl's gown, or the glint of chain armour on some exquisite youth, or the jewelled splendour of pontifical copes, and all the daintiness of fairyland in the Borgia apartments! And indeed it is not seldom we seem to find Bonfigli and Fiorenzo di Lorenzo as his earliest masters. For if it was from Bonfigli he learned the charm of the fashionable costume of his day, it was perhaps from Fiorenzo he learned the necessity of making his women so pretty; pretty after one pattern almost. How like to the innumerable virgins, and the gayer, more happy girls of Pintoricchio's pictures at Spello, at Rome, at Siena, is that Madonna of the Nativity attributed to Fiorenzo di Lorenzo in the Perugia Gallery! And yet when we find Pintoricchio painting for Sixtus IV. in the Sistine Chapel, it is almost as an independent painter, a painter whose work has for many years been mistaken for that of Signorelli or Perugino. We know but little of Pintoricchio at any time of his life, and nothing at all before the time of the frescoes in S. Maria in Aracoeli and in the Sistine Chapel. It is strange, considering the importance of the Florentine school of painting, its excellence, its vitality, to find so much Umbrian work in the Sistine Chapel. But it is well to remember that Sixtus IV. was della Rovere, an Umbrian of Urbino; that Melozzo da Forli, the pupil of Signorelli, was a man of no little importance in Rome; and that for these reasons, even apart from the excellent fame of Perugino, Umbrian Art would receive favour and consideration. However that may be, we find Pintoricchio at work in Rome so early as 1482, and ten years later he had begun the Borgia apartments. His work in the Sistine Chapel—two frescoes, the Baptism of our Lord, and the Journey of Moses—might seem, even with all the rest of his work to choose from, the best he ever did. In a landscape full of great rocks in whose crevices grow many a delicate tree, in the manner of Fiorenzo, Pintoricchio has painted certain scenes from the life of Moses. In one corner of the picture a great valley steals away between soft mountains, and in the foreground a host of people is assembled, shepherds and children, and many women and a bright angel. Zipporah is intent on the ceremony of circumcision, while Moses, a figure so like to Christ as almost to be mistaken for Him, looks on, a little sadly. Again we see this figure stopped by an angel who seems to be delivering some urgent message. A little further off shepherds dance, and a company is assembled as though for some ceremony, a marriage or a funeral. Long given to Luca Signorelli, there is, to our eyes at any rate, but little of Luca's strong work in the Peruginesque fresco now rightly given to Pintoricchio. That angel who so strenuously stops the great prophet, those two women who are so intent on the circumcision of Gershom, might well be the work of Perugino, who would not be unlikely to help his pupil in a task so important as work in this chapel, among so many illustrious painters, must have been. And indeed in Pintoricchio's other fresco, the Baptism of Christ, the hand of Perugino would seem to be even more visible. More conservative than the Journey of Moses, we find here the *mandorla* of cherubim, the isolated groups, each with its own dramatic interest, that were just then being discarded by the Renaissance. And was it from Fiorenzo that Pintoricchio learned to paint so many portraits in his pictures, or did Fiorenzo learn it from him ? The figure of

Christ, so reverent, so humble, the profound quietness of
the figure of the Baptist, are perhaps the finest achievement
in figure-painting that Pintoricchio ever reached. But it
is rather in the exquisite landscape, and in those flying
angels who lean towards the Eternal, that we see the
influence of Perugino most surely. And yet as a piece of
'space-composition' how far short of Perugino's work in this
chapel, the Delivery of the Keys to St. Peter, are these two
frescoes! It is, as I think, very obviously not the master
but the follower, the imitator, that we find in these paintings,
which are full of Perugino's desire for space and light and
yet so crowded. It is true that we have in Pintoricchio
a master of 'space-composition'; but how much less spiritual,
how much less religious is its effect on us in his pictures
than in those of Perugino and Raphael! And yet in spite
of any fault that we may, perhaps a little inconsequently,
find in work so sincere, so eager for a certain sort of success,
as the work of a youth of twenty-eight years of age it
must surely have dazzled the painters of that day. For
even beside the work of Botticelli it is by no means contemptible, promising as it does quite another sort of success—
a success which, as it seems to me, never came to Pintoricchio,
who concerned himself rather with certain trivialities than
with the enthusiastic and passionate art that was just then
dawning in the world. The whole of the rest of his life
would seem to have been a kind of enlargement and multi-
plication of the more charming successes of these early
works. He paints a whole city of pretty women, whose
dresses fall in those unforgettable folds, as though he had
lingered with delight on the thought of the gracious attitude
of some woman he had loved. Again and again you find
his fields bright with spring flowers, his valleys white with
daisies or starred with campanulas. In his skies you will
find so many little birds, that you will be sure he must have

loved them, and everywhere he lingers fondly over the
innocent, trusting life of animals: dogs which look up at
his figures so intelligently, gentle deer, and a snowy brood
of rabbits. And at last in the Borgia apartments you come
upon a whole delightful country, a kind of Garden of Eden,
where the animals are friends with man—man and woman
being always so dainty, so charming there; so that they
play among the tall flowers unafraid, and the birds sing
under the soft sky, or build in the strange, fantastic
trees.

It might seem that here at last was an Umbrian painter,
from Perugia, too, who was not in captivity to religion; who
had, as it were, thought of the world, of beauty, as of
more value, or at least more valuable, to Art than Faith.
But it is no such attitude of mind, I think, that we find in
Pintoricchio's work, but rather a certain faculty for narrative,
a delight in the story that a picture unfolds with so many
accessories, pretty aids to the decoration of a tale, which
for us at least have their value, not æsthetic, perhaps, but
historical. To him as to Perugino the scene is of importance,
is full of an incisive and delicate reality, but it awakes in
him no spiritual exaltation; space is to him a kind of
dimension with which his master has taught him to conjure,
it is never fulfilled with that light and air and largeness in
which Perugino so often painted some scene poor enough
in itself. Some poetical or religious sense—something, I
know not what, is wanting. As you wander through the
Libreria at Siena, how poor seems the fulfilment of the
promise in the Sistine Chapel. 'Almost perfect as archi-
tectonic decoration,' Mr. Berenson has said of these careless
works. It is hardly possible perhaps to express better their
one virtue. He could compose with space well enough to
deceive us as to the badness of his work as a figure-
painter.

It was in 1501 that Pintoricchio went to Spello, where a bishop of the house of Baglioni had determined to decorate his cathedral. Ruined as they are to-day, these frescoes possess a charm that in spite of every fault is delightful. What a pretty world this painter has created! How much more charming than Italy is, or stony Palestine, or any country that ever was in the real world! It is his curse this obsession by a continual desire for prettiness, and yet it is so sincere withal, so evidently well meant, that it is difficult to be angry. Besides, his life was none too happy. Vasari, always a little contemptuous of those who were born neither in Florence nor in Arezzo, or who had not won the applause of the Florentine masters as Perugino had done, suggests that his death came almost through a contemptible piece of avarice. A certain Sigismondo Tizio, however, a writer of his own day, and an historian of Siena, tells another and a sadder story. As he lay sick it seems, his wife, who never loved him, locked him into his room, and passed the time until his death with one she found more to her mind. His cries appear to have attracted the notice of certain neighbours, who afterwards told Tizio the story he relates. And it seems that owing to the neglect of his wife, whom Tizio accuses of making a deliberate attempt to starve her husband, Pintoricchio died in 1513. 'The little painter,' with, it would seem, so many physical disadvantages, had yet managed to gather sufficient glory to keep his memory green. Indeed, he is the first ornamental painter of Italy. To write of him as a 'decorative' artist is to give the reader a false impression. He is by no means a great decorative artist. Not decoration but ornament—sumptuous, gay, and always charming ornament—was his aim. The Borgia apartments, the Libreria at Siena, are not monuments of decorative art, but are possibly the most sumptuously ornamented rooms in Italy. To speak of him as in the first rank, as it seems

R

certain writers of our time have done, or as a great 'master of decoration,' seems to me impossible. He is, as Dr. Ricci has so well said, 'wholly destitute of passion,' and to think of him as anything but a minor painter with those words after his name should be for ever impossible.

UMBRIA MYSTICA

XXV

JOACHIM DI FLORE

IN the eleventh and twelfth centuries when the romantic
spirit, the spirit of chivalry, was everywhere, certain
Italian poets began to imitate the songs of the troubadours.
It was a moment of crisis in the history of Europe; Italy
was awakening from her long sleep that had been so full of
terrible dreams, and with the fall of the Hohenstaufen we
find a real and living poetry, wholly national, beginning to
supersede the imitative sense of those obscure poets who
found their inspiration in the Provençal songs.

An age of frightful, unforgettable disaster was just passing
away. Beginning with the decay of the Roman Empire and
the coming of the Barbarians, it was in the first place the age
of the spread of Christianity, that Oriental religion which,
in the midst of every sort of political catastrophe, it was
necessary for Europe to assimilate. Out of the chaos of
those terrible years, blazing with every sort of sensuality
and cruelty, one beautiful and splendid figure had arisen,
the forlorn hope of the world—the Catholic Church. And
indeed, though for no other cause yet for this, is she Holy
and Divine, that through all those centuries of misery and
barbarism, in spite of the brutal lust and cruelty of the
North, the suicidal madness of the Latin world, the devastation within, the devilish wars without, she kept safe for us
Humanism and Law, controlling the new Faith in its excesses,
calm and composed amid all the destruction and madness.

gradually building up stone by stone, fortress by fortress, tower by tower, pinnacle by pinnacle, that invincible and everlasting city of light that has survived every attack, every disaster, every passion of humanity; that has educated the world, preserved its treasures of learning, held in reverence the old great masters, recreated Art and protected Humanism, in the early days as in the Renaissance, from the barbarism of the Reformation as from the vulgarity and vandalism of to-day.

In the decaying Roman Empire misery had been common enough, but the coming of the barbarian peoples, Goths and Germans, without laws or morals, overwhelmed Italy under an army of devils. Physical torture, everlasting devastation and war, were their delight and their daily life. Under that wave all culture was lost, civilisation ceased to exist, and Rome, the capital of the world, that in the time of Trajan had possessed a population of nearly two millions, was in 546, when Totila, King of the Goths, had done with her, during the space of forty days utterly devastated, without a single inhabitant. Nor was this her last trouble; for three hundred years later the Mohammedans sacked Rome and plundered the treasuries of St. Peter and St. Paul, leaving their indelible mark on Italy in many a castle and watch-tower by the sea. She who was eventually to rise again and master the world, as of old, by the power of her intelligence and her art, the indestructible genius of the Latin race the virtue and authority of her civilisation, was a ruin.

Nor was the intellectual life of the Middle Age less terrible than the physical. Rome it seems had not yet had time to civilise Christianity. Every sort of brutality was practised in that name. Antiquity with its tolerance and its beauty was swept from men's minds, and instead ignorance reigned, with fear and credulity, a mighty trinity, damning indiscriminately all the poets and philosophers, with the exception it may be of Virgil—that divine poet whom the Barbarians were unable to understand, since they regarded him not as a poet but as a kind of magician not unfriendly to their frightful religion, of which of course he knew nothing.

In the year 529, St. Benedict, the first great educator of the modern world, destroyed on Monte Cassino the last Temple of Apollo; and those doctrines of love and equality that might seem to have been lost sight of by the barbarian zealots of the new religion gradually came to be preached throughout Europe. 'My Order,' he said, 'is a school where men learn to serve God.' It was that and much more. It was for some hundreds of years the only school in Europe that touched the mass of the people. Where the Benedictines brought the Cross, there also they took the plough, and so gradually brought Europe under cultivation; reclaimed the swamps and marshes, drained the wet lands, and dammed the springs for the use of themselves and the people. Founded on Silence and Obedience, his Rule was naturally rather the means of doing work than of suppressing heresy or producing the arguments of the schoolmen. It was, too, the friend of the Arts, almost their foster-mother. The work of the Order was, however, necessarily gradual, and for more than five hundred years the most terrible ignorance and brutality continued to torture humanity. Terrified by its sins, driven mad by the fear of Hell, a kind of gloom fell upon the world. Men, caring nothing for any human affection or relationship, flogged themselves to death in the mountains. I do not suggest that all the world took part in such excesses, but that all men saw in this madness, this self-torture, a kind of ideal. All Europe appears to have been in a state of melancholia. Suddenly, with a kind of immense relief, she thinks to purge herself of all her sins at the very tomb of Christ; and so, one after another during two centuries, the Crusades devastate Europe; wave after wave of fanatic heroism, army after army, are dashed in pieces against that stone which Joseph placed before the tomb of Jesus.

Meanwhile that Church which had crowned Charlemagne as Emperor was indefatigably building her Empire in the hearts of men. And in thinking of those terrible years it is as the Saviour of the world she appears to us, calm and inscrutable upon her everlasting hills. For hundreds of years the Emperors strove to snatch her power from her; many armies were hurled against her in vain; indestructible and victorious, she was busy creating the modern world, restoring to us Humanism and Art and Beauty, angry if some eager mind threatened to attain her end before she was ready to advance, for the whole world was as it were in her keeping; loving best that profound and reverent intelligence which alone was capable of understanding her, since she demanded from her soldiers a duty of reverence, of fidelity toward the old as toward the new ; to the past as to the present; assured in her heart of her victory, since she would save the world not by revolution but by development and remembrance.

And it is really into that world, as it were, of the twelfth and thirteenth centuries that we come when, passing through Arezzo, we approach Cortona, where Brother Elias lies buried. By the time that Joachim di Flore announced to the world the advent of the kingdom of the Spirit, the coming of St. Francis, Rome was mistress of the soul of man. That spirit which had so hardly conquered the world, and brought a kind of order out of all the chaos of the Middle Age, was about to renew itself—not without a certain fear and pain. And so it was not altogether without protest that Joachim and the Franciscans restored something of the spirit of

Jesus of Nazareth to a world that by its own extravagance and brutality had rendered the letter so necessary and so tyrannical.

The immense unrest of the twelfth century, its desire for expression, its profound dissatisfaction with its own achievement, may be found in the life of one of the most mysterious personalities of that age of mysticism. Joachim di Flore was a dreamer, a revolutionary thinker, rather than a man of action. He seems to have foreseen the achievement of St. Francis, the immense power of poverty over the hearts of men, though himself incapable of any such victory of Love. We discern in him a kind of poet who was in sympathy rather with mysticism than with government; and, unimportant though his Order of Flore proved to be, he at least attained to a certain authority in that religious dream which was about to become aware of itself; so that we find his influence still living many years later, partly in his prophecies, those strange, enigmatical sayings so likely to achieve a kind of fulfilment; partly in the passionate vitality, that was rebellion almost, against fate, as it were, in so great a man as John of Parma, and that remnant of the Franciscan Order which remained loyal to the ideal of St. Francis. That after Joachim's death a certain doubt of his orthodoxy appeared, is really an acknowledgment of his importance in the history of mystical Italy, where he lives as a kind of anarchist, anxious, above all, about the freedom of the spirit of man; so that at one time the Greek and Latin Churches seem to him just Sodom and Gomorrah, while at another he professes his faith in humanity. And so to us as to Dante he appears as a prophet brooding over the immense and shapeless future of the world, of humanity, of the soul of man.

Born at Colico near Cosenza about the year 1130, he became a monk of the Cistercian Order, and towards the end of
that century we find him an abbot of a monastery of that
Order in Calabria. Something mysterious, inexplicable,
seems to have surrounded him from his birth, so that his
ancient biographers tell us that there was nothing more
wonderful and strange in the birth of St. John Baptist than
in that of Joachim; and, indeed, it is as a kind of St. John,
a forerunner of St. Francis who is so like to Christ, that we
think of him now, as his followers seem to have done. Before
he was seven years old he had lost his mother, and, as was
not uncommon in that age, in spite of the stories of his
youthful piety, he was not baptized until his eleventh year.
A kind of beauty expressed very delightfully in the stories
concerning him seems always to surround him, as when we
find him praying on a great rock in the midst of the woods
near his father's house. Some curious influence which those
near him always felt in his presence, in a kind of allegory, as
it were, softened the hardness of the rock, perhaps, as indeed
the legend suggests, by reason of the daily contact of that
body 'very pure and chaste,' so that a wonderful flower
with healing in its petals grew there, nor was this wonder
long hid from the people round about. At last a woman
who had often watched him praying plucked the flower to
cure some beasts that were sick, and it might seem to be
characteristic of that time, differing as it does so profoundly
from our own age, that we read that the people were discon-
solate at the loss of this flower, and went to the young
Joachim in tears and besought him to pray yet once again in
that place; and not without a certain shame he agreed, and
suddenly there was seen not the same flower but a spring,
which could not be stolen away, and which 'ceased not to
flow till his death.' That story in its simplicity might stand
for an allegory of his life. He seems to have touched life so

rarely as almost to have left it unregarded. So when he became page to Roger II., Duke of Calabria, it is really only a moment before he is disgusted with court life and on his way with a certain Andrea to Palestine, and having passed through many adventures, in which he is marvellously saved from drowning, from robbers, and from the plague, he returns to Italy to his father, from whom at last he wins permission to embrace the monastic life, retiring very gladly to the Abbey of Sambucin of the Cistercian Order. And was it as a kind of explanation of his indifference to life, his preoccupation with the Scriptures, or as a vision that he had really encountered of what his life must be, that he has told us of the youth of exquisite beauty who came to him one day of sunshine saying, 'Joachim, drink this, for it is divine. And when he had drunk so much as he thought he had need of he gave back the cup, but the youth refused it with indignation, saying, 'If you had drunk it all, there is not a science in the world in which you would not have been perfectly instructed, but now you will only have knowledge of the Scriptures.' A little later we find him taking the life vows and entering the Abbey of Curace, where he became first prior and then abbot. And it was during his life at Curace that he became famous as a preacher and a prophet, foretelling, as is said, the sufferings of Pope Lucius III.; seeing on the walls of St. Mark's, during a journey to Venice in 1185, the images of St. Francis and St. Dominic in the habits of their Orders; assuring those who heard of this vision that these were two prophets whom God would send to the help of His Church. It was, it would seem, almost like a second Jonah that he came to the city by the sea, preaching repentance, that strange sad cry that has echoed out of the wilderness deafening the world. In the midst of his encounters with the world he retired from Curace, going to Cascmar, after a meeting with Frederic

Barbarossa, whose ideas and government pleased him as little as those of the churches he had perhaps too hastily condemned. It was during his retirement at Casemar that he composed one of the few authentic works we possess from his hand, the *Psalterium decem chordarum*. It seems that on the Day of Pentecost he was before the altar intending to recite certain Psalms in honour of the Holy Ghost, when suddenly he began to doubt the Mystery of the Holy Trinity. Throwing himself to the ground, he invoked the Holy Spirit to dissipate his doubts, at the same time reciting those Psalms he had proposed to himself, and in a moment the figure of the Psaltery with its ten strings came to him as in a vision, and in some subtle way he thought that he had found in that instrument of music an emblem as it were of the Holy Trinity. In his wonderful mind, so sensitive always to sensuous impressions of beauty or fitness, all his doubts were dissipated ; nor could he forbear from crying out, ' It is Thou, Lord, who doest all wonders ; is there a God comparable to Thee ? ' It was thus that he composed the work, dividing it into three books which correspond to the Three Persons of the Holy Trinity. In the first he treats of the body of the instrument itself, which is the source of all the melody it produces, and this is the Person of the Father, from whom all things proceed. In the second he speaks of the number of the Psalms which are sung upon the instrument, and these under the name of Wisdom represent Him, *per quem omnia facta sunt*. In the third he explains the method of Psalmody, which by reason of its sweetness and melody represents the unction of the Holy Spirit, that Lord and giver of life, in whom are all things hid.

It is perhaps in this book that we find the first suggestion of that famous saying ascribed to him through many centuries, though but doubtfully his own : ' The kingdom of the Father is passed, the kingdom of the Son is passing, the kingdom of the Spirit is to be.' And it is indeed chiefly as the prophet of this kingdom of the Spirit in all its freedom and perfection that Joachim di Flore is of importance to us. Whether or no he was the author of the 'Eternal Gospel,' he was at least the forerunner of a new age, which used his ideas and expressed his thoughts in action. It is, as he himself says, the 'etiquette of a doctrine' that he gave to the world. And he is capable of a vision of history so serene that he can say, 'The Holy Spirit saved the Greeks, the Son works the salvation of the Latins, the Eternal Father watches over the Jews, and shall save them from the hatred of men without its being necessary for them to forsake Judaism.' And as though in an ecstasy of optimism very rare in that age, he says, 'The Old Testament, the work when the Father governed, may be compared to the ancient or original sky, to the light of the stars. The New Testament, the work of the time when the Son reigned, to the second sky, to the light of the moon. The Eternal Gospel, the work of the time which shall be governed by the Holy Spirit, to the light of the sun. The first was a starry night, the second was the dawn, the third shall be the broad day. The first bore nettles, the second roses, the third shall bear lilies. The first is represented by Septuagesima, the second by Lent, the third by the joy of Easter.'

For him even Christ and his disciples came short of perfection in the contemplative life. For it is there, in all the quietness of thought, that he foresees the future of humanity. And so when certain miracles ascribed to him, perhaps a little hastily, for he himself never claims them, bring great crowds to his monastery, he retires to Flore and establishes there the first monastery of his reformed Order. In comparison with this new Order, says his old biographer, the Cistercians appeared 'comme un Ordre relâché qui avait déjà besoin de réforme.' Yet he foresees the persecution, the misunderstanding, and destruction to which his ideas will be subject, rejoicing for the most part only in those strange visions of St. Francis which come to him from time to time, and which it might seem impossible to explain. Nor is he, in spite of his severity towards himself, without a certain Epicureanism, for we read of the magnificent gardens that surrounded his abbey, and of his delight in beautiful churches. And he is friends with kings; foretelling, as it is said, to Richard Cœur de Lion of England his misfortunes and his death, and chiding Frederic Barbarossa for a certain indifference towards spiritual things, not necessarily religious, which he discerned in him.

For himself he will not claim any gift of prophecy, finding in himself rather a kind of intelligence, a little rare and subtle, which enables him to understand mysteries in the Scriptures hidden from the vulgar, and even from those who appear so learned. He died on Passion Sunday, March 30th, 1202, aged seventy-two years. And in his Will we find the reason, perhaps, of the defeat of his Order, of his ideas, and of his own personality in conflict, more or less open, with the Catholic Church. 'I have achieved,' he says there, 'as far as I have been able, and as it has pleased God to inspire me, the work on the Two Testaments in five books; an Exposition of the Apocalypse in eight parts; the Psaltery with Ten Strings in three volumes, and some smaller works against the Jews or the enemies of the Catholic Faith. I reject all that the Holy Catholic Church rejects. I accept all that she accepts, believing firmly that the gates of Hell cannot prevail against her.'

Hardly a Christian at all in middle life, looking for a new Order, a revelation less limited, a freedom of spirit beyond anything to be found even in the early Church, he submits himself at last to the only power capable of defeating him—the Catholic Church. He died a Christian, but his ideas could not die. His dreams had so stirred the hearts of men in that strange and beautiful country of Central Italy, that when St. Francis began to preach in 1209 many of those who heard him understood him. For St. Francis was the true son of Joachim, though it is possible he was unconscious of his parentage. He too failed as did Joachim, and yet at one time it seemed possible the world might become Franciscan rather than Christian, so powerful was that idea of freedom which these dreamers offered to men. All, or almost all, which they dreamed and desired has been achieved for us by means how different, by intelligences how prosaic, in comparison with these poets of the twelfth and thirteenth centuries.

It was a divine madness that they wished to thrust upon the world—a dream of reaching some ill-defined goal, which they only knew in a vision, by some short cut or byway. And for this cause the Roman Church crushed them; because in her keeping lay all the work of the old great masters, the precise and necessary order of the world along whose indestructible highways she was determined to march. Ever of the centre, holding as strictly to the temperate judgment, the hardly achieved civilisation and art of the world, as to the dreams of Jesus of Nazareth, she was at once the heir of Roman Law, of Roman Religion, of Roman Art, of all that so great civilisation, and of the new religion of Love which had come into the world so late. Already she had seen the enthusiasm of the ignorant peoples sweep away a very precious civilisation; in her heart for centuries she had kept safe for us all that they had sought utterly to destroy, and now that she was mistress of our world, responsible for everything that lifted man a little above the beasts with whom he still shares the world, she found it necessary to crush all those who, as it were, hampered her in her untiring march towards a goal that only she had really seen. So she destroyed Joachim and St. Francis, both of whom she understood and loved. The victory of either meant not only her own destruction but the loss of order, of certain success, in a kind of enthusiasm, an excitement that was dangerous, seeing that it was founded neither on the intellect nor on faith, but on a certain imaginative faculty so capable of seeing visions and of dreaming dreams, so liable to change, as to be almost at one with it; so poetical, not always in the best sense, as to be led away by beauty or tears; so terrible as to acquiesce in its own annihilation.

It was perhaps a new religion that Joachim and his followers, John of Parma and Gérard, tried to found; a religion having much in common with the later Lutheran movement in its most engaging form, in that the appeal was ever to the individual conscience, to the spirit rather than to the letter, to the personality rather than to society. The Eternal Gospel which influenced certain minds in the thirteenth and fourteenth centuries so strongly, if it ever had any real existence as a book, seems to have been a kind of harmony or collection of thoughts, perhaps, from the works of Joachim. 'Spiritual men,' he says, 'are not obliged to obey the Roman Church, nor to acquiesce in its judgments in matters pertaining to God'; nor does he appear to see in his enthusiasm for liberty the impossibility of dividing the spiritual, who need not obey or acquiesce, from the worldly, who must do so.

In a world that has forgotten Joachim for many a dreamer less bold, for many a personality less lovely, his ideas are by no means dead. A kind of anarchy in spiritual things has for centuries been the normal condition of Northern Europe and America. And there we may see that the soul which insists upon meeting God as it were haphazard, without introduction, and in no immemorial way, has not attained to greater freedom than the Catholic who seems to be so fettered.

Bound by its indifference, or lonely in the immense solitude of love, if it seeks for God it knows not where to find Him; and if it seek Him not, to whom else should it go? At least in that beautiful and ancient way, seeking Him, we may ever find Him in the Mass; Himself the reason for, the beginning and the consummation of that ancient and beautiful service which, like some divine hostel, gives us the Bread of Life just for love. And if one may find Him there whose service is perfect freedom, where else can there be liberty that we should seek it out, or why should we come to Him through distracting byways, or do anything but hasten towards Him along the great highway as our fathers have told us?

And again, in thinking of St. Francis of Assisi, it is necessary for us to keep Joachim di Flore in continual remembrance. For though St. Francis was perhaps unconscious of the humanist who divined the modern world in the midst of mystical Italy, at the last his most loyal followers were captured by a philosophy at once so revolutionary and so divine. The Eternal Gospel consumed the simple divinity of him who went barefoot and shared his life with the birds and the sun, to whom man was merely the best-beloved of the thoughts of God. Coming to us then with the most perfect simplicity, with an appeal scarcely less certain than Jesus Himself, St. Francis in his claim to be a son of God only repeats the divine message of Christ. Like a child he sees God and understands the secret of His love. His achievement was neither consciously revolutionary, nor in any sense hostile to the Catholic Church, for he himself was ever her most loyal son; and yet in the perfection of his simplicity, in the clearness and sensitiveness of his conscience, in his immense love for the whole world, he accused her of a kind of compromise, not with evil, perhaps, but with indifference. It seems to have been with a sort of surprise that the Church saw him take Christ at His word. That mediocrity

S

which is the almost certain fate of governments and societies was impossible for him, he was never in danger from it. He is the Jesus of the Middle Age; neither does he hesitate to sweep away the intervening centuries and to take Christ by the hand. He alone of all men dared to understand Him. It has been said of him that he is himself one of the most powerful reasons for believing Jesus to have been divine. For in the love of everything that surrounded him, which claimed the birds as his sisters, and would have rescued even the worms from the indifference of man, which overcame the most brutal natures and made them burn with love, which saw everywhere beauty and intention, and accepted the flowers as not the least of God's gifts, we find the true achievement for once of the teaching of Christ—that perfect love which was to overcome all things and to be a divine wisdom. And it is just here that St. Francis himself, if ever, touches Joachim di Flore. For Joachim the Spirit was of more importance than anything beside; it was the third kingdom, a kind of Paradise that was to be built in the hearts of men freed from the immense superstitions of the intellect. Well, St. Francis in a moment has attained to this state and has conformed his life to it. And he has achieved this victory not by means of knowledge, as Joachim seems to suggest, but by means of love—a love that is free from the possession of anything whatever. For him and his brothers it is a sin to possess anything, not merely because Christ said it was better to be poor than to be rich, but chiefly because those who think they possess things are really always possessed by them. He divines a life fuller and more enjoyable in this perfect liberty; those things which are worth having being not only indivisible but impossible of appropriation. And so by his love, by his acquiescence in the mere rules of the Church, by his humility and simplicity, he achieves all that Joachim had dreamed, in a way how much more lovely. Art, which is the child of Poverty, began to flower on his tomb. And it is almost to that sacred place, as holy for the Humanist as for the Religious, that we may trace all that is really worth having in the ages which have followed his death. Pietro Cavallini and his school, Giotto and his pupils, recreated Italian Art in his honour and because of him. Dante was his son. What is there to be said in religion that he has not understood and expressed in his life?

And to-day in England, for instance, how absurd would his life appear to us! Indifferent alike to the kingdom of the Spirit that captured the imagination of Joachim, and to Poverty whom St. Francis married, we, immersed in business, not for its own sake but for the sake of gain, in order that we may accumulate trifles; our material needs increasing every moment, our spiritual sensitiveness decreasing ever faster and faster as we. gain riches; in that little yellow desert of gold which we have created as our indestructible prison, look on St. Francis as a kind of lunatic. But the beauty which surrounds him always, the art which sprang from his tomb, we shall never possess. Bankrupt in spirit, without art, without a peasantry, without an aristocracy, but with an ever-increasing multitude happy in their mediocrity, as we walk over our hills black with smoke, while still Umbria is golden in the sun, or down the streets of our trumpery and hideous cities, it is not love but hate that possesses our souls. Kings and princes, poets and monks, republics and peasants, having in the past created our world, built up our civilisation, given us our art and our history, it might seem that we, grubbing for gold, lying and cheating, and immersed in business, may destroy it utterly in our con-tempt of anything that is not mediocre, or to be bought with money. This is an age of business men, an age of grocers and clerks, and I have yet to learn that such have given us anything worth having. As we walk over the Umbrian hills in a country still blessedly poor, among a people still noble, that has not forgotten how to fight, or to suffer, or to pray, it is strange to think how natural St. Francis would seem even to-day in Assisi, how impossible in London or New York, contented in their desperate mediocrity with that part of life which, since they never see the sun, is scarcely worth having at all.

XXVI

ST. FRANCIS OF ASSISI

IN M. Sabatier's life of St. Francis of Assisi there is much
which only an exquisite and loving care, a patient and
profound scholarship, could have divined, as it were, in the
lovely but fragmentary legend of his life. During many
years devoted to the study of the life of the little poor
man of Assisi, M. Sabatier has gradually made clear for us
those things which were hidden and obscure, throwing a new
light on that life of peculiar perfection, so that he seems to
suggest that under all the beauty and sweetness that have led
men to think of St. Francis as an imitation of Christ there
lies the revolutionary, the progressive reformer, intent on his
own freedom of spirit and the liberty of the hearts of men.
And whatever we may think of so new a reading of the
parable of St. Francis's life, we are from the first surprised to
find one whom we had always considered as the most humble
of saints suddenly converted into a kind of divine schismatic,
an amiable Martin Luther at least in his intention, accusing
the Church, rather by his conduct, it would seem, than by his
teaching, of the betrayal of mankind into a kind of slavery
from which he, the little poor man, would set it free. Words
of his trenchant enough to justify this impression are not
recorded, and would have been out of keeping with a genius
of which one characteristic is its supreme obedience. It
would seem that he never exercised his own judgment without a certain hesitation, or if he did, how many times he

has reproached himself! And, indeed, if we are to accept M. Sabatier's view of this saint of an alien religion, we must ever after think of St. Francis as really a failure, seeing that he was able neither to overthrow the authority of the Church which established his Order, nor to take a single step without her approbation. But, to an eye less keen, a criticism less revolutionary, St. Francis might seem to be the last man to create schism. Out of his austerity and strength came sweetness, not destruction; not denial, but the lovely affirmation of the promises of Christ. He was not concerned with the tremendous politics of the Catholic Church, but in the dust and dirt he found the lilies of her love. For the real revolution, for which St. Francis worked, was a resurrection of love among men. He, too, with St. John, seems ever to repeat, 'Little children, love one another.' If this ancient and orthodox teaching may confound the Church, then, indeed, St. Francis was her enemy; but he who loved even the poorest and the most wretched would have been the last to embrace that Mother who had taught him all he knew, and introduced him, as it were, to Him who was ever his pattern, in any hasty or ridiculous anathema.

The Middle Age, that poetic period—poetic as we see it, perhaps, a little ideally—really comes to an end, is, as it were, summed up, in St. Francis. It was an age of great passions, of the most splendid enthusiasm, profoundly humorous and merry, too, in a way that the Reformation and Renaissance, in the North at any rate, have for ever made impossible. And even as Raphael seems to sum up, and by a certain divinity in his nature to save the age of the Renaissance from itself almost, so St. Francis is, as it were, the saviour of those dreamy years that went before him; in him they seem to find their true interpreter; by him they are saved from a charge of brutality that without his life it might not be easy to deny. So we seem ever to find him passing up and down those Umbrian roads, in the vineyards, or in the olive gardens, or upon the mountains, singing his French songs by the way, laughing and weeping a little in the sunshine, at one with Nature and with God; since in every flower of the field there was some divinity, in every delicate, serene day a suggestion of His perfection, while the crested larks ceaselessly praised Him, and the cool beauty of the night was, as it were, only a fragment of that silence which surrounds Him always.

Born in 1182, the son of wealthy parents, St. Francis was named Giovanni at the font of S. Rufino, the Cathedral Church of Assisi, while his father was away on a journey, possibly to Lyons, to sell cloth or silk; it was only on his return that he was renamed by him 'Il Francesco,' the little Frenchman. Educated by his father, not only as became a merchant, but to some extent as became a fine gentleman of the day, Francis appears first to have turned his thoughts towards Heaven from a world that he ever found gay, after a long illness. It was from this time that we find him with 'no relish but for solitude and prayer.' A sudden dislike of all that rather brutal life which had so fascinated him—the encounters in the streets, the vanishing loves of the twilight, itself not less swift in its passing than those facile affections, the brightness of war, the long days full of just amusement —seems to have come to him in his convalescence, so that those first days in which he was free from physical suffering were a kind of purification, or new birth. The past seems to have fallen away from him, to have receded into a dim perspective, and in his first encounter with Nature, with the woods and the fields, after so helpless a time in the dark, he was cleansed, returning to the simplest things, as indeed one is so ready to do in those mystical days of recovery from sickness, when the heart opens so frankly to the sunlight and all the delicate things of spring, the rain and the flowers.

But it would appear that with perfect health something of the old desire for life, for what he understood life to be, returned to him, and it is as on the eve of departure for some entrancing adventure that we see him suddenly stopped by a vision, as it is said, so that he had only gone as far as Spoleto when he determined to return, making his way back to Assisi to the surprise of every one. It is as though he has suddenly heard a voice calling him, calling him, so that after many hours of seclusion he is observed by his friends to be pale, and attentive, as it were, to some invisible friend or companion, and ever after he is strange to them. In their happy, inconsequent, thoughtless lives, it is only love, they think, some fantastic passion less fleeting than usual, that can have absorbed him so from the life about which he used to be so eager.

'Thou art in love,' they tell him. 'Go to, Francesco is about to take a wife.' But it was a wife more mysterious and lovely by far than any they had dreamed of for him that he is about to wed. 'Yes, I shall take a wife,' he says, 'more beautiful and more pure than you can imagine.' But he spoke of Lady Poverty. And, indeed, in those silent fields about Assisi, littered with flowers and musical with many waters, a mind less mystical than St. Francis's might well have been charmed with the thought of a wandering life, the freedom of just that; that not here but in heaven have we any place of abiding, any real treasure worth having; it is there, perhaps, that we come upon the true impulse of his life, as it was certainly the one revolutionary idea in his simple rule. And we find this joy in a life of wandering, the delights of the road, the surprise always to be found in that sort of life in the word 'to-morrow,' the love of strange sights and men, manifest in him in a pilgrimage he appears to have made about this time to Rome. He went, or at least returned, as a simple pilgrim begging his way, and in this real encounter with poverty, an intercourse voluntary and made for love with those who depend for very life on the 'charity or caprice' of the passer-by, he seems at last to have found happiness, so that the gloom which had over-shadowed him ever since his illness is finally dispersed, and ever after we think of him as possessed of a great cheerful-ness, which later did so much to transform Christian asceti-cism, giving it something of his own, something perhaps that it really lacked until his day, and has lost since.

It was one day in St. Damian's Church without the walls of Assisi, that, kneeling before a Crucifix, he heard again a voice—that voice which creeps into the lives of all the saints as that mighty river winds through the valleys of Umbria—saying thrice over: 'Francis, go and repair my house which thou seest falling'; for even in those days the church was very old and frail, haunted by innumerable unavailing prayers and unworthy petitions. And coming home he, without thought of evil, overwhelmed by that implacable voice, 'took a horse-load of cloth out of his father's warehouse, and sold it together with the horse' at Foligno, a town some twelve miles from Assisi. So he came back to St. Damian's Church with the money, which he offered to the priest, who, however, refused it, laying it on the window-sill; but the priest, though old and poor, seems to have seen something divine in the young man after all, for he permitted him to stay with him and loved him. But Peter Bernardone, the father of Francis, came to St. Damian's Church angry because of the loss of his cloth and of his horse, but finding the money laid on the window-sill he grew calmer, though he did not forbear to denounce his son as a madman, in which the townspeople seem to have agreed with him. And later Bernardone, attracted by the noise of the children pursuing a beggar through the streets with cries of 'Pazzo, Pazzo,' discovers his son in that wretched one whom they persecute. So he compelled him to come home, and having bound him, he locked him into a closet, but his mother set him free when his father was gone. Thus the story of St. Francis begins with an unusual touch of everyday humour, none the less charming on that account, since the saints as a rule early put humour away from them with life.

And St. Francis, freed by the love of his mother, returned to St. Damian's straight, where after a time his father found him; and when he had found him he demanded that he should return home, or forgo his inheritance. For a moment that patience which so rarely deserted him seems to have been insufficient for him, for he replied that he was no longer under the government of his father. M. Sabatier seems to suggest that he may at this time have already received minor Orders, but he has no evidence to support his view; and, indeed, it might seem that St. Francis meant that he was already in the service of God, and must be about his Father's business. However this may be, we find him appealing to the ecclesiastical power. Before the bishop, who, as well may be, was astonished no less at the severity of the father than at the eagerness of the son for poverty, and appears therefore to have hesitated, St. Francis, impatient of delay, 'stripped himself of his clothes and gave them to his father, saying cheerfully and meekly, "Hitherto I have called you father on earth, but now I say with more confidence *Pater noster qui es in cœlis*, in whom I place all my hope and treasure."' The good bishop, somewhat overcome by the remarkable action and fervour of the youth, and for the sake of Lady Modesty, gave Francis his cloak for the moment, and later procured that of his servant for him, which Francis signed in chalk with the Holy Cross and cheerfully accepted as his first alms. Thus St. Francis renounced the world and set out for heaven, being about twenty-five years old.

And it was now in the wonderful spring, which is so loth

to go in Umbria, that he took to the hills singing on his way. In the sunshine of that silent world what dreams, poetical and mysteriously sweet, came to him we may not know. Only that they were of a certain strange beauty is most sure; for while in the mountains, he fell among thieves, who demanded of him who he was; and he made answer, 'I am the herald of the Great King, but what is that to thee?' And, having stripped him, they cast him into a ditch, saying, 'There is thy place, poor herald of God.' And when he had come to himself he went on his way, all naked as he was, singing through the forest till he came to a monastery, where he was permitted to serve in the kitchen; but they gave him nothing, so that he left them, and having a friend in Gubbio across the mountains, he journeyed so far, and received some clothes and at once set out for St. Damian's.

St. Francis now began to beg money to repair St. Damian's; and having collected a little, he with his own hands helped to carry the stones, and so repaired the church. It was about this time that he began to visit the lepers, whom even as a youth he had so pitied. And it was at this time also that he went to La Porziuncula, a little chapel nearly two miles from Assisi, belonging to the Benedictines of Subiaco. When St. Francis came there on that morning in 1207 he found it in an utterly ruinous condition, almost unfit either for service or dwelling. He immediately set himself to repair it, which he did before the year was out. And it happened that as he knelt one morning in that little chapel while a monk from Subasio said Mass, the words of the Gospel were those with which Christ sent forth His disciples; and for the second time he heard that voice, loving and mysterious with so great a sweetness and yet not without a certain severity: 'Take nothing for your journey, neither staves nor scrip, neither bread, neither money; neither have two coats apiece.'

And it was this one coat, girt.with a rough cord, that in the next year, 1208, he gave to his disciples as their habit, when first Bernard, a rich man of Assisi, and then Peter, and then Giles, 'a person of great simplicity and virtue,' joined him as his brethren in his cell at Porziuncola. Nor was it in any melancholy spirit that these simple persons came together and separated themselves from the world and its possessions, but rather with a great cheerfulness. They went singing through the fields, so that they came to be known as Joculatores Domini—God's joyful ones, or jesters—as they laboured with the peasants in the fields or praised God at evensong. He who thus with so much joy had penetrated into the most secret places of the hearts of men preferred always happiness to unhappiness, the simple delight in the beauty of the world to the mysterious dislike of earthly things, since heaven was so much the more splendid, which overtook so many of the Saints. Well, it is not perhaps a mark of anything but Catholicism, that 'making a fool of oneself for God,' which is not infrequent in St. Francis's life. In the service of the world his sons despised what they served, and yet loved it too because they served it. Nor in spite of their antics had they anything in common with Puritanism, that most hateful of all heresies; for the sign and mark of true vocation was a certain *joie de vivre*, not without its tragic moments, which we so often find in the lives of his followers.

It was in 1209 that St. Francis set out for Rome, and obtained there a verbal approbation of his Order from Innocent III. This great Pope had at that time already sat for twelve years upon the throne of St. Peter. A man of immense authority, he had brought low the King of England not less easily than he had humbled King Pedro of Aragon, who had laid his very crown upon the tomb of the Apostle in token of his submission. The first Latin perhaps of the modern world to raise the cry 'Italia! Italia!' he was not less great as a reformer of the Church than as a statesman; for even as he made the Papacy a great political power, 'in some sort the suzerain of the Emperor,' so by 'his indomitable firmness in defending morality and law' he was able to gain a certain moral strength which was both useful as a weapon of political warfare and lovely for its own sake. A great Pope of a great ambition, certainly the greatest statesman in Europe in his day, he was by no means the mere politician certain Protestant historians of the life of St. Francis have tried to prove him. That he did not immediately approve of the somewhat vague Rule which St. Francis submitted to him, consisting as it did of certain texts from the Gospel, is not surprising. For many years he had been busy suppressing ecclesiastical disorders, and when suddenly asked to approve of a new congregation which must, so far as he could see, subsist by mendicancy—as indeed it came to do, since it had no possessions of any sort, desired none, and forbade the possession of any property whatsoever, either by the congregation itself or by any individual member of it—Innocent III. may well be excused for a certain hesitation.

It may be well here to traverse certain statements made by M. Sabatier in his *Vie de S. François d'Assise.* While protesting my admiration at the devotion and scholarship of this Protestant writer, it is yet with a certain hesitation one accepts his conclusions, seeing that he so evidently fails to understand Mysticism and the Catholic religion. St. Francis, for him, is a kind of rebel against authority, a kind of heretic whom the Catholic Church thought best to conciliate and afterwards to destroy. Words of his, strong enough to warrant this conclusion, may be found in his book, *Vie de S. François.* It is there he says that it would have needed very little for the Franciscans to meet the same fate at the hands of Innocent III. as the Waldenses had from Lucius III. But we find that from the first moment in which St. Francis was introduced into the Pope's presence by Cardinal Giovanni di S. Paolo, he met with nothing but sympathy from Innocent. 'My dear children,' the Pope said, 'your life appears to me to be too severe; I see, indeed, that your fervour is too great for any doubt of you to be possible, but I ought to consider those who shall come after you, lest your mode of life should be beyond your strength.' It was in these words, surely not without a certain fatherly kindness, that the Pope suspended judgment. Nor is it surprising that no definite decision was come to at once. In every question of importance, Rome, realising her immense responsibility, has refused to decide on the instant; it was the same with the Dominican Order, with the Society of Jesus, and with the Franciscans, and although M. Sabatier can see little but defiance in St. Francis's parable of the woman who was very poor but beautiful and the great king, to a mind less prejudiced against the Catholic Church there might seem to be less defiance than humility. Nor does the account we have of St. Francis, prostrate at the Pope's feet, 'promising the most perfect obedience with all his heart,' seem consistent with any attitude of defiance that the enemies of the Church Catholic, as of him, have sought, as we may think in vain, to find in his heart. And we see the Pope, who was so powerful and strong a shepherd of the Church, blessing him, saying : 'Go, my brethren, and may God be with you. Preach penitence to every one according as the Lord may deign to inspire you. Then when the All-powerful shall have made you multiply and go forward you will refer to Us ; We will concede what you ask, and We may then with greater security accord to you even more than you ask.'

Nor was it in any spirit of hostility to the Priesthood that St. Francis conceived his mission to the world. That he himself never became a priest argues his humility rather than his contempt or hatred of those who alone could administer the Sacraments, things of very little account to Protestant or Agnostic to-day, but of an immense importance to all Christians in the twelfth and thirteenth centuries. Francis claimed no freedom for himself or his companions from the duty of confession, as Molinos, the unhappy Spaniard, did later. He himself, like S. Teresa, must ever have been under the direction of a confessor; and, indeed, the respect due to the clergy was the subject of his frequent counsels to his disciples, so that we find him telling them that a priest should not be met except they kiss his hands. And so it is a little confusing to find a scholar like M. Sabatier, to whom we owe so much, suggesting that the religion of St. Francis was, as it were, quite independent of the priest; summing up his argument in an unhappy and confused comparison, a little rhetorical, of Christ who first ordered that high dignity, that so chargeable office, to the little Saint of Assisi; finding the likeness of Him who was the Son of God to him who was so perfect an imitation of Him in the strangely sentimental heresy that Christ 'came to preach a worship in spirit and in truth, without priest or temple, or rather that every fireside shall be a temple and every believer a priest.'

Nor is it only in an attitude of mind a little unsympathetic towards government and authority, those splendid and classical virtues of the Roman Church, that we seem to find M. Sabatier at fault. His apprehension of Mysticism is imperfect, for we find him making a statement so extraordinary as the following must of necessity appear to any student of the lives of the Saints. 'Francis, he says, 'is of the race of mystics, *for* no intermediary comes between God and his soul.' It would be sufficient to examine very briefly the experience of so mystical a soul as St. Teresa to expose the superficial reasoning, the profound fallacy of such a statement. It might seem that since all action is the result of ideas, whether consciously apprehended or not, it is necessary if we would understand the lives of the Saints to make sure of what their ideas were, of what they believed. And since, indeed, I find no phenomena in any other company of those who call themselves Christians comparable for a moment to the lives of the Saints, it might seem that some idea peculiar to the Catholic Church informed their minds— an idea strange and lovely and altogether different from those which have led in the end to any other form of action, religion, science, or philosophy. And I find this idea so full of vitality, from which beauty so naturally ensued, to have been the claim of the Catholic Church to be in possession of a supernatural religion. To her, absolute truth is revealed; nor is she, since she remembers the promises of Christ, amazed at the miracle. To believe, is for her and for her children an act of submission to authority, while to any other Christian is it not a kind of conscious choice, among many astonishing possibilities, necessarily subject to all the ailments of the reason to which in the end man becomes the slave, howsoever imperfect it may be? And so at last we understand that while the Catholic is content with the authority of the Church, believing indeed that it is sufficient for all occasions since Christ has promised He shall not fail her, the Protestant or the Agnostic is dependent either on the indestructibility of a book that is already falling to pieces, or on his reason warped by its own inherent deformity after centuries of struggle and prejudice, by innumerable circumstances that have enslaved it, by to-day's delight or to-morrow's sickness; and at last when he is conscious of the merely brutal and destructive capabilities of this imperfect instrument, he is compelled to take refuge in a kind of spiritual nihilism, eager to deny that he knows anything but

that he must die, that he apprehends anything save that
tedious journey from the brute, which he is even now in the
midst of, travelling as he is from no whither that he may
know, nor even yet in any place of abiding, since even now
he is stepping forward to some goal, to some resting-place, of
whose satisfaction he is not sure; inexplicable alike to himself and to his fellows, finding in that brutal confusion a kind
of delightful mystery, an irresponsibility, which seems to
place him a little further from the final achievement of the
simplicity of all those things that yet await the hand of the
creator, a little nearer to that brute creation with whom he
shares the world.

And indeed, since such an one is not sure of God Himself,
how is it possible that he should apprehend even for a
moment that 'annihilation in God,' which is the informing
desire of all the Mystics? It is just there that M. Sabatier,
who for the most part has shown us so exquisitely St.
Francis as he lived, fails us. His own reason is his enemy,
so infirm that it is incapable even of apprehending anything
contrary to experience; he is unable to concede the intervention of God, Whom he prefers to call the 'first cause,' in
any particular case at all. It is not surprising that he
falters over the story of the Stigmata; indeed, it is only
surprising that he should have attempted to deal at all with
a life so full of that 'intervention of God' as the life of
St. Francis. And so when we find St. Francis glorified as a
kind of rebel, a little scornful of the clergy, anxious to
approach God in any way rather than by means of the
Church, or eager to withstand a Pope so strong and excellent
as Innocent III.,[1] we shall understand that so beautiful was
his life, so full of humanism and love, so altogether lovely,
that the officers of every rebel sect or schism in Christendom
are anxious to claim him from the Church which signed him

[1] 'A Pontiff so just,' says Piccotti, 'that neither friend nor foe
has ever said a word against him.'

T

with the Cross at the font, gave him his first prayers, fed him with the Bread of Life, taught him all he knew, aided him in his work, comforted him in his sorrow, upheld him at the last, and buried him with tears when he died, setting him among her Saints; and to-day as for hundreds of years she invokes his prayers, while his sons are her sons, his daughters her daughters, his God her God, now as then, nor shall the avarice of a thousand starving heresies ever deprive her of him or him of her.

For indeed to understand the spirit of this man—so like to Christ as to have seemed to be almost a reincarnation of Him, so that the legend tells us that he was born in a stable as was our Lord, and other things too they had in common— is to possess oneself of one of the most beautiful things in the world. His body we are told he called Brother Ass, because it must bear great burdens and be beaten, and rest but of necessity. Everything and every sort of animal in the world were to him brethren or sisters. Thus the sun, the moon, and the stars, the fishes, the birds, and the flowers, are as it were only perhaps more attentive members than ourselves of the family of God. A profound humanist in the best sense of the word, he in that rough and rude age had in more than one way, as it were, anticipated the Renaissance. 'Know, dear brother,' he says to his companion, 'that courtesy is one of the qualities of God Himself, Who of His courtesy giveth His sun and His rain to the just and the unjust; and courtesy is the sister of charity, the which quencheth hate and keepeth love alive.'

It was in March 1212 that St. Francis met Clare, the daughter of Favorino Sciffi, a knight of noble family, she having run from home to Porziuncula, where St. Francis dwelt with his companions. Before the high altar St. Francis gave her the penitential habit, and there being as yet no Franciscan convent, he sent her to the Benedictine nunnery of St. Paul. Thus was founded the congregation of Poor Clares so famous throughout the world.

It was about this time too that St. Francis set out for Palestine, thinking that the Gospel had but to be 'announced' to the Saracens who held the Holy City and they would be converted. But this strange mission was to come to nothing, St. Francis being wrecked on the coast of Slavonia; and having come to shore he returned to Italy, landing it would seem at Ancona, where he began to preach on his way back to Assisi. And coming to the lake of Perugia, called Trasimeno, he passed Lent there on an island alone. The author of the *Fioretti* tells the tale very simply and beautifully.

'It befell on a time,' he says, 'that St. Francis, on the day of carnival, being hard by the lake of Perugia in the house of one of his devoted followers, with the which he had lodged the night, was inspired. of God that he should go and keep that Lent on an island in the lake; wherefore St. Francis besought this devoted follower that, for the love of Christ, he would carry him across in his little boat to an island on the lake, wherein no man dwelt, and that so he would do upon the night of Ash Wednesday, so that none might be ware of it; so he for love of the great devotion that he had unto St. Francis, with diligence fulfilled his request and carried him across to the island aforesaid, and St. Francis took with him naught save two small loaves. And being come unto the island, and his friend parting himself to go back home, St. Francis besought him tenderly that to no man would he reveal in what guise he there abode, and that save upon Holy Thursday he would not come to him; and so he ran away. And St. Francis remained alone: and sith there was no dwelling-place whereunto he might betake him, he entered into a close thicket which many a thorny bush and shrub had fashioned like a cave or little hut:

and in this place he gave himself up to prayer and contemplation of the things of heaven. And there he abode all the Lent, nor eating nor drinking aught save half of one of those small loaves, even as was found by his devoted follower on Holy Thursday what time that he came back to him; who found of the two loaves one still entire, but of the other, half. So men believe that St. Francis took no food from reverence for the fast of Christ, the blessed one, who fasted forty days and forty nights without partaking of any earthly food; but in this manner with that half a loaf chased far the venom of vain glory from him, and after the pattern of Christ kept fast for forty days and forty nights; and thereafter in that place where St. Francis had wrought such wondrous abstinence, through his merits did God work many miracles; for the which cause did men begin to build houses there and dwell therein; and in brief space uprose a hamlet fair and great, and therewithal a house for the brothers, the which is named the House of the Island; and even to this day the men and women of that hamlet have great reverence and devotion for the place where St. Francis kept the aforesaid Lent.'[1]

During that same year, 1213,[2] he appears to have been in Romagna, where he met a certain Conte Orlando dei Cattani, who being moved as much, it might seem, by the personality of St. Francis as by the words that he spoke, gave him a certain mountain, 'especially favourable to contemplation,' called La Verna, in Tuscany. It may be that St. Francis was not able to visit this lonely and beautiful place till 1224, as the author of *Fioretti* gives us that date, though he states that it was in that year too that Conte Orlando gave La Verna to St. Francis.

---

[1] *The Little Flowers of St. Francis*, newly translated out of the Italian by T. W. Arnold, London, 1900, pp. 23-25.

[2] Sabatier, *op. cit.*, p. 400.

However that may be, this period of his life is confessedly obscure. A certain pessimism and despair seems to have obscured his vision of life for a time, for we read of him as doubting what he ought to do; whether to give himself wholly unto prayer, or whether, at least in part, to devote himself to preaching. A certain desire for the contemplative life, as he found it among the Benedictines, seems to have possessed him, and it was only at the earnest entreaty of St. Clare and Father Silvestro that he continued his work of preaching and evangelisation. For it is God's will, they tell him, that he shall go throughout the whole world to preach, 'since He hath chosen thee not for thyself alone, but also for the salvation of others.' So he seems to have set out in no little haste, and coming to Bevagna, preached to the birds, as may be seen in many a pleasant fresco up and down Italy. A profound pantheism and love for all God's creatures, in whom since He created them the seeing eye may discern something of the Creator, is one of the chief characteristics of St. Francis. Nor was his love for these creatures of God confined to those among them whom we in our dull vulgarity alone think of as living. He had a great love for fire. 'Brother Fire, noble and useful among all the creatures,' as he says when, being nearly blind, the physician is about to burn his eyes, 'be gentle to me in this hour, for I have always held thee in love, and shall ever do so for love of Him who created thee.' And his praise of the sun is surely one of the immortal verses in the great poetry of the world. 'Praised be thou, Lord, for all thy creatures,' he says, 'and especially for my Brother the Sun which gives us the day, and by him thou showest thy light. He is beautiful, shining with great splendour; and of thee, O Most High, he is the symbol.'

His life was a great romance, full of a profound Humanism, that he had attained not by means of the intellect, but by Love. He is a triumphant vindication of the truth of

Christian ethics. Hardly able to read, unlearned in any way, ignorant alike of music and of painting, he is yet a complete Humanist—wise enough, temperate enough, to own at last that it may well be he has been less than fair to his Brother the Body. 'He had ever a tender pity for all gentle creatures,' one of his old biographers tells us. It is the burden of his whole life; so that he speaks of the birds as his sisters, and of the wolf as his brother. Nor was he without an understanding of Nature in her less kindly moods, for he feels the terror lurking in a great forest, the fear of loneliness among the shadows of the great musical trees, or upon the mountains, and is only really happy among the byways, where he goes singing his French songs fulfilled with joy in the sunshine and in the rain.

It may well be that St. Francis met St. Dominic in Rome in 1215. They can have had but little in common. For St. Dominic the earth has already ceased to exist; he finds there no beauty at all, only a kind of prison from which the soul is ever striving to be free—that soul for which in the end he will sacrifice everything, in whose service he will torture the body, or burn the very world, that it may attain a kind of cold perfection under authority. It is rather a new system of education that he introduces into the world than a new idea, a reconciliation of all that old Asiatic asceticism with learning, so that in the end the soul may have, as it were, even more to renounce. And poet though he is, it is of Heaven and the Blessed Virgin he sings rather than of the sun or the birds, or the happiness of life. He is a true Spaniard. Those arid and tawny deserts, perhaps the most terrible and ardent country of the world, have robbed him of everything but a great desire for slavery; and so when he meets St. Francis, it is as one who has already submitted to authority with a kind of voluptuous joy. And while we may regard St. Francis as a Humanist, as a joyous knight in the service of humanity, simple and unconscious of anything but love, we find St. Dominic, already a little dazed with visions, a little mad with the sensuality of words, looking on mankind as a herd of desperate souls who must be enslaved by the promises of Christ, by the immense future of the Church. And yet they had thus much in common, that they were both dreamers—the one absorbed in the future of Christianity, the other in the future of man; and it is told how that as they were about to part from one another in Rome, St. Dominic, anxious it might seem for one more submission, begged St. Francis that he would give him the cord wherewith he was girded, the which he ever after wore under his habit. 'At length the one did place his hands between the hands of the other, and each did most sweetly commend him to each in mutual farewell greeting. And St. Dominic said unto St. Francis: "Brother Francis, I would that thy Religion and mine should be made one, and that we should live in the Church under equal conditions."' No answer is recorded by the author of the *Speculum Perfectionis* to this strange request. St. Francis perhaps understood the insatiable ambition of St. Dominic, an ambition that was by no means personal or unworthy, for conquest. Profoundly as the Dominicans transformed the Franciscan Order after the death of St. Francis, in his lifetime they were powerless to influence it. Had St. Francis agreed to that strange request how much poorer the world would have been, how much less various the centuries!

In 1219 was held at La Porziuncula the great Chapter called 'of Matts,' because, being very numerous, it was impossible to find a building in which it might assemble, so tents and booths were set up in the fields. So great had the Order grown that it is said more than five thousand friars came to this general Chapter. It would appear that it was about this time that certain disorders and modifica-

tions of the Rule began to show themselves. St. Francis
who was in the East is reported dead, a messenger is sent
to him imploring his return. He appears to have arrived
at Venice, July 1220.¹ Something of these disorders may
be found in the *Speculum Perfectionis*, and M. Sabatier gives us
a letter, found in Cap. 6 of the Rule of the Damianites, in
which St. Francis again asserts his purpose.

'I, little Brother Francis, desire to follow the life and the
poverty of Jesus Christ, our most high Lord, and of His
most holy Mother, persevering therein until the end; and
I beg you all and exhort you to persevere always in this
most holy life and poverty, and take good care never to
depart from it upon the advice or teachings of any one
whomsoever.'

And at last his life of action is over; ever after he is
compelled to be just a kind of peacemaker among his own
children. It was such a crisis as the Pope had foreseen,
perhaps, when St. Francis first asked him for an approbation
of his Rule. How is it possible, many had begun to ask,
to live without possessions? The freedom which St. Francis
had understood was only attainable through poverty, that
immense influence in the hearts of men, to be acquired by
possessing nothing, was really gone for ever. The next
few years are devoted to an attempt to fix his idea upon
his Order. We see him in many an exquisite moment
with St. Clare, with the mysterious and beautiful 'Brother
Jacoba,' that sorrowful Roman lady who loved him, with
Brother Leo and the rest, always a little overcome by the
passionate strength of that which he had created. In
those years he becomes almost a contemplative, condemned
by his own thoughts, dreaming of the Passion of Jesus
Christ, the divine figure that had inspired and sustained
his whole life.

¹ Sabatier, *op. cit.*, p. 229.

It was about the time of the Feast of the Exaltation of the Holy Cross in September 1224, that St. Francis made his retreat on Monte La Verna, and there received the Stigmata from our Lord Jesus Christ. Conte Orlando had given that mountain to him as early as 1215, and so it was that St. Francis came to make his retreat there in the sorrowful years of his life, before the Feast of the Exaltation of the Cross.

He being alone was wont to say Matins with Brother Leo, who, in order to see whether or no St. Francis wished his company in prayer, used to cry out, *Domine, labia mea aperies*—'O Lord, open thou my lips'—when he drew near that place where St. Francis was. But on this morning St. Francis made him no answer, and contrary to St. Francis's desire, but with the very best of intentions, dear little brother Leo crossed the bridge over the chasm which you may see to this day, and entered into St. Francis's cell. There he found Francis in ecstasy, saying, 'Who art thou, O most sweet my God? What am I, most vile worm and thine unprofitable servant?' Again and again Brother Leo heard him repeat these words. And wondering thereat, he lifted his eyes to the sky, and saw there among the stars, for it was dark, a torch of flame very beautiful and bright, which, coming down from the sky, rested on St. Francis's head. So thinking himself unworthy to behold so sweet a vision, 'he softly turned away for to go to his cell again. And as he was going softly, deeming himself unseen, St. Francis was aware of him by the rustling of the leaves under his feet.' Surely even to the most doubtful, that sound of the rustling leaves must bring conviction? And St. Francis explains to Brother Leo all that this might mean.

'. . . And as he thus continued a long time in prayer, he came to know that God would hear him, and that so far as was possible for the mere creature, so far would it be granted him to feel the things aforesaid. . . . And as he was thus set on fire in his contemplation on that same morn, he saw descend from heaven a Seraph with six wings resplendent and aflame, and as with swift flight the Seraph drew nigh unto St. Francis so that he could discern him, he clearly saw that he bore in him the image of a man crucified : and his wings were in such guise displayed, that two wings were spread above his head, and two were spread out to fly, and other two covered all his body. Seeing this, St. Francis was sore adread, and was filled at once with joy and grief and marvel. He felt glad at the gracious look of Christ, who appeared to him so lovingly, and gazed on him so graciously ; but on the other hand, seeing him crucified upon the Cross, he felt immeasurable grief for pity's sake. . . . Then the whole Mount of Alvernia appeared as though it burned with bright shining flames, that lit up all the mountains and valleys round as though it had been the sun upon the earth ; whereby the shepherds that were keeping watch in those parts, seeing the mountain of flame and so great a light around, had exceeding great fear, according as they after-wards told unto the brothers, declaring that this flame rested upon the Mount of Alvernia for the space of an hour and more. In like manner at the bright shining of this light, which through the windows lit up the hostels of the country round, certain muleteers that were going into Romagna arose, believing that the day had dawned, and saddled and laded their beasts : and going on their way, they saw the said light die out and the material sun arise. In the seraphic vision, Christ, the which appeared to him, spake to St. Francis certain high and secret things, the which St. Francis in his lifetime desired not to reveal to any man ; but after his life was done, he did reveal them as is set forth below ; and the words were these:

"Knowest thou," said Christ, ' what it is that I have done unto thee? I have given thee the Stigmata that are the signs of my Passion, to the end that thou mayest be my standard-bearer. And even as on the day of my death I descended into hell and brought out thence all souls that I found there by reason of these, my Stigmata, even so do I grant to thee that every year on the day of thy death thou shalt go to Purgatory, and in virtue of thy Stigmata shalt bring out thence all the souls of thy three Orders, to wit, Minors, Sisters, Continents, and likewise others that shall have had a great devotion for thee, and shalt lead them unto the glory of Paradise, to the end that thou mayest be conformed to me in death as thou art in life." Then this marvellous image vanished away, and left in the heart of St. Francis a burning ardour and flame of love divine ; and in his flesh a marvellous image and copy of the Passion of Christ. For straightway in the hands and feet of St. Francis began to appear the marks of the nails in such wise as he had seen them in the body of Jesus Christ the Crucified, the which had shown Himself to him in the likeness of a seraph : and then his hands and feet appeared to be pierced through the middle with nails, and the heads of them were in the palms of his hands and the soles of his feet outside the flesh, and their points came out on the back of his hands and of his feet, so that they seemed bent back and rivetted in such a fashion that under the bend and rivetting, which all stood out above the flesh, might easily be put a finger of the hand as a ring : and the heads of the nails were round and black. Likewise in the right side appeared the image of a wound made by a lance, unhealed and red and bleeding, the which afterwards oftentimes dropped blood from the sacred breast of St. Francis, and stained with blood his tunic and his hose.'.

It was thus that St. Francis received the Stigmata. Nor

is there any reason to doubt the writer of the *Fioretti*. That St. Francis actually received the Stigmata is as certain as any other fact of history, and far better attested than most. 'Ces paroles,' says M. Sabatier in defending the authenticity of Fra Masseo's letter, in which are found these words of St. Francis: 'Farewell, thou mountain of God, thou holy mount,—Mons coagulatus, Mons pinguis, Mons in quo beneplacitum est Deo habitare,'—'Ces paroles ont dû véritablement être prononcées par lui.'

No long time after St. Francis came to die—lame from the sacred wounds, and ill and weary at last. No longer as in his youth could he sing those French songs in the byways and olive-gardens around Assisi. We catch a glimpse of him in the convent garden of St. Clare, under the shade of the olive-trees in a summer of drought; and again carried in a litter by his companions on the way from Assisi to S. Maria degli Angeli, he bids them halt that he may bless the city before he dies. It is ever thus I seem to see him, broken and feeble and yet beautiful withal, turning to bless the city that had laughed at him so long ago.

Was it at evening or in the dawn that he saw the little city at the foot of the beautiful mountain for the last time? And indeed the words in which he blessed her are not the least lovely of his life: 'Blessed be thou of God, O holy city, seeing that through thee shall many souls be saved, and in thee shall dwell many servants of the Lord; and out of thee shall many be chosen for the kingdom of eternal life.' And they carried him to St. Mary of the Angels.

Of the three women who loved him, Pica his mother, Clare Sciffi the nun, and the Lady Jacoba, but one was with him when he died—the Lady Jacoba. That she loved him, who will doubt? Have we not all loved him in our fashion? Is he not dearer to us than any other hero of romance? And it is, as I think, while she held his hands, having kissed him many times, that he was content to let his spirit go free, while those crested larks he had so loved sang him up to heaven and praised him to the angels. 'Lady Jacoba di Sentensoli of Rome, who was the greatest lady of her time in Rome, and had a great devotion unto St. Francis, both before he died and after his death, both saw and kissed these wounds many times with much reverence, because by divine revelation she came from Rome to Assisi for to be present at the death of St. Francis, the which befell in this wise. . . . For St. Francis called unto him one of his companions and said unto him: "Brother, most dear, God hath revealed to me that from this sickness on such a day I shall pass away from this life; now thou wottest that the beloved Lady Jacoba di Sentensoli, who is so devoted to our Order, would be sore grieving if she heard of my death and had not herself been present: whereby send her word that if she would see me alive again, let her come here straightway." Replied the brother: "Father, thou hast well said; for of very sooth for the great devotion that she bears thee, it would not at all be fitting that she should be absent at thy death." "Go then," quoth St. Francis, "and bring me inkhorn and paper and pen, and write as I shall tell thee." And when that he had brought them St. Francis dictated the letter after this manner: "To the Lady Jacoba, the servant of God, Brother Francis the poor little one of Christ, greeting and the fellowship of the Holy Spirit in our Lord Jesus Christ. Know, dear lady, that Christ the Blessed One hath of His grace revealed to me that the end of my life is shortly at hand. Wherefore if thou desire to see me still alive, when thou hast seen this letter, do thou arise and come unto Saint Mary of the Angels, for if thou art not come by such a day thou wilt not find me still alive: and bring with thee a shroud of hair-cloth to wrap my body in, and the wax that is needed for the burial. I pray thee likewise that thou bring me some of the food that thou wast wont to give me when I lay sick in Rome." And while this letter was writing, it was of God revealed unto Saint Francis that the Lady Jacoba was coming unto him and was even then come nigh the House, and was bringing with her all the things he was asking for by letter. Therefore, having this revelation, Saint Francis said unto the brother that was writing the letter, that he should write no more, seeing that there was no need, but should lay the letter aside : at the which thing the brothers marvelled much, in that he finished not the letter and desired that it should not be sent. And after a little space there was a loud knocking at the door of the House, and Saint Francis sent the porter to open it. And the door being opened, behold! there was the Lady Jacoba, the most noble lady in all Rome, with her two sons that were senators of Rome, and a great company of horsemen, and they entered in; and the Lady Jacoba went straight to the infirmary and came unto Saint Francis. And of her coming Saint Francis had exceeding great joy and comfort, and she likewise, beholding him still alive and having speech of him. Then she told him how God had revealed unto her in Rome as she was at prayer the near end of his life, and how he would send for her and ask for these things, all of which she said she had brought with her; and she let bring them to Saint Francis and gave him to eat. And when he had eaten and was much comforted, the Lady Jacoba kneeled down at the feet of Saint Francis and took those most holy feet, marked and adorned with the wounds of Christ, and kissed them and bathed them with her tears in such a rapture of devotion, that to the brothers that stood around it seemed they saw the very Magdalene herself at the feet of Jesus Christ, and by no means could they draw her away. And at length after a long space they lifted her up thence and drew her aside; and they asked her how she had come at a time so fitting and so well provided with all things that were needed for the sustenance and for the burial of Saint Francis. Replied the Lady Jacoba, that as she was praying in Rome one night, she heard a voice from heaven saying: "If thou desire to see Saint Francis still alive delay not to go unto Assisi, and take with thee the things thou wast wont to give him when he was sick, and the things that will be needed for his burial"; and (quoth she) "even so have I done." So the said Lady Jacoba abode there until such time as Saint Francis passed away from this life and was buried; and she paid great honours unto his burying, she and all her company, and she bore the charges of whatsoever was needed. Then returning to Rome, after a short time this gentle lady died a holy death; and of her devotion to Saint Francis she decided and desired to be carried to Saint Mary of the Angels and be buried there, and so it was done.'[1]

St. Francis died one day of October 1226, and it was Saturday. In St. Mary of the Angels, the Lady Jacoba weeping beside him as Sasseta has told us, he lay listening to the song of the birds he loved best, when Christ caught him away from our earth, which has ever been the poorer since we spared him.

It is said of him that Death, which is to all men so terrible and hateful, he praised, calling her by name: 'Death, my sister, welcome be thou'; and that one of those best-loved brothers saw his soul in the manner of a star, 'like to the moon in quantity and to the sun in clearness.' And however we may think of him, whether he is to us one of the most precious saints in all that splendid calendar, or whether he is merely a delightful figure a little ailing, a little mad from the Middle Age, he went honourably upon the stones, like Him who was called Stone, as de Voragine reminds us. 'He gadryd the wormes out of the wayes, by cause they should

[1] She lies under the pulpit in the Lower Church at Assisi.

not be troden with the feete of them that passyd by.' He
called the beasts his brethren ; and in all that age of passion
and war, of immense ambition and brutal love, he loved us as
Christ has done, and was content if he might be an imitation
of Him. 'He beheld the Sonne, the Mone, and the Starres,
and somoned them to the Love of their Maker.' And so while
Joachim comes to remind us, not without a very sure appeal
to the modern world, that the letter killeth but the spirit
giveth life—his beautiful life, so little understood in his own
day, has been hidden for us behind the more perfect loveliness of St. Francis. Of St. Francis who may now speak
well ? His best biographers were those who had something of his spirit, the author of the *Fioretti*, or those three
companions who had heard his voice. Full of the lust of
gold and sensuality and ugliness, how can we, who desire to
possess everything, understand one whose chief claim on the
love of mankind was that he possessed nothing whatsoever,
and having nothing, he gathered all things to himself ? He
has been a stranger in the world for many centuries. That
he proved to us the reality of the life of Jesus, that in his
perfect appreciation of the beauty of the world he recreated
art, that he loved mankind as we may dream God has loved
us—what are these, since he is dead ? His spirit lives only
as a beautiful flower pressed between the pages of life.
And if, as has been said, all men wear mourning for the
perfect Emperor, how much more may those who have not
the learning or the wealth or the capacity to understand
a soul so winsome and so discontentedly in love with
contentment, mourn continually the little poor man of
Assisi who went barefoot and was hungry, and lifted the
worms out of the way that they should not be trodden
under foot, and understood the birds and all other angels.
That he, too, was the slave of his own ideas, as when he
turned even the sick out of that house at Bologna which

had been given to the friars, because 'Poverty is the way to salvation'; that he failed to understand Frederick ii. and the splendour of his paganism and his culture, are merely the limitations of his genius; as well might we complain that Jesus failed to understand the Roman Empire.

Ah! as we pass up and down the Umbrian ways, it is this figure which goes ever before us, whispering to us in the night in the great rivers that are ceaselessly moving in the valleys, and in the daytime in the manifold voices of all those things which he loved. He was aware of the love of God, since the sun shone, and divined the whole of His tenderness for us in the beauty of a single flower. And though it has been said that his life was a kind of failure, that his dream was overwhelmed by the materialism of the Church, it is impossible to think of failure in his company; for he himself is a figure of immortal beauty, as great in a certain diviner fashion as the greatest emperor, seeing that he was a poet as it were in the rhythm of life. Finding life, which he took as his material, hard and arid as iron, he burned and melted it with the fire of his genius, and created out of what seemed so unfortunate a priceless and immortal story, his own life, that still in all the ages since his death remains unequalled in love and beauty, a possession for ever for the sorrowful who, like him, only possess the sun, the sky, and the flowers.

XXVII

ST. CLARE

IT is impossible to think of St. Clare apart from St. Francis, because she loved him. All the sour discretion of the historians has not been able to deceive us in this, for her love is the pillar of fire that guides her whole life. In that noiseless convent of St. Damian she seems to pass through the rooms among the virgins exercising a careful authority, exciting a wonderful devotion, but her eyelids have fallen over her eyes, hiding the love that burned in them always from those who could not understand. Sometimes they remark a certain radiance in her face, and ever after think of her as one who has seen God; sometimes it is a kind of ecstasy they see, and so they speak of her as attentive to some angel or dream; but in reality it is only of Francis she dreams, it is to his thoughts she is for ever attentive, nor for her is there any angel half so divine as the divine adventurer.

Born at Assisi in 1194, she was the eldest daughter of Favorino Sciffi, a noble knight of considerable wealth. The usual somewhat melancholy stories are told of her youth: how that she devoted all her time to prayer; and seeing that the Rosary was as yet unknown in Italy, she, in imitation of certain ancient anchorites, counted her *Paters* and *Aves* with little stones in her lap. However this may be—and it is perhaps a little distressing to think of a childhood so serious, without a thought of the flowers, or the romance of to-morrow—it was in the early spring of the year 1212 that

St. Clare first heard St. Francis preach in S. Rufino, the Cathedral.Church of Assisi. In that magical hour everything seemed easy and plain under the eloquence, passionate and insistent, of one who was about to capture the world. It was springtime and the nights were long and still. As she lay in her bed and saw the moon shine through the window, and heard the nightingales sing in the garden, and listened for the soft whisper of the wind in the trees, the wind that had passed through the great forests and over the mountains, did she suddenly realise what her life must be? or was it only after the deep, long thoughts of many days of youth that she knew 'she never might have rest in her heart till she was come to him and that to him she had opened her heart?' We shall never know; but on that night of Palm Sunday a little towards dawn she arose and dressed herself in fine clothes and ran to St. Francis over the valley. In all that spring night, soft with the promise of summer, there was nothing more exquisite than St. Clare, her beautiful hair streaming behind her, fleeing to St. Francis in the dawn. She came to Porziuncola as the friars were singing Matins, and they went out to meet her with lighted tapers and began to sing the hymn *Veni Creator*. And St. Francis took her, and after Mass he read again to her the words Christ spoke to His disciples, and before the altar he dressed her in the penitential habit and cut off her hair; and because as yet he had no convent of his own in which to place her, he sent her to the Benedictine nunnery of St. Paul, near to Bastia, that she might be in safety. But her father and her friends came in anger to bring her home again, not without violence; but she, uncovering her head that they might see the havoc of the shears, besought them to leave her, since Christ had called her to His service and she would have no other Bridegroom. So they let her alone, and presently St. Francis removed her to the convent of S. Angela in Panso belonging

to the Benedictines in Assisi, where to her joy she was joined
by her sister Agnese, who was but fourteen years old. But
when her kinsmen heard that Agnese also was gone to dwell in
a convent, they came in great numbers to carry her off. And
they 'made no force of St. Clare for to draw her out, for they
knew well that they should nothing exploit of their intent,
but they turned to Agnes and said to her: What makest
thou here? Come out with us home to thy house. And she
answered that she would never depart from the company of
St. Clare. And a tyrant, a knight, took and drew her by
the hair, and the others took her by the arms and carried her
forth afar. And she which deemed that she was among the
hands of a lion began to cry, and said: Fair, dear sister! help
me and suffer not that I be taken from the holy company of
Jesu Christ. But the felons drew this virgin against her
will over the mountain, and rent her clothes and drew and
rased her hair. And the holy sweet virgin St. Clare kneeled
down and put herself to prayer, and prayed our Lord to give
her sister a strong heart and a stable, and that she might by
the puissance of God overcome and surmount the puissance
of the people. And anon her body became by the power of
God so pesant and heavy that it seemed that her body were
fixed to the ground in such wise that for all the force and
power that they could do they might not bear her over a
little brook. Then the Lord Mouvalt, her uncle, lift up his
arm for to beat her cruelly, but an ache and pain took him
suddenly and tormented him a long time right cruelly. After
that this said St. Agnes had suffered this long wrestling of
her kinsmen and friends, came St. Clare and prayed them for
God's sake they should leave this battle with her sister and
go their way and take heed of themselves. And she received
the cure and charge of Agnes her sister, which lay there on
the ground in great disease, and finally her kinsmen departed
in great anguish and sorrow of heart.'

So de Voragine in the *Golden Legend* tells the sorrowful tale. And not long afterwards St. Francis gave Agnes also the habit, and placed the two sisters in a little house close to St. Damian's, that little church not far outside the walls of Assisi which he had rebuilt with his own hands. And we find St. Clare made superior of what is really a second Order, for while her mind is intent on St. Francis, and occupied with his ideas—ideas that at that time, at any rate, were not concerned with the foundation of an Order at all but rather with a certain liberty of spirit—she has unconsciously founded the Congregation of Poor Clares, she being about eighteen years old. Soon she is joined by her mother Hortulana and several ladies of her kindred to the number of sixteen, and then in Perugia, in Arezzo, in Spoleto, in Siena, and Venice, in Padua, Mantua, Bologna, and Rome convents spring up looking to her and to St. Francis for guidance and direction. Agnese, daughter of the King of Bohemia, founds a convent of her Order in Prague, she herself becoming a nun; and in Germany also women came under her rule with a kind of eager joy, as though they discerned a new sort of liberty in this rule of poverty, silence, and obedience.

It was an age of great enthusiasms, an age of ideas. Pope Innocent III., a great statesman and patriot, seems to have been possessed by them no less than Frederic II., St. Dominic, and St. Francis. And it is perhaps in the Franciscan ideal, concerned as it was with liberty and joy, the joy that is only to be found in a certain light-hearted freedom from the care of material things, that we find a really valuable idea, a paradox that has confounded the experience of the centuries, that would have led us by quiet and orderly ways to a new world of labour and love. In that rule of poverty, silence, and obedience we may find almost everything that is necessary for life: a freedom from the slavery of material things, which claim us so eagerly; a quietness in which we may find God and all beautiful things; an authority which will correct our enthusiasm, and save us from the bitter dregs of that liberty we are so eager to drain to the end. And so we find St. Clare, when at her father's death she is possessed of her fortune, giving it wholly to the poor; in spite of the Pope's protest, she strips herself of everything in order that she may give herself more perfectly to love. She sacrifices everything so that she may possess her pearl of price, St. Francis. 'Dispose of me as you will,' she says to him, 'I am yours; to God I have consecrated my will, it is no longer my own.' And he, the little poor man, delights to see her at work on beautiful things—fine linen for the service of the altar, fair corporals, and the like, which he distributes among the churches of Assisi. The long sickness that consumed twenty-eight years of her life has begun, she can do little but spin and give her body to the devouring spirit; but at times her face is so bright that it dazzles the eyes of them that behold her. Suddenly into the quietness of her life comes the noise of battle. Frederic II., at war with the Pope, is ravaging the valley of Spoleto with his army of brigands and barbarians. They come to take Assisi, and first St. Damian's, since it stands without the walls a little way towards Rome. Amid all the noise of that brutal assault, the unreality of all that, she, already a kind of exile from heaven, intent on no earthly business, has herself carried to the gate of the convent, while in a pyx the Blessed Sacrament, like a beautiful and splendid Knight, invisibly guards her. When they come upon her, she is lost in prayer, or is it just a divine conversation with that heavenly Knight who surrounds her with His invincible peace? 'Ah, fair Lord God,' she whispers, 'please it you then that they that serve you and be disarmed, whom I nourish for your love, be brought into the hands and power of the paynims? Fair sweet Lord, I beseech thee that thou keep thy handmaidens and servants,

for I may not keep them in this point.' And in a moment
He says to her in a gentle voice, strong and beautiful, 'I
shall keep you always.' Something of the strange beauty
that seems always to have surrounded her, the terror of the
barbarian at the sight of anything beautiful, fell upon the
assailants and they fled Two Popes visit her, Gregory IX. at
any rate out of a very real affection for her whom he had known
from her youth; and seeing her so ill and so poor he tries
to absolve her from the vow of Poverty that was St. Francis's
Bride, but suddenly weeping, she says, I will be assoiled of
my sins, but the vow of poverty I shall keep unto death.
Even to her death it was ever for the voice, the thought, of
Francis that she listened. We catch a glimpse of her one
day in that long idyll woven between the convent of St.
Damian and Porziuncola, in the *Fioretti*.

'Whenas St. Francis was at Assisi, oftentimes he visited
St. Clare and gave her holy admonishments. And she
having exceeding great desire once to break bread with
him, oftentimes besought him thereto, but he was never
willing to grant her this consolation; wherefore his companions, beholding the desire of St. Clare, said unto St.
Francis: "Father, it doth appear to us that this severity
accordeth not with heavenly charity, since thou givest not
ear unto Sister Clare, a virgin so saintly, so beloved of
God, in so slight a matter as breaking bread with thee; and
above all, bearing in mind that she through thy preaching
abandoned the riches and pomps of the world. And of a
truth, had she asked of thee a greater boon than this, thou
oughtest so to do unto thy spiritual plant." . . . Then spake
St. Francis: "Since it seems good to you, it seems so, likewise, unto me. But that she may be the more consoled,
I will that this breaking of bread take place in St. Mary
of the Angels; for she has been so long shut up in St.
Damian, that it will rejoice her to see again the house of

St. Mary, where her hair was shorn away and she became the bride of Jesus Christ; there let us eat together in the name of God." When came the day ordained by him, St. Clare with one companion passed forth from out the convent, and with the companions of St. Francis to bear her company came unto St. Mary of the Angels, and devoutly saluted the Virgin Mary before her altar where she had been shorn and veiled; so they conducted her to see the House until such time as the hour for breaking bread was come. And in the meantime St. Francis let make ready the table on the bare ground as he was wont to do. And the hour of breaking bread being come, they sat themselves down together, St. Francis and St. Clare, and one of the companions of St. Francis with the companion of St. Clare, and all the other companions took each his place at the table with all humility. And at the first dish, St. Francis began to speak of God so sweetly, so sublimely, and so wondrously, that the fulness of the divine grace came down on them, and they were all rapt in God. And as they were thus rapt, with eyes and hands uplifted to heaven, the folk of Assisi and Bettona and the country round saw that St. Mary of the Angels, and all the House, and the wood that was just hard by the House, was burning brightly, and it seemed as it were a great fire that filled the Church, and the House, and the whole wood together: for the which cause the folk of Assisi ran thither in great haste for to quench the flames, believing of a truth that the whole place was on fire. But coming close up to the House, and finding no fire at all, they entered within and found St. Francis and St. Clare.'

And again we see her during a week of passion and sorrow in the convent garden, under the old great olives in a summer of drought, drinking the tears from the almost blind eyes of St. Francis, quenching her thirst for him in their bitterness, lifting up his soul in her hands.

That she loved him I will not doubt. She is the woman in his life, and yet it is strange that it was Lady Jacoba who came to him as he lay dying at Porziuncola, while St. Clare might only kiss him when he was dead, on his way to burial.

Ah, but his most joyful and his most sorrowful hours were spent with her! If she heard him sobbing when he was blind and helpless, it was in her garden, too, that he composed the Canticle of the Sun while she sat at his feet, and her love brought him joy as a great gift. Did she not long for him as she lay sick in her bed on the eve of Christmas, 'in the hour of the nativity of Jesus Christ; when the angels and the world made feast, and sung and enjoyed of little Jesus that was born,' and she was alone? And suddenly on the wings of her longing desire she is carried to Porziuncola, and of all those friars who sang the Matins it is St. Francis she hears, and 'the melody of his song,' till she is a little satisfied.

And when at last she must die, she will not consent to leave the world until the Pope has approved of the Rule St. Francis made for her. She has called herself 'the little flower of St. Francis,' and indeed it was for him she looked up into heaven, for him she was sweet by the wayside, for him she unfolded the petals of her heart that he might rejoice and be comforted on the way to death, and be no more alone.

And if in her we see the spirit destroying the body, as is so frequent in the lives of the saints, it was her love that kept her even so long from heaven, since Francis loved our world. He, too, was not quite fair to Brother Body, should she be fairer than he saw fit to be? For her whole life is like a great beautiful lily, towering at the feet of St. Francis, that he might drink of her fragrance and be glad of her immaculate beauty. As a child almost, this immense love swept into her life, and found her ready to give everything in exchange for it. And at last when all was accomplished, in spite of the tears of her sister and of those who loved her, it is alone in all the precious silence and solitude of love that she sets out for heaven, to find Francis there among those clouds and clouds of saints, not far from the Son of Man whom he had taken at His word.

XXVIII

BROTHER BERNARD

OF all those who followed him with so much loyalty and love, St. Francis seems to have had an especial affection for Brother Bernard, his first disciple. A man of a certain age, one of the 'noblest and richest and wisest' of those who ruled in Assisi, his chief characteristic seems to have been a love for, a faith in, St. Francis, a perfect apprehension of his idea, the liberty to be attained by poverty. This capacity for the reception of ideas in one who was no longer young is perhaps a little surprising, and yet it was no rare thing in the mission of St. Francis. For we find that Silvestro also was a priest, with a certain experience of the world, of life, when on that morning St. Francis loaded him with Bernard's gold, and taught him suddenly the worthlessness of material wealth. Hortulana, too, and how many others, had passed their first youth when the dreams of the adventurer assailed them, and carried them away into that romantic life of the Spirit where St. Francis had founded a new kingdom.

It was while St. Francis was still in the secular habit, that, held in scorn of all men, pelted by the children through the streets of Assisi, Bernard of Assisi, one of the governors of the city, 'began wisely to take heed unto him, how exceeding strong his contempt of the world, how great his patience in the midst of wrongs.' So it is even thus early we may discern that one who 'through subtlety of intellect flew up even unto the light of the divine Wisdom.' He alone, immersed in all the petty affairs of state and city government, the frightful quarrels of the age, enslaved by convention and the authority of government, is able to find in St. Francis something divine. Full of a certain curiosity, he called the fantastic mountebank, the fool of Assisi, the mad son of Bernardone to sup with him, and St. Francis consented, and supped with him and lodged. There is no record of what passed at that strange supper, but Bernard was evidently excited by the ideas of his guest, for he set a lamp in the chamber and determined to watch his sanctity.

'And St. Francis,' says the author of the *Fioretti*, 'And St. Francis for to hide his sanctity, when he was come into the chamber incontinent did throw himself upon the bed and made as though he slept: and likewise Bernard after some short space set himself to lie down and fell to snoring loudly, in fashion as though he slept right soundly. Whereby St. Francis, thinking truly that Bernard was asleep, in his sleep rose up from his bed and set himself to pray, lifting up his hands and eyes unto heaven, and with exceeding great devotion and fervour said: "Deus mi et omnia, Deus mi et omnia." And praying thus and sorely weeping he abode till morning, always repeating "My God, my God," and naught beside.' So through all that long night St. Francis prayed and Bernard wondered. And in the morning Bernard said to him, 'Brother Francis, I am wholly prepared in my heart to leave the world and follow thee in whatsoever thou mayest bid me.' It might seem that St. Francis was surprised that one who was so securely in possession of this world's goods should suddenly desire to be free, and so we find him explaining the difficulty of the way, the greatness of the task, the inevitable weariness that was not altogether obliterated by the freedom and the joy of life, the romance of the world; it was not till after they had heard Mass and the priest had

taken the missal, and having signed it with the sign of the
most Holy Cross, had opened it thrice in the name of Jesus
Christ, that hearing the words the priest read he was convinced
of the vocation of Brother Bernard. At the first opening
appeared the words that Christ spoke in the Gospel to the
young man that had great possessions, even as Bernard had :
'If thou wilt be perfect go and sell that thou hast and give to
the poor and follow me.' And again the second time the priest
opened the book at these words which Christ spake to his
apostles when he sent them forth to preach : 'Take nothing
for your journey, neither staves, nor scrip, neither bread,
neither money ; neither have two coats apiece.' And again
the third time he opened the book almost at the same
place and read : 'If any man will come after me, let him
deny himself and take up his cross daily and follow me.'
And immediately Bernard went out and sold all that he had,
for he was rich ; and together with St. Francis he distributed
the money 'to orphans, to prisoners, to monasteries, and to
hospices, and to pilgrims.' Then came Silvester, a priest
who afterwards was a Brother of St. Francis, and said to
him : 'Thou hast not paid me altogether for the stones to
rebuild the church, then pay me now since thou hast riches.'
St. Francis wondered at his greed, and putting his hand into
Bernard's bosom loaded him with money, promising him
more if he were not satisfied.

Reading that valiant tale, shall we wonder that Bernard
was oftentimes caught up to God, or that St. Francis loved
him and said that it was he who had founded the Order. He
was the first to leave the world in order that he might possess
it the more abundantly ; he gave away all his possessions,
apprehending in a moment that in reality they possessed
him ; he understood St. Francis when all mocked him—is it
wonderful that St. Francis loved him ? For of all those
Brothers who later came to St. Francis and gave up all

and followed him, Bernard alone, it seems to me, had understood the true Franciscan ideal. For that idea he sacrificed everything, content if he might in peace and quietness enjoy the liberty he had bought at a price so great.

We see him later in Bologna, this noble of Assisi, mocked by the children, spattered with mud, weary and in rags, yet always with a joyful countenance, always possessed of a serene patience. And again on the banks of a great river met by a beautiful youth who greets him with the words, 'God give thee peace, good brother'; and Bernard marvelling to hear his native tongue so far from home, asked, 'Whence art thou come, good youth?' And he told him, from the place where St. Francis dwells. 'But wherefore dost thou not cross over?' the youth asked. And Bernard said, 'Because I fear the danger for the depth of the waters that I see.' And the angel, for so he was, answered, 'Let us cross over together and be not doubting'; and he took him by the hand, 'and in the twinkling of an eye set him on the other side of the stream.' And having told him his name, which was Wonderful, he vanished out of sight.

In St. Bernard's life we find none of those tricks, those fooleries, that in Brother Juniper are a little boisterous but a joy for ever. He was a man of grave intelligence who had rather understood the Franciscan idea than been carried away by its spirit, its irresponsible freedom and liberty. For him it might seem that liberty was rather intellectual or spiritual than emotional.

And so when St. Francis comes to die it is for Brother Bernard he sends, that he may partake of a certain 'dainty dish' that had been made ready for himself. All Bernard can do in that hour of sorrow is to beg for his blessing, for he thinks that if St. Francis gives him his blessing, 'God Himself and all the brethren will love me better therefor.'

'The Blessed Francis could not see him, for that by the

space of many days before he had lost the sight of his eyes, but stretching forth his right hand he set it upon the head of Brother Elias, that was the third brother, believing that he had set the same upon the head of Brother Bernard that sat next him. And straightway perceiving the same by the Holy Spirit he said: "This is not the head of my Brother Bernard."

'Then Brother Bernard drew him nigher yet, and the Blessed Francis setting his hand upon his head gave him his blessing, saying unto one of his companions: "Write that which I shall say unto thee. The first brother that the Lord did give unto me was Brother Bernard, that did first begin and did most perfectly fulfil the perfection of the Holy Gospel by giving all his goods unto the poor, by reason whereof and by reason of many other prerogatives I am bound to love him better than any brother in the whole Order. Whence I will and enjoin, so far as I am able, that whosoever shall be Minister-General shall love and honour him as myself. Let the ministers, moreover, and all the brethren of the whole Religion, hold him in my stead."'

In spite of the neglect into which he fell after the death of St. Francis, he has not wanted for champions, the chief of which after all is St. Francis himself. He was one of the great men of the Kingdom of Heaven, as St. Francis had perceived. And so we read that as he too lay a-dying, Brother Giles said with a certain joy, 'Sursum corda, Brother Bernard, sursum corda.' Well, it was his right that, having lived long, not without joy, at the last he should greet death not less cheerfully than he had met life. And being at the last hour he spoke these words to the brothers that were with him:—

'O brothers most dear, I desire not to speak to you many words, but ye should bear in mind that the life of Religion that I have had, ye have still now, and this that now I have ye shall have also. And this I find within my soul, that for a thousand worlds the like of this I would not have served any other Lord than our Lord Jesu Christ: and for every fault I have committed I do accuse myself, and confess my guilt unto my Saviour Jesu and to you. I pray you, my brothers most dear, that ye love one another.' And so he died. It was St. Francis who compared him to St. John, it is strange that he should have used his very words at the last. In him we find a certain strength seldom expressed Was it not to him that St. Francis called when nearly blind and weary with the way he had comforted himself with the assurance that he should find Bernard at the end of the journey? And when he found no Bernard but only a great silence in answer to his call, did he not weep, even he, St. Francis, for very need of that first disciple, that strong and silent brother? 'Bernard, come, speak to me, I am blind. I want you. I need you.' Yes, we have heard St. Francis crying those words; and it is that cry too we seem to hear for years after his death, when, distracted and undone, the Brotherhood of St. Francis desired a strong and steadfast soul to lead it in the way he had pointed out; and found none.

XXIX

BROTHER ELIAS

TO write of Brother Elias is to encounter the tragedy of the Franciscan Order, and not of the Order alone; for in thinking of the life of a man so full of vitality, so irresistible, and so strong, we are face to face with the tragedy of St. Francis himself, that failure of understanding which Jesus suffered too at the hands of his disciples—a blindness in men, almost wilful it might seem, and yet so inevitable, to the perfection of his simplicity, the beauty of just that, its power over the hearts of men, which is perhaps less fatal to the master than to those who will not understand. And so, when we have disregarded the hatred of centuries, the abuse of those who tried to remain loyal to the Rule of St. Francis, it is really a very great and a very sorrowful figure that we see, ever immersed in work, never free from toil for a single moment, when we think of Brother Elias, that Bombarone whom St. Francis loved, who revolutionised the Franciscan Order, and to whom we owe the beautiful church of San Francesco and much of the splendid work on its walls.

It is the fate of some men to be attracted by what they cannot understand. It was so with Brother Elias. St. Francis, whom he appears to have met in his youth, overwhelmed him with his genius, his exquisite temperament, and the beauty of his simplicity. His real tragedy was that he never understood the little poor man of Assisi. The immense talent of Elias for affairs, for government, for patronage,

X

made any understanding of the profoundly Christian, almost anarchical, ideas of St. Francis impossible. He has been called by those who hated him the Judas Iscariot of St. Francis, but in reality he is his St. Paul. His immense practical ability made Franciscanism really an international power, and while we discern in him the same want of understanding of the ideas of the founder as we find at a greater moment in St. Paul, it is to him as to St. Paul that we owe the great success of the religion, its power in the world, its practical success. He too, like the Apostle of the Gentiles, was not among the first followers of his master, yet after his death we find him in almost undisputed command ; and again, like St. Paul, he is certainly the second great figure in the history of the movement, usurping in the first ' Life ' of Thomas of Celano a place we might have expected to see filled by one of those who were with St. Francis from the beginning, as Brother Bernard or Brother Leo. Lacking the charm of those dreamers and saints, he is a figure greater by far, more human perhaps, without their divine simplicity, more tragic in his failure than they in their exquisite success, since he succeeded well enough to ruin himself.

Born at Beviglia, near Assisi, it is said in the same hour as St. Francis, and at any rate about the year 1180, he was the son of very poor people who earned a bare living by mattress making. He himself even in early youth seems to have possessed remarkable intelligence, for we find him as a schoolmaster in Assisi, leading, as we may think, a very quiet life, consumed even in those days by a kind of insatiable restlessness and ambition. It is difficult to imagine anything more different than the youth of St. Francis from the youth of Elias. With every advantage of wealth and rich companions, the son of Bernardone took Poverty for his bride, while Elias, who during all those long years of youth was the servant of every one, desired above all things power

and riches, the which he too compassed before he was old;
and, indeed, these two great men—the one a saint of genius,
the other a statesman of immense talent—are alike only in
their death, which was for both full of sorrow and disappointment, coming almost as a relief after assured failure.
That merciful death which we may believe rases out all the
bitterness of disappointment from the soul and introduces
her to yet another illusion, found St. Francis a blind old
man, scarcely able to walk, regarded even in his own
Order as a kind of ineffectual saint, divine but impossible,
unpractical as we might say, loved by all but unregarded,
the great distinction of the new Order, and yet its most
embarrassing possession; and the reason for this was for the
most part Brother Elias: it found Brother Elias excommunicated, received at the last, it is true, back into the Church,
but in a manner so hurried, so irregular, that a searching
inquiry was held as to the correctness of his reception. Poor
and without friends, with enemies everywhere, death came to
him at last as a great deliverance from men whom he had not
loved as St. Francis had loved them, but whom he had known
how to govern; from the Church whom he had served, but
whom he too had failed to understand; from his own hatred
and contempt of a world, so ungrateful and unsatisfying, in
whom he had trusted. After all, in a way very different, he
was as great a dreamer as St. Francis, without any such
compensation as the love of the whole world.

M. Sabatier suggests that it was he who watched outside
the cave while St. Francis prayed. However this may be,
it is certain that Elias was early attracted by St. Francis,
and that the Saint loved him. Perhaps St. Francis discerned in him those qualities of practical statesmanship
which he himself lacked; but we may remember that while
many of the early Brothers were wealthy, and used, as
St. Francis himself was, to the luxuries of the material life,

Brother Elias was born poor; and it is not unlikely that one so in love with poverty as St. Francis would be naturally attracted to one who, while he possessed by right of birth the quality of poverty, was yet of great intelligence and by no means ignorant or altogether unlearned. That he was utterly without vocation for the Franciscan life St. Francis never perceived. To the last he trusts Elias almost beyond any of the others. Very near the end, when he was nearly blind and is about to submit to the rude healing of the day, it is for Brother Elias he sends that he may be with him. 'When he had come to the hermitage of Fonte Palumbo, near to Rieti,' says the *Speculum Perfectionis*, 'for the cure of the infirmity of his eyes whereunto he was compelled on his obedience by the Lord Bishop of Ostia and by Brother Elias, the Minister-General, one day the leech came unto him, who, after examining his infirmity, said unto the Blessed Francis that he wished to make a cautery over the cheek as far as the eyebrow of the eye that was worse than the other. But the Blessed Francis would not that he should begin the operation save Brother Elias was there, for that he had said he would fain be present when the leech should begin that operation, for the Blessed Francis was afraid, and right grievous was it unto him that he should have so great solicitude about himself; wherefore he would that the Minister-General should be the one to have everything done as concerning him.'

And again in the Chapter of 1221, when we first see Elias as Minister-General and President of the Chapter, we find St. Francis, just returned from Rome where he had met St. Dominic and Frederic II. (who appears to have loved him), sitting at Elias's feet and plucking at his robe 'when there was anything that he wished to have put before the Brothers.' Had St. Francis understood the danger his ideas were in from Elias, it is not in such an attitude we should find him. But the rule of Elias proved, in outward seeming at least, most beneficial to the Order, for we find a large increase in the number of Brothers soon after his appointment as Minister-General. And, indeed, Elias was the statesman of an Order that till he came had no need of anything but saints. He founded the Franciscan Order upon the Brothers Minor. He gave it its innumerable churches, its convents, its great monasteries. He found it a divine society, as it were, which possessed nothing but a great love for mankind; he left it immersed in its splendid possessions. Even so early as this we find him undermining those ideas of Poverty as the way of salvation. For when St. Francis retired 'into a certain mountain' to make the Rule of 1223, many ministers came to Elias and said to him, 'We have heard that this Brother Francis maketh a new Rule, but we be feared lest he should make it too harsh in such sort that we cannot observe it. Wherefore we will that thou go unto him and tell him that we will not be bound unto that Rule. Let him make it for himself and not for us.' Unto whom Brother Elias made answer that he would not go without them, whereupon they all of them did go together. And when Brother Elias was nigh the place where Blessed Francis was standing, Brother Elias called him; who, making answer, and beholding the ministers aforesaid, the Blessed Francis said: 'What would these brethren?' And said Brother Elias: 'They be ministers that have heard how thou makest a new Rule, and being afeared lest thou make it too harsh, do say and protest that they will not be bound thereunto. Make it for thyself alone, and not for them.' Thereupon Blessed Francis did turn his face towards Heaven and spake unto Christ on this wise: 'Lord, said I not well when I told Thee they would not believe me?' Then all did hear the voice of Christ that made answer in the air: 'Francis, naught is there of thine own in the Rule, but

whatsoever is therein is all. Mine own, and My will it is
that thus shall the Rule be observed to the letter, to the
letter, to the letter, without gloss, without gloss, without
gloss.'

Whether or no this strange incident is an invention of
the zealots in their hatred of Elias, it is certainly founded
upon the fact that, long before the death of St. Francis,
Elias was working with the intention of suppressing the
troublesome Rule of Poverty, about which St. Francis was
so insistent.   Around the death-bed of St. Francis many
stories have gathered.   It is impossible to believe the
malicious tales that certain of the zealots have told of
Elias.   He loved St. Francis; that he did not understand
him was not altogether his fault.   How many understood
him in his own day? how few since!   Whether St. Francis
gave his blessing to Leo or Bernard or Elias, it was Elias
who really took over the government of the Order after
St. Francis's death.   It was he who conceived the idea of
building San Francesco; it was he who wrote that strange
letter to Brother Gregory of Naples, Provincial of France;
it was he who managed the temporary burial in San Giorgio.
It is from this point his real career begins.   And in spite of
the fact that he destroyed the fundamental idea of St.
Francis upon which he had built the whole of his life, his
first plans were for the honour of the dead saint.   Whether
he saw the indispensable value of the life of St. Francis for
the success of his own plans, or whether indeed the Pope
and the Church, a little suspicious of so literal a following
of certain words in the Gospel, were too strong for him,
we may not know; at least he raised that church, the glory
of Assisi, and one of the loveliest Gothic buildings in all
Italy, splendid with the work of so many artists, to
guard the body of his friend.   And if he spoiled that work
of St. Francis which as an idea he could not understand,

he was able to translate something of the beauty that shone
in the soul of the saint into everlasting stone, that we too
might understand it and catch some reflection of what his
eyes had seen. Nor was he content with such a monument,
but with a knowledge of men worthy of him, he selected
Thomas of Celano, a Brother who had doubtless loved St.
Francis, and an artist in letters, to write his biography,
producing in this way a book scarcely surpassed in any
literature for its style, its enthusiasm, and the immense
number of its readers. The Bollandists used it for the *Acta
Sanctorum*, and it remains to this day a work of the utmost
importance in the study of the life of St. Francis, and
almost the only authority we have for the life of Elias
himself.

In 1227 John Parenti had been elected Minister-General.
Though such a choice must have disappointed Elias, it
would appear that he was unmoved by it. In 1228 the
Pope—that Gregory who had known and loved St. Francis
—came to Assisi to canonise him. In 1229 the life of
Thomas of Celano had been written. In 1230 the body of
St. Francis was translated from S. Giorgio to the new
church in San Francesco, of which Elias was master of the
works. He determined to assert his power. Gathering
his friends together, invoking the aid of the authorities in
Assisi, who were naturally impressed by the power of the
man who was the friend of the Pope, and who had built
the mighty church on the Colle del Inferno, he took the
body of the saint from S. Giorgio, and secretly by night
buried it in San Francesco, where till our own day it
remained hidden. Thus he declared war on John Parenti,
who meantime had gathered the regular assembly at
Porziuncola. But the friends whom Elias had brought to
Assisi stormed the assembly, and in a moment had placed
Elias in the chair of the Minister-General, only a little

later to be themselves expelled and Elias with them, by the enraged Brothers. The General appealed to the Pope, who threatened the secular powers with excommunication, and placed the new church and convent under an interdict. This was no doubt a terrible blow to Elias. He seems to have retired rather in anger than in any sort of repentance, only the more determined to succeed when another opportunity occurred. Possessed by his idea of making the Franciscan Order a power in and for the Church, he was really at one with the Pope, although the means he employed were those rather of a soldier than a Brother Minor. He appears to have remained in a kind of exile for some time, while his ideas were inevitably undermining the whole Order. 'John Parenti,' says Miss Macdonell in her delightful book, *The Sons of Francis*, 'was no very strong rival. A good man of beautiful nature, and if we were to accept the view of Père d'Alençon concerning the authorship of the *Sacrum Commercium*, of a charming fancy; but perhaps lacking the strong personality that would make his views growingly accepted.' However that may be, and that he was a good man is not open to doubt, it seems to me that nothing short of a second St. Francis, perhaps a continual generalship by men of the greatness of St. Francis himself, could have saved the Order from the ambition of the Church. It was almost impossible that any society could maintain itself within, or indeed in those days without, the Church, and at the same time by its very character accuse her of a kind of compromise with the world. Certainly the Church took the responsibility of destroying the Franciscan ideal, not because it was impossible, but because it was in its principle of life anarchical, and therefore antagonistic to her government. St. Francis had not understood this, was indeed really incapable of understanding it; and even as he trusted Elias so he trusted the Pope and the Catholic Church, whose son he was. Had he understood the view the Church must necessarily take of his movement, the revolutionary appeal behind her to the text of Scripture, he would, as I think, have submitted himself, since the whole character of his teaching and of his life may be said to be non-resistance, even evil being better overcome by good than resisted openly.

In September 1230 Gregory signed the Bull *Quo elongati*, and a little later John Parenti resigned and Elias was elected in his stead. A great change is at once to be found in the Order. Hitherto, it had been a pure democracy, in which the virtue of obedience was taught as a kind of spiritual gymnastic. It now became an army led by a great general who claimed obedience as a right, whose aim was not so much the salvation of man—though ultimately that might be said to be his object—as power over the hearts of men, power in the government of the Church, power in the government of nations, power—more power than for instance the Order of St. Dominic might win—in everything. There were many who remembered old days and rebelled. That idea of Poverty as a bride, as the great Liberator—even then Liberty being the mistress, perhaps a little bashful, secretly in the hearts of men—was difficult to slay. Elias dealt with the zealots as a general might deal with mutineers. Cæsar of Speyres, his own convert, he killed, it is said accidentally; many he scourged, and others he exiled.

His chief need was money to complete San Francesco—that monument which is to-day certainly as much his as St. Francis's. It was he, probably at the Pope's suggestion, who employed those Roman painters under Pietro Cavallini to paint the roof of the upper church. Giunta Pisano also he employed, and about 1236 sat to him for his portrait, which has been lost. His manner of life at this time seems to have been rather that of a lord than a friar. But his health was delicate. In 1238 Gregory IX. sent him as ambassador to Frederic II. He appears to have impressed the Emperor as a man of great ability. Perhaps the Pope suspected him of intriguing with his enemy, or perhaps his rule was stirring up too much strife; however that may be, in 1239 the Pope for the first time listened to the complaints of the zealots against him. It was an Englishman, Symon of Faversham, who spoke against him. Among other somewhat futile charges, he accused him of heaping up money for himself. This Elias indignantly denied, and the Pope suggested that he should place his case in his hands as Head of the Church. But Elias would not. Then the Pope in anger told them all how he had chosen Elias from among them because he loved St. Francis, and such an one he thought would please every one of them. If it were not so, then they might proceed to elect another general. They chose Albert of Pisa. Thus fell a great man whose tragedy was to have loved St. Francis rather than Frederic II. He went to Cortona. Nor would he listen to the Pope, nor to the new general. He went to the Emperor, who employed him gladly. Gregory excommunicated him. It is said that he wrote to the Pope stating his case, which he appears to have thought, perhaps not without justice, had never been heard. He sent the letter to Albert of Pisa, in whose pocket it was found after his death.

In 1241 Gregory died, and with him all hope of pardon for Elias. We see him at the court of Frederic still wearing his habit, sometimes going on long journeys for the Emperor, and in return winning certain distinctions for the city and people of Cortona, where he had made his home. Later, they granted him land and built for him a great convent. But in 1250 Frederic died, and his employment was gone. He retired to his convent in Cortona, and seems to have followed the ways and tastes, the sunless pleasures, of one who had been defeated. He was no rebel; he had been used to command rather than to suffer discipline and listen to the orders of others; his excommunication weighed heavily upon him. So he sent for the local clergy and made his submission, and they in his last hours gave him absolution, consoling him, if it might be, for all his disasters with the Blessed Sacrament which he, in all simplicity, still held to be divine indeed.

In the life of this great man we see the profound inability of the world to understand St. Francis. The Franciscan ideal failed to touch Elias. He loved St. Francis, but he did not understand him; at all times they who loved him have been more than they who understood him. Elias, though born poor, perhaps because of it, was dependent upon the material possessions of the world. Without them he was almost nothing. With them St. Francis had amused himself, without them he in some sort conquered the world. It is the difference between two ideas of which the one is no longer heard of. Henceforth the Franciscan Order was a Society differing but slightly from the Dominican or the Benedictine Orders. It existed for the service of the Church rather than for the service of men. Perhaps that was the inevitable fate of a movement, very lovely in itself, which taught rather by vision than knowledge, preaching a kind of divine philosophy which, in those who sought to keep the Rule of St. Francis, degenerated into something very like heresy under John of Parma. The mysterious prophecies of the Eternal Gospel, rather than the simpler teaching of the Gospel of Jesus that had so filled the life of St. Francis, appealed to them. And we come to think of them as we think of any other order of friars, finding there indeed little to differentiate them from the rest, seeing that St. Francis was in heaven and there was no one on earth who understood and remembered him.

CONCLUSION

WHAT is that Angel, splendid, shy, elusive, whom we pursue sometimes with so much haste and vulgarity, and always in vain, on our travels through dead or living cities, over the immense miles of the deserts, or through the horrid limitations of space strangled in mean streets, but the Spirit of Place? Sometimes, as in some great city antique and wonderful, this white Angel is strong and full of vitality, and splendid amid dead or dying things; sometimes, as in the brutal highways of some trumpery modern capital, he is shy and timid, so elusive, that it is perhaps only for a moment, gone while we try to apprehend it, that we feel the wind of his wings or catch one breathless half-word whispered as he vanishes.

Yet it is always in vain that we pursue him, he is not to be hunted by even the cleverest among us. If we find him it is always on some fortunate day when we least expect it, when we are thinking of other things. He who sets out to bring him home in triumph is bewildered by shadows or reality. To visit some ancient, indestructible city with difficulty, after much longing, perhaps at night, to be forced to leave after one intoxicating look, is to catch a miraculous glimpse of that swift Angel brooding over the immemorial splendour and ruin of the world, in the hours when he knows he need not fear the pursuit of the vulgar.

It is so one might look on the Roman Campagna for the first time, with eyes a little weary for some great spaciousness, and so suddenly an indestructible memory of profound beauty would impress itself on the imagination : the image of the lonely majesty of the Campagna, littered with the monsters of old forgotten religions ; full of the dead things of Paganism and Christianity, the bones of saints, the mighty trunks of forgotten gods.

But perhaps it is really only in words that we possess our heart's desire. Words are visions. Italy herself was never half so gracious as the dream which is eternal in her name. And if her wrongs are written in ashes, we may find all her splendour in the word Rome. Is it not so with everything ? Was any woman, howsoever beloved, half so radiant as she who hides for ever in the name ? And if I say the word Princess, it is not any mortal royalty I see. For the fairest girl is less fair than Helen of Troy, the loveliest woman how much less lovely than Cleopatra, and she who has given us all has yet not loved us as Isoud loved. Have we ever really seen a bleeding topaz, even on a Pope's finger, or in any Queen's ear those rubies cut in the shape of drops of blood ? It is really only those things which we have not seen that we possess, since all the gold of Ophir will not buy Eldorado. For who, having heard the name of Athens, may be content with any other city ? And since this is so with Perfumes and Jewels and Women, how may we reconcile the world with our expectations of it ?

There is but one escape from the immense disillusion of reality, but one medicine that will cure us of our disappointment. It is in Art that all beauty lies, and there is nothing perfect upon earth but man has made it. It is that breathless half-word that the Angel whispers as he vanishes, and it is with this purification that all that is best in the world must come to us. To see anything as in itself it really is, is to understand what it might have been, what it may be.

Thus there is more truth in Poetry than in History, and the only reality we may know is that which has been conceived by man.   Achilles lives since Homer sang of him, but who has remembered the princes of Egypt, or the lovers that walked by the Phœnician Sea ?   So Agamemnon remains the king of kings,while Lycurgus is as a forgotten dawn.   What were Francesca and Paolo Malatesta if Dante had passed them by, or Cleopatra if Shakespeare had not told us of her, or even Jesus of Nazareth without the perfect syllables of the Gospels ?   Names that come to us in dreams, ghosts that wander in the abyss of time, words that are lovelier than the roses.   And so it is that the night of Christmas is the only one in all the centuries that we really remember ; and the dawn of the first Easter is fairer far than any that broke the blossoms white and red in the gardens of Babylon.   While for those who may see, every ancient altar in the world is still green with bays and grey with olive.

In Umbria, perhaps, we miss those everlasting garlands less than anywhere else in the world.   Here, we have not yet banished the gods, those indestructible witnesses to the wisdom and beauty that is from of old ; still, still, they laugh in the woods, or in the reeds beside the river whisper together, a little fearful of our approach.   And if you have seen April all in red and white dancing through the valleys, you have seen a goddess, and are happy : remember then, how few are the seasons she will go by before you too will not know whether her white feet come swiftly, or linger by the Eastern Sea.   Ah, be wise, love her while you may, for she is still the fairest in the world.

And that you should fail to understand my book, it is but a little thing : but that you should fail to love Umbria, it is a disaster for you, since she gives you what you bring to her, and her angel is ever gracious to those who come to her quiet places not hurriedly at all, but with a certain reverence.

INDEX

Printed by T. and A. CONSTABLE, Printers to His Majesty
at the Edinburgh University Press

Lightning Source UK Ltd.
Milton Keynes UK
UKOW04f1929230215

246773UK00001B/61/P